Dunkirk: The British Evacuation 1940

Robert Jackson

Dunkirk: The British Evacuation 1940

Arthur Barker Limited
London
A subsidiary of Weidenfeld (Publishers) Ltd

Published in Great Britain by
Arthur Barker Limited,
11 St John's Hill, London SW11

420194738

ISBN 0 213 16598 8
Printed in Great Britain by
Butler & Tanner Ltd,
Frome and London

Contents

A*

Maps

Acknowledgements

I have been indebted to many sources in the preparation of this book. Foremost among them, as always, is Roderick Suddaby, keeper of the department of documents at the Imperial War Museum, whose enthusiasm and helpfulness never ceases to astonish. The various branches of the Dunkirk Veterans' Association, too, have been most co-operative, as have military museums throughout the country.

But it is the individuals who make up the story of Dunkirk; hundreds of them, who have delved into their memories for snippets of valuable information. To them all go my heartfelt thanks, and to newspaper editors all over the United Kingdom through whose pages my appeal for material was broadcast.

Here are just a few of those individuals who contributed their written recollections or tape-recorded stories:
J. Roy Adern, A.V. Allinson, K.D. Anderson, Ronald Avey; Phil Back, Bob Barlow, A. Bates, C.S. Best, Mrs B. Bowden, Les Boyce, A.T. Bridge, A. Bruce, J. Buchanan, Tom Byers; F.E.J. Carey, Ken Carter, I.R. Casley, E. Clark, T.W. Coatsworth, T. Collins, Charles Crisp; D. Glyn Davies, Mrs N. Dennis, J.F. Duffy, Mrs J.E. Dunbar; W.T. Elmslie DSM, D. Embury; Edward Faulkes DCM MM, Mrs A.E. Fisher, Jack Flanagan, E.A. Frorey; J. Gallagher, D.P. Glanville, R. Godfrey; R.A. Hague, T. Hogan, John P. Howard, A. Hughes, Mrs Hazel Hughes, F.G. Hutchinson; Captain N.D.G. James, C.I. Jones, Tom Jordan; Robert W. Lee, Major Rhydian Llewellyn MC DL; J.A. Matheson, H.F.H. Matthews, W. Mills, Sam Morne, F.B. Morris, R.T. Morris; Vincent Ord; R.L. Pointer MM, Mrs P. Poulton, Bill Priest, Peter Pring, H. Pritchard; W.T. Richardson, G.J. Roberts, G. Robertson, Reg Rushmere; R. Simpson, W.H. Smith, Major A.E.G. Steede, D. Stone; J.M. Thorpe, J.L. Todd, Mons Trussler; T. Urwin; W.J. Walker, Charles White, Mrs J. Wilkinson, W.E. Williams, E. Wilson.

1 Battle Situation, 20 May 1940

Captain Victor Veniel was desperately tired. He had flown five sorties since dawn; now, at six o'clock in the evening, grimy and unshaven, his body clammy with the sweat that had poured from him as he sweltered under the hot May sun in the cramped cockpit of his Bloch 152 fighter, he wanted nothing more than to bathe some of the tension away, snatch something to eat and fall asleep.

His day's work, however, was not yet done. He still had to wade through the stack of documents on his desk, the mound of forms and orders that seemed to grow bigger every day. They all had to be filled in: combat reports, statistical returns, observations of mechanical defects – defects such as the continual jamming of the Bloch 152's cannon, a perpetual and deadly nuisance that showed no signs of being rectified because no one higher up appeared to be interested in signing the necessary authorization. That very day two pilots of Veniel's unit – No. 3 Squadron, Fighter Group II/I of the French Air Force – had been shot down when their cannon jammed in the middle of a dogfight with Messerschmitts.

Wearily he brushed a hand over the stubble on his face and resigned himself to his task. France might be crumbling in ruins around their ears, but the staff at group HQ still insisted on having the paperwork done on time. Providing replacement aircraft and pilots, apparently, was of secondary importance.

Veniel looked up as his office door opened. It was Captain MacMahon, the group's adjutant. MacMahon told Veniel that he was to report to the group commander, Captain Robillon, immediately. It seemed that there was some sort of urgent mission in the offing; the order had come in just a few minutes ago, direct from French Air Force GHQ.

Thankfully Veniel left his papers and went to the operations room, where Robillon was waiting. The latter, a highly experienced fighter pilot with icy blue eyes and a whiplash voice that brooked no question of his authority, put Veniel in the picture as far as he was able. At 06.30 the following morning, 20 May, Veniel was to fly to Le Bourget, on the outskirts of Paris, with three flights of fighters. He was to report to Commandant Daurat, the co at Le Bourget, who would give him further instructions. The fighters were to provide an escort for an aircraft carrying a vip whose identity Robillon did not know.

The next morning, Veniel took off from Buc – the group's base – at the head of eight fighters. The ground crews had worked all night to make them serviceable, repairing battle damage. Fifteen minutes later they landed at Le Bourget, on schedule. As he climbed from the cockpit, Veniel was greeted by Commandant Daurat, commander of the GHQ Air Transport Flight. The two were old acquaintances.

To his consternation, Veniel learned that Daurat had no information at all about the proposed mission. He had been awakened at 2am by a telephone call from a GHQ staff officer, who had told him to prepare a fast bomber for a vital mission in a few hour's time. The problem, as Daurat had soon discovered, was that no bombers were available. Finally, in desperation, he had telephoned the Air Force test centre at Saint-Inglevert and asked the co there if he could spare a machine. There was only one: a twin-engined Amiot 354, France's latest and fastest bomber. It had not yet entered service and was still undergoing its trials. Nevertheless it would have to do.

A messenger roared up on a motor cycle and addressed Daurat. A general had arrived on the airfield; he was waiting in Daurat's office and he was not, it seemed, in a pleasant mood. Daurat jumped on the motor bike and sped away towards the operations room; Veniel and his pilots stayed where they were, wondering what was going to happen next.

While they waited, they watched with interest as a brand new Amiot 354 landed and taxied in. It parked close to the fighters, the polished metal of its wings and fuselage contrasting sharply with the dark grey camouflage of the other machines. Three crew members climbed from the Amiot, and the pilot came over to introduce himself to Veniel. His name was Captain Henri Lafitte, and he was a test pilot. Like Veniel, he was completely in the dark about the true nature of the mission.

Veniel cast an eye over the bomber, and was reassured by the sight of twin machine guns protruding from its rear turret. Lafitte smiled wryly. The guns were wooden dummies, fitted at the last moment. It was unlikely that they would fool the German fighter pilots.

A staff car approached and halted a few yards away. Commandant Daurat got out and opened the rear door. Veniel brought his pilots to attention as he glimpsed the gold braid of a general's kepi.

The man who emerged was old, but bore himself stiffly erect as he returned their salute. Veniel immediately recognized him from photographs he had seen: the piercing eyes, the hollow cheeks, the mouth set in a firm line. Their VIP was General Maxime Weygand, commander-in-chief of all French forces on land, at sea and in the air.

Weygand. Despite his seventy-three years, despite his obvious tiredness, he bore himself with pride and youthful vigour. He might have been one of Napoleon's generals, stepping from a page of history when all Europe lay at France's feet, instead of an old man summoned from across the sea in a desperate bid to rally the tottering French armies and exhort them to stand firm against the panzers that were debouching across the plains of Flanders. This was the man who, nearly a quarter of a century earlier, had been the shadow of the great Marshal Foch; it was Weygand who had been at Foch's right hand on that fateful day in November 1918, when the Armistice terms had been presented to the defeated Germans in the Marshal's special train at Compiègne.

His critics – and there had been many – had often cast doubt on his powers of leadership, drawing strength from the fact that he had never commanded troops in battle. In 1920 he had been sent to Poland as France's representative on an Allied mission whose task had been to advise the Poles in their fight against the invading Russians, and there were those who claimed that he had been the mastermind behind the Polish success. Two years after his return to France he had been appointed high commissioner in Syria, and 1931 had seen him elevated to the post of commander-in-chief of the French Army.

In 1939, after four years of retirement, he had been recalled to the colours and sent back to Syria as military commander. He was still there on 10 May 1940, when the Germans launched their offensive against France and the Low Countries. On the eighteenth he had been in Cairo, conferring with General Wavell, the British commander in Egypt, when an urgent signal arrived from French Premier Paul Reynaud summoning him to Paris.

He left immediately, hoping that his aircraft would reach Paris that same evening after refuelling at Tunis. The machine, however, encountered strong headwinds and the pilot was forced to turn back and refuel at Mersa Matruh in Egypt, losing three precious hours. His homecoming seemed to be dogged by misfortune; when the aircraft finally touched down in France on the morning of the nineteenth, at Etampes airfield, its undercarriage collapsed and Weygand had to scramble clear through a gun turret, shaken but unhurt.

He arrived at Vincennes, the French GHQ, at 15.30 that same day, and had an interview with the commander-in-chief, General Maurice Gamelin – the unhappy man who was about to be made the scapegoat for the series of military disasters that had overwhelmed the French armies in the field during the past week. It was only now, in the course of Gamelin's briefing, that Weygand began to appreciate the full magnitude of these disasters and the dire peril that confronted his nation.

Briefly, the situation outlined by Gamelin was as follows. When the Germans struck on 10 May, the formations on the left of the Allied defensive line – the French First and Seventh Armies and the British Expeditionary Force – had swung forward into Belgium to confront the armoured spearheads of the German Army Group B under Field Marshal Fedor von Bock. By the fourteenth, after preliminary fighting, the situation appeared to have stabilized, with the Belgian Army defending the line from Antwerp to Louvain, the BEF in position along the river Dyle between Louvain and Wavre, and the French First Army on their right between Wavre and Namur. The Seventh Army meanwhile had pushed on up the coast and crossed the frontier into Holland.

The Allies, in fact, had acted precisely as the Germans had hoped and anticipated; for the decisive battle was not to be fought in

Belgium. The main effort was to be made in the centre by von
Rundstedt's Army Group A, whose divisions – including nine
armoured – were to break across the river Meuse and establish
bridgeheads for a drive to the sea.

During the first forty-eight hours of the campaign, while the Allies
raced forward to counter the threat from Army Group B, the armoured columns of Army Group A – led by two panzer corps under
General Ewald von Kleist – had been pushing steadily on over the
twisting mountain roads of the Belgian Ardennes, across terrain that
French military strategists had claimed could not be negotiated by
tanks. By Whit Sunday, 12 May, the left wing of Kleist's panzer
group – XIX Panzer Corps, under General Heinz Guderian – had
reached the Meuse on either side of Sedan, and the following day it
launched its attack across the river in the wake of a massive air
bombardment. Sedan was the weakest point of the French defensive
line; it was in this sector that the right flank of the Ninth Army
joined the left flank of the Second, and there was little cohesion between the two. Moreover the French divisions were manned for the
most part by untried reserve troops.

By the morning of the fourteenth Guderian had succeeded in
establishing a strong bridgehead on the west bank of the Meuse in
Second Army territory, and the French were crumbling rapidly
before the onslaught. Further north, at Monthermé, the right wing
of Panzergruppe Kleist – Reinhardt's XLI Panzer Corps – had met
stiffer resistance, but here too a crossing of the Meuse had been
forced by the 7th Panzer Division led by a dashing and as yet unknown general, Erwin Rommel.

Throughout the fourteenth the French Air Force and the RAF
attempted to bomb the Meuse bridgeheads; the damage they caused
was insignificant and they suffered appalling losses from the
20-mm flak and the prowling Messerschmitts. By nightfall both the
French Second and Ninth Armies were collapsing before the mount-
ing German pressure; the panzers were breaking through everywhere, flooding through a sixty-mile breach in the defences. On the
fifteenth both XIX and XLI Panzer Corps broke out of their bridgeheads and began to drive rapidly westwards, pausing only to let
their supporting infantry catch up. On the sixteenth Rommel's 7th

Panzer, decimating the French 1st Armoured Division *en route*, raced on fifty miles to Avesnes. That evening XLI Panzer Corps reached the river Oise near Vervins, while to the south XIX Panzer Corps pushed on to the river Serre. By the morning of the seventeenth French resistance on the upper Oise fell apart and the westward plunge of the panzers continued; it was still not yet clear whether their primary objective was Paris or the Channel coast. What was apparent, however, was that the speeding panzers were driving a dangerous corridor between the Allied armies; to the north of it lay the Belgian Army, the French First Army and the British Expeditionary Force, in contact with von Bock's advancing Army Group B, while to the south the battered French armies that had recoiled before the shock of Army Group A were desperately trying to regroup along the river Somme and form a defensive shield against a German drive southwards.

Such, broadly, was the battle situation described to Weygand by Gamelin on that afternoon of 19 May. Gamelin, to give him credit, had realized that the rapid advance of the panzers had left the German flanks dangerously exposed; on the eighteenth, air reconnaissance had confirmed that the enemy tanks were once again a long way ahead of their supporting units. Winston Churchill, newly appointed British prime minister, summed up the situation in picturesque fashion early on the nineteenth in a cable to Gamelin:

'The tortoise has protruded its head very far from its shell. Some days must elapse before the main body can reach our lines of communications. It would appear that powerful blows struck from the north and south of this drawn-out pocket could yield surprising results.'

It was a time for decisive action, for Gamelin to take a firm hand in the conduct of the battle. So far he had been content to leave the burden of decision on the shoulders of General Georges, the French C-in-C North-East, and now, at this crucial stage in the battle, he showed no inclination to alter this policy. At 09.45 on the nineteenth, he shut himself away and penned his one and only operational directive to Georges. Under the heading 'Personal and Secret Instruction No. 12', it ran:

Without wishing to interfere in the conduct of the battle now being waged, which is in the hands of the Commander-in-Chief of the North-East Front, I consider that, at the present time:

1 There are grounds for extending the front of our Eastern Armies and those covering Paris towards the west, and for maintaining the link with No. 1 Army Group. [Author's note: Comprising the French First, Seventh and Ninth Armies in the north.]

2 That, as regards No. 1 Army Group – rather than let it be encircled, we must act with extreme audacity; first by forcing, if necessary, the road to the Somme, and secondly, by throwing in particularly mobile forces against the rear of the panzer divisions and the motorized infantry divisions which are following them. It seems that there is, at present, a vacuum behind this first echelon.

3 We must prepare with all our might for a Second Army offensive, also involving the Sixth Army's right, striking towards the Mézières bridges.

It was immediately clear to General Georges that this 'instruction' was nothing of the sort; rather, it was a series of personal observations and suggestions. Nevertheless Georges decided to act upon it and at once set about translating it into operational terms.

It was at this juncture, in the afternoon of the nineteenth, that Weygand arrived on the scene. After his briefing by Gamelin, he went to see Georges at La Ferté-sous-Jouarre, GHQ North-East, returning to Paris at 18.30 for a meeting with Reynaud and Marshal Philippe Pétain, who at Reynaud's invitation had joined the government as deputy premier twenty-four hours earlier. At this meeting Reynaud asked Weygand to take over the reins from Gamelin. After a lengthy discussion, Weygand said: 'Very well. I accept the responsibility you are putting on me. You will not be surprised if I do not promise victory, or even give you hope of a victory.'[1] On this far from optimistic note, he retired for his first real sleep since leaving North Africa.

He was back in the C-in-C's office at Vincennes early the next morning, looking much refreshed. There was a brief, cool meeting with Gamelin, during which the latter formally handed over to his replacement. Afterwards Gamelin left Vincennes for ever, a solitary and pathetic figure, bidding goodbye to no one.

Weygand's first act as generalissimo was to cancel Gamelin's 'Instruction No. 12', a move which he considered prudent given the lack of firm intelligence on the enemy's movements, but which in fact served only to add to the confusion already surrounding General Georges and his subordinate commanders. Nevertheless Weygand took another immediate decision which, when it reached his commanders in the field, brought sighs of relief: the roads leading to the front were to be cleared at once, and civilians were to be permitted to move only between 18.00 hours and midnight. Had Gamelin made this decision several days earlier, its influence on the early stages of the campaign might have been considerable; at least part of the German success so far was due to the fact that Allied reinforcements – particularly armour and artillery – had lost much vital time in forcing their way along roads congested with streams of refugees.

Weygand believed, rightly, that the Allied forces north of the corridor driven seawards by the panzers were now in a critical position; it was becoming clear that the enemy planned first to eliminate these forces by crushing them between the hammer and anvil of Army Groups A and B before swinging southwards into the heart of France. Weygand's main problem was that all direct communication with General Billotte, commanding Army Group One, had been severed by the speeding panzers; any news he received from the north came very much secondhand, via London. A visit to Georges at La Ferté that morning strengthened his belief that a personal call on the commanders in the north was imperative if he was to make a clear assessment of the situation, and he advised Reynaud of his intention that afternoon. His original intention was to journey to Abbeville by train, but Reynaud dissuaded him. It was just as well; unknown to Weygand, Abbeville was at that moment within sight of Guderian's leading tanks. Instead, the c-in-c agreed to make the trip by air and asked the Air Force to provide a fast machine. He also sent messages to King Leopold of Belgium, Lord Gort and General Billotte, requesting a meeting in Ypres on the afternoon of the following day, 21 May.

Weygand considered a meeting with Lord Gort to be of prime

importance; the intentions of the BEF's commander had to be clari-
fied with all possible speed. Weygand's concern stemmed from news
of a telephone call made by Gort's chief of staff, Lieutenant-General
Pownall, to the War Office in London on 19 May. Gort had just had
a visit from a depressed General Billotte; the two men had discussed
the possibility of closing the dangerous gap created by the panzers
by means of strong counter-attacks, but Gort soon realized that:
'Clearly he had little hope that they would be effective ... I was
unable to verify that the French had enough reserves at their disposal
south of the gap to enable them to stage counter-attacks sufficiently
strong to warrant the expectation that the gap would be closed.'[2]

In Gort's view, this left the Allied armies in the north with two
alternatives. Either they could fall back on the line of the river
Somme – a move that might have disastrous consequences, for it
would mean that the Belgian Army would have to abandon its own
territory to fall in with the plan or else go on fighting alone, with the
certainty of early defeat – or they could retreat towards the Channel
ports and there form a secure bridgehead from which the British
Expeditionary Force could be evacuated if the situation demanded
it.

These were the proposals telephoned to the War Office by
Pownall; the French Army monitoring service eavesdropped on the
conversation and passed on the information to General Georges,
laying emphasis on the remarks concerning the possible evacuation
of the BEF. It was the French General Staff's first inkling that the
British were seriously considering such a move.

What the French did not know was that even at this stage the
British Government, still failing to realize the gravity of the situ-
ation, had already rejected Gort's proposal for a withdrawal on the
Channel ports. The chief of the Imperial General Staff, Field
Marshal Lord Ironside, had told a meeting of the War Cabinet late
on the nineteenth that he was flatly opposed to any such plan,
advocating that a retreat southwards from Belgian territory offered
the best solution. Churchill's War Cabinet agreed, and within hours
Ironside was on his way to France with the appropriate instructions.
He arrived at Boulogne in the early hours of 20 May, and reached
Gort's command post at Wahagnies at 06.00. By 08.00 he was in

conference with Gort, and it was only now that he realized the impossibility of a swing to the south; the Germans had advanced faster and further than anyone had anticipated, and it was too late. If the seven divisions of the BEF abandoned their defensive positions along the river Escaut – to which they had retreated from the Dyle in the past few days – and marched south at this juncture they would run headlong into the panzer divisions that were spearing towards the coast, and would in all probability be destroyed.

It was not yet too late, however, to hope that a major French counter-offensive from the south might sever the neck of the German 'tortoise'; neither Gort nor Ironside yet realized the complete chaos that attended the French armies south of the panzer corridor. They felt that if the French were in a position to mount a counter-offensive, the BEF could assist it greatly by striking a blow southwards with the Expeditionary Force's two remaining divisions, the 5th and 50th, supported by tanks. The attack would preferably be launched around Arras, against which a German advanced guard was thought to be moving. In fact, the 'advanced guard' was Rommel's 7th Panzer Division, supported by the ss Totenkopf (Death's Head) Motorized Infantry Division, although the British did not know this at the time. The overall plan, therefore, was to extend the British defensive line southwards past Arras, cutting through whatever enemy units were encountered and at the same time relieving the threat to the town's garrison. It was clear that any British effort along these lines would be strictly limited, but Gort resolved to implement the plan in the absence of any further orders from the French.

After his conference with Gort, Ironside – accompanied by General Pownall – set off to find General Billotte at the latter's headquarters under Vimy Ridge, near Lens. After a tortuous journey over roads crammed with refugees they located both Billotte and General Blanchard, commanding the French First Army. Ironside was horrified to find that the French generals appeared to have lost their nerve completely. Billotte, in particular seemed to be on the edge of a nervous breakdown, his whole body trembling; he was in the grip of deep despair. Ironside, towering head and shoulders over the Frenchman, seized him by the tunic in exasperation and shook him in an effort to bring him round. He finally persuaded the reluctant Billotte to agree to a French counter-attack towards Cambrai in support of the British push at Arras, but he left Lens shortly afterwards without much conviction that the French would lend much support, if any.[3]

Gort agreed completely, and went ahead with the plan for an independent British attack at Arras. To co-ordinate the operation he selected Major-General Harold Franklyn, commanding the 5th Division. On paper the troops at Franklyn's disposal consisted of his own 5th Division and Major-General G. le Q. Martel's 50th, together with the 1st Army Tank Brigade, but in reality Franklyn's command – known as 'Frankforce' – was much smaller. For various reasons each of the infantry divisions could field only two brigades each instead of the usual three, while the Tank Brigade – which had a hundred tanks on its inventory – could muster seventy-three. Of these, only sixteen were Mk II 'Matildas', armed with a two-pounder gun; the rest were Mk Is, armed with medium machine-guns.

The planning went on throughout the twentieth. Franklyn was not told that the primary object of his attack was to support a possible French counter-offensive from the south; his orders were principally to 'support the garrison in Arras and to block the roads south of Arras, thus cutting off the German communications (via Arras) from the east'.

During Ironside's earlier visit to Billotte at Lens, the commander of Army Group One had promised that French support for Frank-force's mission would take the form of an attack towards Cambrai by two divisions of General René Altmayer's V Corps, but by 18.00 on the twentieth no liaison officer from V Corps had arrived at head-quarters to discuss co-ordination. In fact shortly after Ironside's visit Billotte had sent an emissary to Altmayer to urge the latter to co-operate fully with the British, but the emissary – Major Vautrin – had found Altmayer prostrate on his bed, in tears.

Altmayer pulled himself together somewhat and told Vautrin that it was impossible to attack on the twenty-first, as the British wished; one of the French divisions scheduled to take part, the 25th Motorized, had no hope of being in position before the twenty-second. Later, Vautrin reported to Blanchard:

In spite of the fact that I had told him of General Gort's insistence
that the attacks should begin next day, since in front of Douai
and Arras there was only the rear of the German armoured
divisions, and that the main body of normal divisions had not yet
entered the area, General Altmayer, who seemed tired out and
thoroughly disheartened ... told me that one should see things as
they are, that the troops had buggered off, that he was ready to
accept all the consequences of his refusal and go and get himself
killed at the head of a battalion, but he would no longer continue
to sacrifice the army corps of which he had already lost nearly
half.'[4]

It was nearly midnight when Gort learned, by letter from
Blanchard, of Altmayer's negative reaction. The best v Corps
commander could do was to provide cover for Frankforce's western
flank with the aid of detachments of the 3rd Light Armoured
Division, under General Prioux. Neither could Gort secure any
promise of air support for the operation; the French Northern Air
Operations Zone had been notified but had not been supplied with
any times or targets, and the RAF's Advanced Air Striking Force in
France was so depleted after the fearful losses it had sustained during
the first week of the campaign as to be virtually ineffective. Nevertheless Gort was determined to carry out the plan. Frankforce would
launch its attack at 14.00 hours on 21 May.

Meanwhile, on the night of the twentieth to the twenty-first,
General Weygand was snatching a few hours' sleep at Vincennes
after having finalized – or so he thought – the arrangements for his
flight north the following morning. It was with considerable anger
that he learned, on arrival at Le Bourget, that no one had been
given details of the mission. Calming down somewhat, he held an
impromptu briefing in a hangar with Captain Lafitte, his pilot, and
Captain Veniel, leading the fighter escort.[5] First of all they would
set course for Abbeville, following the valley of the Somme, then
turn towards Cambrai or Valenciennes. They would then make a
reconnaissance of the Lens-Béthune area, landing at Norrent-
Fontès to refuel. GHQ had arranged for Weygand to be picked up
there and taken by road to Ypres for his meeting with the Allied

commanders. Altitude for the flight was to be 2,500 feet, out of range of enemy small-arms fire and below the level of most medium and heavy flak.

Weygand's Amiot took off at exactly 09.00. The eight fighters of the escort slipped protectively into place above it and on either side. The sky was cloudless, with near-perfect visibility. The formation passed over Beauvais airfield; shortly afterwards there was a nasty moment when the pilots spotted three German Dornier 17 bombers, escorted by a dozen Messerschmitts, above and to the right. The enemy formation, however, maintained a steady course towards the south and quickly disappeared.

Poix slid by on the starboard side, and now the pilots began to see the first real signs of war. The autoroute leading south from the town was jammed solid with vehicles of every description, ranging from heavy lorries to horse-drawn carts; a panic-stricken exodus was under way. The scene of confusion fell behind as the aircraft droned over the lush, dark green landscape of the Somme valley. Ahead of them a haze of smoke hung over the horizon; underneath it lay Abbeville, and heavy fighting seemed to be going on around the town. The sight came as a severe shock to the Frenchmen; they had not realized that the panzers had advanced so far. The roads beneath were once again congested, this time with armour and military transport. The stark black crosses on the roofs and turrets of the vehicles left no doubt as to their identity.

The aircraft turned north-east towards Arras. Tracer drifted up lazily from a concentration of enemy armour, and a moment later clusters of black puffs burst around the formation as the 20-mm flak opened up. Splinters ripped through the Amiot, a few feet from where Weygand was sitting at the navigator's plotting table, intent on his maps. He never even raised his head. Lafitte opened the throttles and the bomber surged forward, leaving the danger behind.

The formation passed to the south of Arras, over more military convoys. Although fires were burning here and there, the town itself was quiet and there was no sign of fighting; Frankforce's counter-offensive in the Arras sector had not yet developed. Cambrai, a few miles further on, presented a different picture. The centre of the town was in flames and fighting appeared to be in progress in the surrounding countryside, although the drifting pall of smoke made it hard to see exactly what was happening. A lot of flak started to come up and the formation turned west, heading for Norrent-Fontès, near the Belgian border.

The Amiot touched down without incident on Norrent-Fontès airfield while the fighter escort circled watchfully overhead. Then the fighters came in; one's undercarriage refused to come down and the pilot made a belly landing, climbing unhurt from the cockpit. He would continue his journey in the bomber.

Captain Veniel went over to where Weygand and the bomber crew were standing. The general was in a towering rage. GHQ had informed him that an Air Force group was still based there; it turned out that the group had departed three days ago. Norrent-Fontès' only inhabitant was a small and incredibly scruffy private, who now stood off to one side looking overawed by the close proximity of so much gold braid. When the group left, he had been told to stay behind and look after the airfield's fuel dump pending further orders. The orders had not arrived, but he had stolidly remained at his post. Veniel accompanied him to the fuel dump; it contained 20,000 litres of petrol, stacked in 20-litre drums. The pilots descended on it and were soon hard at work refuelling their machines.

Meanwhile Weygand and his aide had set out in search of a telephone, driven by the little soldier in a broken-down truck that was the airfield's sole remaining transport. In a nearby village they found a post office, from where Weygand eventually managed to get through to Army Group One. Over a badly distorted line, he learned that General Billotte had sent out cars to search for him – but no one knew in which direction.

Back at Norrent-Fontès, the pilots were awaiting Weygand's return. Suddenly, a car drove up in a cloud of dust and a French army officer jumped out. The man seemed panic-stricken.

'What are you doing here? The Boches are only ten kilometres away, and they're advancing at sixty kilometres an hour. Get out, while you still can.'

Veniel asked the man if he had seen anything of Weygand. The officer became even more agitated.

'How am I supposed to recognize anyone in this muck-up? If he's gone towards Hazebrouck he's been taken prisoner, that's for sure. Go on, get out! You haven't much time.'

The officer ran back to his car and drove off at high speed. The pilots looked at one another, torn by uncertainty. What if Weygand had been taken prisoner, and the Germans were as close as the staff officer had indicated? At any moment the Stukas might appear overhead and blast their aircraft into smoking wreckage.

They waited for twenty minutes, their nerves in knots. Veniel was about to give the order to take off when a vehicle came lurching round the hangars; it was the little soldier's truck. Weygand and his aide got out, the general in obvious distress.

'Captain,' he said to Veniel, 'the situation is lamentable. I had never dreamed that such chaos existed. The roads are so clogged that movement is almost impossible. We must keep cool, or we're finished.'

Weygand pondered for a few moments, poring over his map. Finally, he decided to take off for the airfield at Saint-Inglevert, near Calais. It was just possible that the transport sent out by Billotte might be waiting for him there.

The formation was airborne by noon. A few minutes later they sighted the Channel, with Boulogne over on the left. Veniel noticed a forest of barrage balloons over the port. With Calais dead ahead the formation let down slowly towards Saint-Inglevert, the Amiot landing first. It was only when Veniel taxied in that he saw the bomb craters that pitted the airfield. The Stukas had been here; it was a miracle that the Amiot and its escorting fighters had landed safely.

Weygand came over and shook each pilot by the hand. He instructed them to wait for him until 19.00 hours; if he had not returned by that time they were to fly back to Le Bourget. Then the general set off into Calais in a car his aide had somehow managed to commandeer.

The pilots pushed their aircraft into the shelter of some bombed-out hangars and settled down to wait, smoking nervously. From time to time formations of German bombers cruised overhead, their passage followed by the drum-roll of explosions in Calais. 19.00 hours came, and there was no sign of Weygand. The pilots waited for another hour, then took off and set course for Paris. Their mission was over; what had become of the general was no longer their concern. It was enough that they were returning to base in one piece.

On leaving Saint-Inglevert Weygand had, in fact, gone to the *Hôtel de ville* in Calais, which served as the Allied headquarters. There he found General Champon, head of the French Military Mission to the Belgian Army, who told him that King Leopold would be waiting for him in Ypres town hall at 15.00 hours. Weygand completed his journey in a staff car over roads fearfully congested with refugees, finally arriving at Ypres shortly before 16.00. King Leopold was there, together with members of his general staff and some cabinet ministers, but both Lord Gort and General Billotte were absent. The only British representative present was Admiral Sir Roger Keyes, who was attached to King Leopold but who had no military authority.

In the course of the next four hours Weygand held three separate meetings with the Belgians. The first took the form of a confrontation between Weygand and Leopold, the latter supported by his ADC, General van Overstraeten. Weygand insisted that the Belgian Army's defences along the river Escaut were too thinly stretched and urged the Belgians to retreat further west as soon as possible, taking over and strengthening part of the line held by the British Expeditionary Force. This would enable the British to release two divisions to take part in Weygand's projected offensive southwards. Leopold objected on the grounds that his army was exhausted after the strenuous forced marches it had made over the past few days; through General van Overstraeten, he put forward a tentative plan to fall back on Ostend, where his forces would form 'a vast bridgehead'. Once again Weygand tried to persuade the king to change his mind, stressing that in 1914 the Belgian Army had successfully fallen back and put up a stout defence on the line of the river Yser; they could do so again. This, however, would mean abandoning all but a few square miles of Belgian territory, and would create a tremendous logistics problem in that all the Belgian Army's stores would have to be moved to new depots at short notice. Then there was the problem of the refugees, who had brought the movement of military traffic to a virtual standstill; food supplies were also becoming critical, with sufficient stocks of flour in Belgium to last only another two weeks.

This first meeting ended with no decision having been reached; Leopold promised merely to consider Weygand's proposals and advise the general of his decision later. Weygand had the distinct impression that the king had already resigned himself to defeat, and according to the Belgian premier, M. Pierlot – who saw Leopold a few minutes later – 'The king considered the position of the armies in Flanders almost, if not quite, hopeless.'

At this juncture General Billotte arrived, having spent several hours on Weygand's trail. He was accompanied by General Fagalde, commander of the French XVI Corps. Weygand lost no time in outlining his scheme to Billotte; it involved a drive southwards by the French First Army from Cambrai in conjunction with an offensive northwards by French forces from the Somme, the two arms of the pincer to meet in the region of Bapaume. Billotte, harrassed and weary, pointed out that the First Army was in no condition to launch a major attack; indeed, it could barely hold its own against the German onslaught. In Billotte's opinion, only the British Expeditionary Force was still sufficiently battleworthy to carry out a large-scale offensive operation.

Everything now hinged on Lord Gort's attitude and appraisal of the situation; but Gort had still not appeared. Weygand waited for the British commander until 19.00, and was debating whether to stay the night in Ypres when Admiral Abrial, commanding the French Naval Forces (North), arrived with the warning that it would no longer be possible for Weygand to fly out because of heavy enemy bombing attacks on the few remaining serviceable airfields in the area. Abrial had placed a 600-ton torpedo-boat at Weygand's disposal and the general joined it after dark at Dunkirk. An air raid was in progress and the boat had a harrowing passage out of the harbour, travelling at full speed amid geysers of water thrown up by exploding bombs. The boat eventually reached Cherbourg as dawn was breaking, and from there Weygand continued his journey to Paris by road. He arrived in the capital at 10.00 on 22 May.

The previous afternoon, while Weygand was still making his tortuous way north, Frankforce's counter-offensive at Arras had unfolded on schedule. It was carried out by a force much reduced in size from that originally envisaged, consisting of two territorial battalions of the Durham Light Infantry and two tank battalions, with weak detachments of Prioux's Cavalry Corps providing flank cover, the whole supported by a field battery of the Royal Artillery and an anti-tank battery.

Led by Major-General Martel, the force struck southwards round the west of Arras in two mobile columns, its objective to reach the Cojeul river by nightfall. The right-hand column ran into opposition almost at once, coming up against motorized infantry of Rommel's 7th Panzer in the village of Duisans. The village was taken after a stiff fight and two companies of infantry were detached to hold it. The rest of the column pushed on to capture Warlus and Berneville, advancing as far as the Arras–Doullens road; here, the infantry were pinned down by heavy German mortar and machine-gun fire. The Luftwaffe also took a hand, the Stukas bombing the British positions unopposed. There was no Allied air cover. Martel's tanks, however, carried out a manoeuvre round the left flank and swept down on the village of Wailly, where they raced full tilt into the ss Totenkopf Motorized Infantry Division which had just arrived. The sudden appearance of the British tanks sowed panic among the German troops, who suffered heavy losses in the ensuing confusion. Soon afterwards, however, the tanks were stopped by a battery of German 88-mm guns, firing over open sights, and were forced to withdraw leaving several of their number in flames.

The left-hand column, meanwhile, had enjoyed better fortune, its armour virtually wiping out a motorized column at Dainville and leaving the supporting infantry to round up over four hundred prisoners – the largest 'bag' of enemy troops in a single engagement since the campaign began. The column pushed on rapidly and some of its advanced units actually reached the Cojeul, but the main body of the armour – the tanks of the Fourth Royal Tank Regiment – became involved in a fierce fight with Rommel's forces and, without supporting infantry, had to relinquish the ground they had won.

By the end of the afternoon it was clear that the forces committed to the British counter-attack – which had advanced ten miles – were in no position to hold the ground they had gained. Moreover Rommel's armoured division was recovering quickly from its surprise and would soon be driving on around Arras to threaten the British rear west of the town. General Franklyn, therefore, saw no alternative other than to abandon the operation; he had received no orders to the contrary, and in fact had received no instructions at all from GHQ since his meeting with Gort the previous evening.

At the time, Franklyn had no way of knowing the full extent of the impact made on the enemy by Frankforce's relatively puny counter-attack. It was by far the most determined opposition so far encountered by the Germans, and quite apart from the material losses inflicted on Rommel's forces the British blow presented the German High Command with a strong psychological shock, especially as it was generally believed that the British effort had involved no fewer than five divisions. Field Marshal von Rundstedt, commanding Army Group A, later stated that: 'A critical moment in the drive came just as my forces had reached the Channel. It was caused by a British counter-stroke southward from Arras on 21 May. For a short time it was feared that our armoured divisions would be cut off before the infantry divisions could come up to support them. None of the French counter-attacks carried any serious threat as this one did.'

Rundstedt, in fact, was so alarmed by the Arras operation that he ordered a temporary halt to the movement of von Kleist's armoured group towards Calais and instructed the 6th and 8th Panzer to swing back towards Arras to counter a threat that no longer existed. Meanwhile Rommel's supporting infantry were instructed to move up to the Arras area with all speed. The British attack was reflected throughout the German command, even up to Hitler himself, in a new mood of nervousness and caution which was to have a far-reaching effect on the events of the next few days.

As far as Lord Gort was concerned, however, the counter-attack had failed, and failure meant the end of any hope of a breakthrough to the south; he was not aware of Weygand's efforts to contact him. The previous evening he had received a copy of a signal from Churchill to Admiral Keyes, advising the latter that Weygand intended to visit King Leopold, but since then there had been no

further word. Weygand's subsequent messages to Gort appeared to
have gone astray, which was hardly surprising in the general
communications chaos. General van Overstraeten had also tried to
reach Gort by telephone, without any success, and in the end had
set out to search for him by car, together with Admiral Keyes. They
drove to Hazebrouck, where Gort was reported to have his command
post, but it was no longer there; they located it an hour later at
Prémesques, between Lille and Armentières. They picked up the
BEF commander and took him back to Ypres, only to find that
Weygand had departed an hour earlier.

Gort learned the details of Weygand's projected offensive secondhand from General Billotte; the Englishman was far from enthusi-
astic, pointing out that the Arras counter-attack had fallen short of
expectations (or so it was then believed) and that the BEF's reserves
were now fully committed. But the Belgians had reluctantly agreed
to co-operate by withdrawing to the river Lys, and Gort was
strongly urged to lend his support by General Fagalde; the latter had
seen considerable service as a liaison officer with the other BEF of
1914, rising to the post of French military attaché in London four
years later, and he knew enough about the British troops and their
capabilities to realize that their full participation represented the
only chance of success for Weygand's scheme, however slight.

In the end Gort gave in; the only alternative to the march south
was still a general withdrawal to the Channel ports, and this was
likely to be a risky venture. The German tanks had already reached
the sea at Abbeville and were now menacing Calais and Boulogne.
If the Belgians would take over the left of the British line, he con-
ceded, relieving the 44th Division, and the French the right, releasing the 2nd and 48th Divisions, it might just be possible to mount
an offensive – but not before the twenty-sixth, for in his estimation
it would take four days for the Allies to complete their movements.

So the meeting ended, with no satisfactory conclusion having
been reached; the best that could be hoped for was a compromise.
Gort and Billotte set out for their respective headquarters, distinctly
unhappy men who both sensed a tragedy in the making. For Billotte,
the tragedy was more immediate; on the way back to Béthune his
car skidded and crashed into the back of a lorry. Billotte sustained

severe head injuries and died two days later without regaining consciousness. His accident was a mortal blow to the Allied cause, for he was the only senior Allied commander who had been able to discuss the projected counter-offensive at first hand with both Gort and Weygand; with his death, any real hopes of co-ordination were shattered. To make matters even worse, it was another three days before the dithering French High Command appointed a successor to command Army Group One in the shape of General Blanchard, formerly commander of the First Army; his place in that capacity was taken by the able cavalry leader, General Prioux.

Meanwhile in Paris the French Government had at last begun to wake up to the full gravity of the situation. Standing before the Senate in the afternoon of 21 May, the lonely figure of Paul Reynaud had catalogued the disasters that had befallen France's armies in the north to an assembly that seemed torn between horror, bewilderment and stark disbelief. Now the *députés*, who had themselves been wrapped in apathetic slumber for so long, were clamouring for blood like jackals and demanding the summary punishment of those they held responsible for France's grief; men such as General Corap, commander of the hapless and broken Ninth Army, whose principal 'crime' was that he had adhered to a strategy that had become outmoded with the advent of the armoured assault group and the dive-bomber. Reynaud promised justice, and action too; for the honour of France now rested on the shoulders of two great men – Philippe Pétain, hero of the defence of Verdun in 1916, and Maxime Weygand, who possessed 'the secrets of Marshal Foch'. Somehow, these men were to perform the miracles that would rescue France from her position of grave peril.[6]

How the miracle was to be achieved was by no means clear. Nevertheless when Weygand returned to Paris on the morning of the twenty-second – much to Reynaud's relief, for he had feared that the general might have been captured, he seemed highly optimistic as he outlined his plans to the premier. Shortly afterwards Winston Churchill arrived, having flown to Paris together with Lord Ismay, head of the military wing of the War Cabinet secretariat, and General Sir John Dill, who was soon to take over from Ironside as CIGS. In the planning room of the French GHQ at Vincennes Churchill

B

had his first meeting with Weygand, who impressed him greatly. The British visitors listened intently as Weygand described the battle situation as he understood it following his trip to Ypres, and readily agreed with his scheme for a counter-offensive. Weygand accordingly sat down to draft the plan in detail, under the heading of 'General Operation No. 1'. The text ran:

(i) The forces grouped with No. 1 Army Group (the Belgian Army, the BEF and the First Army) will make it their principal task to block the German advance to the sea in order to maintain contact between themselves and the remainder of the French forces.

(ii) The German Army will only be stopped and beaten by counter-attacks.

(iii) The forces necessary for these counter-attacks already exist in the group, the linear defence of which is much too densely held, and they are:

some infantry divisions of the First Army

the Cavalry Corps

the BEF, which must be withdrawn from the line by extending the Belgian sector, and used as a whole.

These counter-attacks will be supported by all the RAF based in France.

(iv) This offensive will be covered on the east by the Belgian Army on the Yser.

The light enemy units which are trying to cause disruption and panic in our rear between the frontier and the Somme, supported by air raids on our aerodromes and ports, are in a dangerous position and will be destroyed.

The draft shows just how far Weygand's appraisal of the situation was divorced from reality. For a start, the Belgians had agreed to withdraw to the Lys, not the Yser, and this manoeuvre could not be completed before the twenty-sixth; and the 'light enemy units' referred to by Weygand were in fact seven panzer divisions, hardly a token force that could be brushed aside lightly.

Once begun, the myth of Allied strength and German vulnerability gained stature with incredible speed – albeit briefly.

Churchill fell for it hook, line and sinker, as is revealed by the telegram he dispatched to Lord Gort that afternoon:

> I flew to Paris this morning with Dill and others. The conclusions which were reached between Reynaud, Weygand, and ourselves are summarized below. They accord exactly with general directions you have received from the War Office. You have our best wishes in the vital battle now opening towards Bapaume and Cambrai.
>
> It was agreed –
>
> 1 That the Belgian Army should withdraw to the line of the Yser and stand there, the sluices being opened.
>
> 2 That the British Army and the French First Army should attack south-west towards Bapaume and Cambrai at the earliest moment, certainly tomorrow, with about eight divisions, and with the Belgian Cavalry Corps on the right of the British.
>
> 3 That as the battle is vital to both armies and the British communications depend on freeing Amiens, the British Air Force should give the utmost possible help, both by day and by night, while it is going on.
>
> 4 That the new French Army Group which is advancing upon Amiens and forming a line along the Somme should strike northwards and join hands with the British divisions who are attacking southwards in the general direction of Bapaume.[7]

But there was no new French Army Group advancing on Amiens. Behind the Somme, along a ninety-mile line stretching from the coast to the Crozat Canal, there were merely five hastily-assembled divisions that constituted the embryo Seventh Army under General Frère, with two badly battered light cavalry divisions and the British 1st Armoured Division, which up to now had seen no action. The 'advance on Amiens', in fact, did not begin until 05.30 on the twenty-third, and it was carried out by a single division – the 7th Colonial – supported by a squadron of tanks. The 7th Colonial was assigned the impossible task of seizing the Amiens bridges, paving the way for a push northwards across the Somme by the 4th Armoured Division under a relatively unknown young officer named Colonel Charles de Gaulle.

Four miles from Amiens, the attack petered out. Of the eighteen supporting tanks, twelve were knocked out by the wicked 88-millimetres that were now being used in the anti-tank role everywhere on the battlefield. So the assault from the south died, predictably, almost before it had got under way. One by one, the plans still being pored over with enthusiasm in the mausoleum of France's past military glory at Vincennes were being torn to shreds.

2 Fateful Decisions, 23–26 May

On the morning of 22 May the attack in the Cambrai sector by units of the French First Army – which General Billotte, under Ironside's urging, had promised would take place in conjunction with the British counter-offensive at Arras the day before – finally got under way. Entrusted to General René Altmayer's v Corps, it was a much-reduced effort compared with the two-division thrust originally envisaged. Altmayer's hastily-conceived plan had called for an attack by General Molinié's 25th Motorized Division, but in the event two of the division's regiments were ordered to stay in their positions and hold the Arleux-Bouchain sector along the Sensée canal, the attack itself being carried out only by the centre regiment, the 121st Infantry, supported by two reconnaissance groups.

With this drastically whittled-down force there was no longer much hope of taking Cambrai, and the plan now was to form a bridgehead two-and-a-half miles deep south of the Sensée; if the initial attack was successful the remainder of the 25th Division would then move over into the bridgehead and consolidate in readiness for a drive southwards through Cambrai.

The attack by the 121st Regiment, conducted by General Molinié himself, began at 09.00 on the twenty-second, the troops striking from east of Douai towards Cambrai and cutting through widely-dispersed units of the German 32nd Infantry Division which had recently moved up to the south of the Sensée canal. By 10.00 the French troops had secured their primary objective, and an armoured reconnaissance group had penetrated as far as the outskirts of Cambrai. There, however, the French tanks were halted by the determined bombing and strafing of Luftwaffe ground-attack aircraft. Despite this setback the French held their positions in the bridgehead all day, encountering only sporadic opposition, and the stage seemed set for the planned move of the remainder of the 25th Division.

Then, at 21.00, General Altmayer sent for Molinié. To the latter's amazement, he was ordered to withdraw his troops from the bridgehead immediately, back to their original start line behind the Sensée; it appeared that German reinforcements had been seen moving up fast to the Cambrai sector and First Army HQ had, to put it bluntly, got the wind up. So the 121st was to pull out, destroying the canal bridges as it went. The operation was carried out in extreme secrecy in the small hours of the twenty-third, and the Germans were unaware that the French had gone. Shortly after dawn, Molinié's troops on the opposite bank of the canal could see enemy dive-bombers attacking the positions they had recently vacated.

When news of the French attack and its negative result reached Lord Gort, who had not been informed of it until it began, the BEF's commander became utterly convinced that there was no longer any possibility of a coherent Allied stand against the Germans in the north. It was a feeling that had been growing steadily over the past three days, particularly since his receipt of the directives from both Weygand and Churchill ordering him to mount a counter-offensive with forces that no longer existed. A counter-attack southwards with eight divisions, as stipulated in Churchill's telegram to Gort following the British premier's meeting with Reynaud on the twenty-second, was completely out of the question, for the whole of the French First Army was able to muster only eight divisions at the outside, and as far as the BEF was concerned the only two divisions that might have been available – the 5th and 50th, which were normally held in reserve – were now fully committed at Arras. To require all these divisions suddenly to swing southwards, literally turning their backs on a powerful enemy, was both ludicrous and suicidal, for the third Allied force confronting von Bock's Army Group B – the Belgian Army – was already on the verge of collapse. Moreover Billotte was dying, his successor had still not been confirmed, and the Allied commanders in the north were moving from one command post to another under continual enemy air attack;

with communications generally in a shambles, the prospects of co-ordinating an operation of any kind were slim indeed.

Yet in his sanctuary at Vincennes Weygand clung to the illusion that Gort and General Blanchard were in full collusion with one another, and that on this very day – the twenty-third – were preparing to launch his mythical counter-attack. On the morning of the twenty-third, however, Gort had received no battle orders of any kind, and he accordingly sent a telegram to the Secretary of State for War, Anthony Eden, voicing his misgivings. He stressed the vital need for co-operation between the British, French and Belgian commanders in the north, and gave the opinion that any Allied advance could only be in the nature of a sortie, rather than a full-scale counter-attack. The forces in the north had not sufficient supplies and ammunition to undertake a serious assault; in fact, the entire BEF had just been placed on half rations.

Gort's telegram appeared to have some effect in stripping away at least part of the aura of false hope that had surrounded the British War Cabinet since Churchill's meeting with the French leaders. It resulted in an immediate protest from Churchill to Reynaud, which was worded as follows: 'Communications of Northern Armies have been cut by strong enemy armoured forces. Salvation of these armies can only be obtained by immediate execution of Weygand's plan. I demand the issue to the French commanders in north and south and Belgian GHQ of the most stringent orders to carry this out and turn defeat into victory. Time is vital as supplies are short.'[1]

Shortly after sending this telegram Churchill reported to the War Cabinet on the situation as he now saw it, pointing out that the success of the Weygand plan depended entirely on the French taking the initiative, which so far they showed no signs of doing. The twenty-third went by with still no sign of any firm instructions from French GHQ to the armies in the north, and no apparent major French activity either north or south of the panzer corridor. The situation prompted Churchill to send off a second telegram on the twenty-fourth, this time to Weygand via Reynaud:

General Gort wires that co-ordination of northern front is essential with armies of three different nations. He says he cannot undertake this co-ordination, as he is already fighting north and south and is threatened on his lines of communications. At the same time Sir Roger Keyes tells me that up to 3 p.m. today (23rd) Belgian Headquarters and King had received no directive. How does this agree with your statement that Blanchard and Gort are *main dans la main*? Appreciate fully difficulties of communication, but feel no effective concert of operations in northern area, against which enemy are concentrating. Trust you will be able to rectify this. Gort further says that any advance by him must be in the nature of a sortie, and that relief must come from south, as he has not (repeat not) ammunition for serious attack. Nevertheless, we are instructing him to persevere in carrying out your plan. We have not here even seen your own directive, and have no knowledge of the details of your northern operations . . .'[2]

At the same time, Gort had at last received some reassurance in the form of a telegram from Eden, which ran: 'Should . . . situation on your communications make this [Weygand Plan] at any time impossible you should inform us so that we can inform French and make naval and air arrangements to assist you should you have to withdraw on the northern coast.'

In Gort's terms of reference, it was the 'get-out clause' for the BEF which, in his eyes, was already long overdue in its implementation. In thirty-five years of military life, ever since joining the Grenadier Guards as a subaltern in 1905, John Standish Prendergast Vereker, sixth Viscount Gort, whatever other faults he may have had, had never shirked making a decision, however hard and however grim its consequences, if he felt that circumstances warranted it. As a fighting soldier, he had two qualities that were to be of immeasurable assistance to him in this dark hour: courage (he had won the Victoria Cross, the DSO and two bars and the Military Cross in France during 1914–18, and had been wounded four times) and a marked lack of imagination that often enabled him to see a clear road through a tangled web of confusion that would have hopelessly ensnared other less forthright commanders. Now, with absolute clarity, he knew that the Weygand plan would never come to fruition, and that the only hope of saving the BEF from encirclement was to order an immediate withdrawal to the Channel coast.

The urgency was underlined by the situation at Arras, where the garrison – consisting of a hastily-assembled body of troops known as 'Petreforce' after its commander, Major-General R.L. Petre, and comprising the 1st Welsh Guards, the 5th Green Howards, the 8th Royal Northumberland Fusiliers, detachments of the 9th West Yorks, supported by artillery and a few light tanks – was in danger of being outflanked and cut off by the 5th and 7th Panzer Divisions, which were once more forging ahead. By the morning of the twenty-third only two roads out of the town remained open, and it would only be a matter of hours before these lifelines were also cut. At 07.00 on the twenty-third, therefore, Gort ordered the withdrawal of the Arras garrison and the abandonment of the town.

Second Lieutenant J.M. Whittaker, i/c the 5th Green Howards' Carrier Platoon, described the last hours in Arras and the withdrawal:

For some three hours of the morning of 23 May the Luftwaffe pounded the city as they had never done before. The damage that they did was considerable. Many buildings were demolished and some were left burning. The transport suffered badly. Vehicles that had been stowed away in garages had buildings brought down on top of them. Those that had been left out in the open suffered some knocks. Some of the carriers, for instance, had been stowed away among trees and bushes in the Square St Vaast. Two hefty trees were brought down across one of them. It was extricated, and it was a tribute to its construction that it would still go.

Our casualties amongst personnel, on the other hand, were light indeed ... D Company, for instance, who with B Company probably felt as much of the attack as anyone, had only nine serious casualties, including two killed. In all, during our three days in Arras the battalion's casualties would be somewhere round about 30, against which we could set a few, but only a few, Boche picked off here and there by riflemen.

Such an air raid seemed obviously to be the prelude to something, and there was great activity when, as soon as it was over, it was reported from D Company that what looked like a reconnaissance party had been spotted making their way down the Doullens road. They were located in a house some way beyond the road-block, whence they were explosively removed by some accurate shooting by the three-inch mortar ...

... At the CO's conference of that evening ... at least we were told 'The city will be held.' That was the position about midnight of 23/24 May, when I set off on a round of the companies. All was quiet on the railway line up at A Company. Somewhere on the railway there was a patrol out, and I met Lord Normanby (2/Lieut the Marquis of Normanby – battalion Intelligence Officer) and Lieutenant Jourd, the French liaison officer, going up to visit them. C Company, behind the Citadelle, was similarly without incident. But as I moved on from C to D Company I got the first hint that something was happening. A dispatch rider on a motor cycle came crashing through the night.

Arrived at D Company I found Captain Fred Chadwick standing in the middle of the road where the dispatch rider had left him holding a message and scratching his head. 'This is a rum thing,' he said, 'Look at it.' We moved over to a building where we could use a torch. It was an order to get out – and get out quickly ...

When I hastened back from D Company to the Palace St Vaast to find out what was happening I found that although HQ had already gone there were still a few vehicles hurriedly loading up in the Place du Theatre. Captain Herbert Dennis was with them and I asked him what was afoot. 'Make for Douai' was all that he could tell me. That seemed to be the sum of all the information that there was to be had. But somewhere, someone had said 'Make for Bailleul'. I don't know where it came from, but somehow, from somewhere, Bailleul stuck in my head. Looking back now it seems that between those two instructions lies a minor tragedy of war – major to those involved in it. But we knew nothing of that at the time; all that we knew was that we had to go and go quickly.

My own exit from Arras I shall long remember. I left the bombed and burning city standing in the front of a Bren-gun

carrier drinking a bottle of champagne. I was not celebrating . . .
I was extremely thirsty after a hectic night, and there was nothing
else to drink. They were strange times . . .

We had come into Arras through Vimy, down the Lens road.
That made it seem somehow natural that we should go out that
way. I did not know, of course, that the Germans had already
reached Lens, sweeping round to the south and west of us. But
even so, the Douai road looked something less than healthy. I
knew that the front was – or had been – along the River Scarpe,
and the main road ran right across that front. But it was possible
to get to Douai by secondary roads via Bailleul, a few miles further
to the north – and safety. Was that what was intended? In any
event, most of us never reached Douai, or got anywhere near it . . .

As we crossed the St Nicholas bridge the column took the right
fork for St Laurent Blangy and the main Douai road. It was after
we had passed through St Laurent and came to the next fork
that there was ground for real anxiety. The column of vehicles
forked right again, towards Athies; something was clearly amiss.

Dawn was just breaking; it was not possible to see far, and down
by the river to the right there was thick early-morning mist.
Through the mist and the half-light there suddenly came a stream
of tracer bullets from across the valley. Over the noise of the
vehicles slowly grinding along there was no sound of firing to be
heard. Perhaps the fire was coming from some distance away. But
what was happening was plain enough – head to tail on the narrow
road, two abreast where the track was wide enough, we were
driving in our trucks straight into the enemy . . .

To turn round a line of heavy trucks on a narrow road in the
half-light and a mist is no easy matter. But a stream of tracer
bullets ahead is a wonderful stimulus, and we had done an about-
turn in less time than I would have thought possible. The first
thing we did was to try to get up the correct Douai fork, towards
Gavrelle. There we quickly found what had happened. The road
bridge over the railway had been blown – presumably by our own
people retreating, but before we had got out. Troops on foot could
scramble down the embankment and up the other side. This was
what the leading troops and the occupants of the leading vehicles

had done. Their vehicles they had sent to do what seemed to be
the only thing possible short of retracing their route altogether –
to go round by Athies and rejoin the main road as soon as they
could. A little earlier they might have managed it, but the time
was run too fine.

The chaos on the road was now complete. Those of us at the
front were pouring back towards Arras; those behind were still
streaming east; troops and trucks, shoulder to shoulder, nose to
tail, were going in both directions at once; and between them
perplexed and perspiring drivers were trying to turn round 3-ton
lorries in a road little wider than their vehicles were long. Actually,
with the exception of the vehicles at the head of the column, the
trucks were extricated with far fewer casualties than might have
seemed possible – though not without some. One driver was
actually shot dead at the wheel of his truck. His companion just
had time to change places with him, and drove for the rest of that
day with a dead man for mate. A few that were disabled were
overrun before they could be got going again.[3]

The column retraced its steps, taking the other route that led north-
eastwards through Bailleul to Carvin. The blown bridge, in fact, had
prevented a massacre; had the column been able to continue along
its original route to Douai, it would have been cut to pieces by
strong German forces at Gavrelle. The infantry following this route
– comprising most of the 5th Green Howards and the 8th Royal
Northumberland Fusiliers – ran headlong into this enemy force and
had to fight their way through. Most escaped the trap, although
125 men of the RNF, together with their CO, were surrounded and
lost. Bringing up the rear, the 1st Welsh Guards encountered the
enemy at Athies, and while the vehicle column was turned around
the Germans were engaged by three Bren carriers under the command of Lieutenant the Hon. Christopher Furness, supported by
six light tanks. The British armoured vehicles attacked head-on in
the face of withering fire, and all were knocked out; but their
sacrifice enabled the column to make good its escape. After the
war, when the full story was revealed, Furness was awarded a
posthumous Victoria Cross.

The withdrawal of the 5th and 50th Divisions from the Arras area to a line behind the Haute Deule canal, fifteen miles to the north-east, left General Altmayer's French v Corps holding a pronounced and dangerous salient along the Sensée canal, and the French reaction to it was bitter. Their attitude was that the sudden British withdrawal, with its abandonment of the start-line for the northern phase of the Weygand offensive, indicated clearly that the BEF wanted no part of it and that this had dealt a severe blow to the morale of the French forces in the area, as well as placing them in a hazardous situation. On the political front, the immediate result was an angry telegram from Reynaud to Churchill:

You wired me this morning that you had instructed General Gort to continue to carry out the Weygand Plan. General Weygand now informs me that, according to a telegram from General Blanchard, the British Army had carried out, on its own initiative, a retreat of twenty-five miles [Author's note: This was an exaggeration] towards the ports at a time when our troops moving up from the south are gaining ground towards the north, where they were to meet their allies.

This action of the British Army is in direct opposition to the formal orders renewed this morning by General Weygand. This retreat has naturally obliged General Weygand to change all his arrangements, and he is compelled to give up the idea of closing the gap and restoring a continuous front. I need not lay any stress on the gravity of the possible consequences.[4]

But the French were not making progress from the south, and it was subsequently claimed by General E.L. Spears, who was sent by Churchill to be his personal representative to Reynaud, that the French were seizing on the British withdrawal as an excuse for the fact that no French forces had advanced from that direction. Nevertheless, there was evidence of genuine alarm in a signal sent by Weygand to Blanchard when the former first learned of Gort's move: 'You have informed me of the withdrawal decided upon and carried out by the British to the canal in the Haute Deule. If this withdrawal makes the operations as ordered impossible to carry out,

try to form as big a bridgehead as possible covering Dunkirk, which
is indispensable for administering the operations.'[5]

The news of Gort's withdrawal caused Churchill not a little
embarrassment.

My telegram last night told you all that we know over here, and
we have still heard nothing from Lord Gort to contradict it. But I
must tell you that a Staff officer has reported to the War Office
confirming the withdrawal of the two divisions from the Arras
region, which your telegram to me mentioned . . . It is clear however that the Northern Army is practically surrounded and that all
its communications are cut except through Dunkirk and Ostend.[6]

Privately, with more than a trace of anger at having been compelled to justify himself to Reynaud, Churchill asked Lord Ironside:
'I must know at earliest why Gort gave up Arras, and what actually
he is doing with the rest of his army. Is he still persevering in Weygand's plan, or has he become largely stationary? . . . Clearly, he
must not allow himself to be encircled without fighting a battle.'

A few hours later a report arrived from Sir John Dill, who had
been dispatched in haste to see Gort. Its content enabled Churchill
to inform Reynaud that:

We have every reason to believe that Gort is still persevering in
southward move. All we know is that he has been forced by the
pressure on his western flank, and to keep communication with
Dunkirk for indispensable supplies, to place parts of two divisions
between himself and the increasing pressure of the German
armoured forces . . . How can he move southward and disengage
his northern front unless he throws out this shield on his right
hand? Nothing in the movements of the BEF of which we are
aware can be any excuse for the abandonment of the strong
pressure of your northward move across the Somme, which we
trust will develop . . . You must understand that, having waited
for the southward move for a week after it became obviously
necessary, we find ourselves now ripped from the coast by the
mass of the enemy's armoured vehicles. We therefore have no
choice but to continue the southward move, using such flank
guard protection to the westward as is necessary.[7]

The Weygand Plan, in fact, was not quite dead even at this late stage; even though Gort believed that the withdrawal of the 5th and 50th Divisions would make a southward drive extremely difficult, he had agreed to work out further plans with the French, and in the evening of 24 May General Sir Ronald Adam, commanding the British III Corps, had met Generals Altmayer and Blanchard to discuss the attack. It was agreed that it might be feasible to mount an offensive with five divisions; the French 25th Motorized, 2nd North African and 5th North African, together with the British 5th and 50th, now reorganizing south of Lille following their withdrawal from Arras. Flank cover would be provided by the French Cavalry Corps and whatever British armoured units could be assembled. The divisions would assemble on the twenty-fifth, establish bridgeheads over the Sensée on the twenty-sixth, and advance towards Bapaume on the twenty-seventh. Both British divisions received their orders; the 5th to man positions on the Deule canal, the 50th to begin its move south to join up with the divisions of V Corps.

The morning of the twenty-fifth, however, brought an alarming deterioration in the general situation. It began with reports that the enemy had broken through the Belgian defences on the river Lys and were driving hard towards Ypres, threatening to cut off the British Expeditionary Force from the Belgian Army and from the coast. On the Belgian right, the commander of the British II Corps, General Brooke, was seriously worried by the rapid advance of von Reichenau's Sixth Army, and commented: 'I came to the conclusion that this was the beginning of a German offensive intended to push right through to our left rear and join up with the armoured divisions ... I am convinced that the Belgian Army is closing down.'[8]

Brooke's alarm compelled him to travel with all speed from his own HQ in Armentières to GHQ at Premesques, where he found that plans for an offensive southwards were still going ahead and that the 5th and 50th Divisions were already moving up to take part in it. Brooke managed to secure the release of the 143rd Infantry Brigade and the 12th Lancers, which were ordered to proceed to Menin, but it was clear that this scratch force would be far from adequate to protect his left flank.

Two separate events then occurred in rapid succession. First of all came the news, via General Blanchard, that General Besson, commanding the French Army Group Three in the south, no longer considered an attack northwards across the Somme to be feasible. The plan now was for the French forces to line the Somme and establish themselves in depth. The second event, at 17.30 in the afternoon of 25 May, was a telephoned report from General Adam to Lord Gort stating that Altmayer's v Corps could now provide only one division for the thrust from the north, instead of the three promised earlier. It was the final nail in the coffin of the Weygand Plan, and as it was hammered home it seemed as though a tremendous burden had been lifted from Lord Gort's shoulders. No longer was he torn between loyalty to his French allies and his overwhelming primary duty of keeping the BEF intact; he saw now, clearly, what had to be done. Summoning Major-General Franklyn, he informed him that instead of attacking southwards his 5th Division was to establish a defensive line along the Ypres–Comines canal, acting as a shield for the further withdrawal of the BEF towards the coast. A few hours later, at 22.30, General Blanchard – after conferring with Gort and the Belgians – issued the following order: 'The First Army, the British and the Belgian Armies will regroup behind the Aa canal, the Lys and contributory canal, in such a manner as to form a bridgehead to cover a large area around Dunkirk.' This effectively meant that the Allied armies in the north would now be confined in a salient bounded by an eastern arc between Bruges and Ypres, held by the Belgians, a southern arc established on the Sensée, and a western arc on the line of canals from Douai to Gravelines. At their backs would be the English Channel. There was no longer any doubt that, consequent to these new orders, only one thing could save the armies trapped in the north: evacuation.

Meanwhile in the south-west other events were taking place and other decisions made which were to have a far-reaching effect on the days to come, and which would contribute directly to the salvation of hundreds of thousands of fighting men in the great exodus that would go down in history as the miracle of Dunkirk.

3 Holding Action: Boulogne and Calais, 19–26 May

On 17 May, with Arras threatened by the rapid advance of two German panzer divisions, it was decided to move the British GHQ from that town to a safer location. The following day GHQ's considerable administrative element entrained for Boulogne, while the operational element prepared to move to Hazebrouck. By the night of 18/19 May the situation on the BEF's front had deteriorated to such an extent that Lord Gort issued an order for the evacuation of all 'useless mouths' to begin immediately from Boulogne, Calais and Dunkirk.

By far the greatest number of these 'useless mouths' – sick and wounded in base hospitals, Pay Corps personnel, surplus chaplains and the like – were in the Boulogne area, and the responsibility for their evacuation and for the defence of the port rested on the shoulders of Lieutenant-General Sir Douglas Brownrigg, Gort's adjutant-general. Establishing his headquarters in Boulogne's Hôtel Imperial, Brownrigg set about making his arrangements with considerable urgency, which was just as well; Guderian's plunging armour was to give him little time for hesitation.

On 20 May, while Rommel's armour was preparing to bypass Arras – unaware of the impending British counter-attack – Guderian's tanks in the south jumped off from the Cambrai–Peronne line before dawn, capturing Amiens at 09.00 and establishing a bridgehead four miles deep on the south bank of the Somme. Meanwhile, on Guderian's right flank, the 2nd Panzer Division had thrust out from Albert through Doullens, Bernaville and Beaumetz; at 07.00 it took Abbeville and pushed out a single tank battalion which reached the coast at Noyelles shortly before nightfall.

There the Germans halted, for Panzer Group Kleist had as yet received no instructions concerning the future employment of its armoured divisions. Guderian's dash to the sea had apparently taken the Oberkommando der Wehrmacht somewhat by surprise, and the whole of 21 May was spent in waiting for further orders. It was not until early evening that Guderian was ordered to continue the advance in a northerly direction, with the capture of the Channel ports as his objective. His immediate plan was to throw the newly-arrived 10th Panzer Division straight into a rapid advance on Dunkirk via St Omer, while the 1st Panzer Division moved on Calais and the 2nd on Boulogne. Then, as a direct result of the British counter-attack at Arras, 10th Panzer was withdrawn from his command on von Kleist's orders at 6.00 on the twenty-second and was held back as Panzer Group reserve. Guderian at once requested that he be given control of all three divisions for the advance on the Channel ports; the request was turned down, and consequently the drive on Dunkirk had to be abandoned.[1]

The modified advance began at dawn on 22 May, with the 1st Panzer supported by the Grossdeutschland Infantry Regiment heading for Calais and the 2nd Panzer moving up the coast towards Boulogne. Neither of the armoured divisions was at full strength, since Guderian had been compelled to leave units of both behind to secure the Somme bridgeheads until the arrival of XIV Army Corps, following hard on the heels of the racing panzers.

It was not long before the 2nd Panzer encountered resistance in the shape of the French 21st Infantry Division, commanded by General Lanquetot. These troops had been on their way south to join the new Seventh Army on the Somme when they found their way blocked by the Germans at Abbeville; Lanquetot at once turned back towards Boulogne, where he received orders from Army Group One to defend a line between Samer and Neufchatel, on the approaches to the port. What followed was a disaster of the first magnitude. At noon on the twenty-second, most of the 21st Division's 75-mm artillery and anti-tank batteries were caught and destroyed by 2nd Panzer as they were striving to get into position south of Boulogne; sweeping on, the tanks caught more French artillery and troops still on their train *en route* to the front and wiped them out also. Two battalions of the division's 48th Regiment, heading for Boulogne from the east, were surrounded and mopped up by German armoured cars and infantry on the morning of the twenty-third, while the last two available battalions – both belonging to the 65th Infantry Regiment – ran into the 1st Panzer on its way to Calais. Both were cut to pieces.

Meanwhile, in Boulogne itself, Sir Douglas Brownrigg – who had moved his HQ to a safer location at Wimereux, three miles north of the port, following a heavy air raid on the night of 19/20 May in which the Hôtel Imperial was hit and several staff officers killed – was still trying to organize a defence with the forces at his disposal. Between 19 and 22 May various Allied units trickled into Boulogne, among them 1,500 men of No. 5 Group Auxiliary Military Pioneer Corps, who had retreated from Doullens under their commander, Lieutenant-Colonel Dean, VC, fighting an action against advance German units at St Pol *en route*. A large number of these men immediately set to work as labourers in the docks area, preparing for the evacuation. Other troops to arrive included about three hundred men of the 36th Infantry Brigade, which had been badly mauled in the St Pol area during the panzers' dash to the sea, and some stragglers from the Durham Light Infantry, cut off from their units during the battle at Arras.

The units actually allocated to the defence of Boulogne were all anti-aircraft, comprising two troops of the 2nd Heavy Anti-Aircraft Regiment with 3·7-inch guns, two troops of the 58th Light Anti-Aircraft Regiment with Bofors and machine guns, and one searchlight battery. There was also a detachment of RAF Balloon Command, but for some reason which has never been satisfactorily explained this received orders to pack up its balloons and return to the UK on the twenty-first – just when it was most needed at Boulogne. Other permanent defences of the port included three French forts, manned by garrison troops; two of them were on the coast to north and south and the third was the Ville Haute, the old walled town which commanded a view of the harbour from the north-east. All French units in Boulogne, including scattered troops who arrived in the town from the fighting elsewhere, came under the command of General Lanquetot following the disaster that overwhelmed his 21st Division.

A desperate plea for reinforcements by Brownrigg to the War

Office resulted in the hasty dispatch of a detachment of the Royal
Marines, who arrived in the early hours of the twenty-first and
immediately undertook patrol duty on the quay, where merchant
ships had begun the embarkation of civilians and non-combatant
troops. Meanwhile at Camberley the 20th Guards Brigade – consisting of the 2nd Irish Guards and 2nd Welsh Guards – also received
embarkation orders on the morning of the twenty-first, only hours
after the troops had returned from a gruelling night exercise. These
units, together with the brigade anti-tank company and a battery
of the 69th Anti-Tank Regiment, embarked at Dover on the night
of the twenty-first to twenty-second in two steamers and a destroyer,
HMS *Whitshed*; neither of the Guards battalions had maps, wirelesses,
mortars or grenades. The brigade commander, Brigadier Fox-Pitt,
had already been told by General Dill that he was to be responsible
for the defence of Boulogne, but he had no idea of the situation over
there.[2]

The ships began to arrive at Boulogne at 06.30 on 22 May and the
troops disembarked, forcing their way through the refugees and
troops on the quay. At one point, the Irish Guards had to clear a
passage with fixed bayonets. After a hasty reconnaissance, Brigadier
Fox-Pitt decided to place the Irish Guards along a two-mile front
to the south and west of the railway line that bisected the town, while
the Welsh Guards were given the task of blocking the main access
roads from west and north – a formidable assignment, for these
roads passed through hilly terrain which even a division would have
been hard put to defend.

The advance of the 2nd Panzer Division, meanwhile, had been
hampered by stiff fighting at Desvres and Samer and to the south of
Boulogne, where it encountered the remnants of the French 21st
Division, and also by determined attacks from Blenheim bombers
of the RAF and the French Naval Air Arm; these were pressed home
without opposition from the Luftwaffe, for Guderian's headlong
advance had taken his armour out of range of the Messerschmitts
Nevertheless the tanks pushed on steadily, and by 15.00 on the
twenty-second the leading elements of 2nd Panzer were in sight of
the town.

No. 1 Company of the Irish Guards, the last to arrive, were still striving to dig themselves in on the left of the battalion when the first German shells landed among them. At first the shelling was only sporadic. Then, at about 17.30, the fire became more intense and in its wake a German tank came slowly up the road, followed be some groups of infantry. The tank was quickly knocked out by the brigade anti-tank company, but the infantry came on and succeeded in penetrating the Irish positions before they were beaten off. The Germans attacked twice more; during the third assault, after dark they overran a platoon of No. 1 Company and captured the only two anti-tank guns, but they failed to exploit their success and the main positions still held at midnight. Nevertheless the situation was extremely perilous, particularly since the battalion had no way of knowing what was happening elsewhere; seven dispatch riders were sent out to find Brigadier Fox-Pitt but failed to contact him. Waiting in their foxholes, the Irishmen could hear heavy firing from the Welsh Guards' sector and deduced that heavy fighting was in progress there; in fact the Welsh Guards had been less seriously molested than their Irish counterparts, although they had been subjected to accurate shellfire and some probing by enemy armoured reconnaissance groups.

By 01.00 on the twenty-third the Panzers had succeeded in encircling the town, closing the road from Calais – along which reinforcements had been expected – and cutting off Sir Douglas Brownrigg's communications with the north. With the panzers now only three miles from Wimereux Brownrigg decided that it was time to evacuate his headquarters staff, and this was accomplished in the early hours. Brownrigg himself sailed for England on the destroyer HMS *Verity* at 03.00, having been unable to inform Brigadier Fox-Pitt of his departure owing to the breakdown of communications.

With the coming of dawn, however, Fox-Pitt quickly worked out for himself that the 20th Brigade was alone, that GHQ had gone and that there could be no hope of further reinforcements. With the threat from the north now apparent the brigadier did what he could to bolster his defences, injecting eight hundred pioneers into a dangerous three-mile gap between the left flank of the Welsh Guards and the coast and allocating a further hundred and fifty pioneers as reinforcements to the Welsh.

All British units stood to at first light, anticipating a dawn attack, but this did not develop immediately. Instead the Germans were completing their encirclement of Boulogne by reducing the French garrison at the Fort de la Crèche, north of the town, and it was not until an hour after sunrise that the British positions were subjected to a further assault. It fell initially on the Welsh Guards, whose outposts on the slopes of Mont Lambert were heavily attacked by enemy armour. Although one Welsh platoon was cut off, the line still held.

At 07.30 the expected attack developed against the Irish Guards, and particularly against a knoll of strategic high ground held by a platoon under Lieutenant Sir John Reynolds. The Irishmen put up a fierce resistance for over an hour, fighting the German tanks with small arms, but in the end this platoon too was surrounded. By midday the Irish Guards battalion had been whittled down to a strength of only two and a half companies and they were compelled to pull back, under continual pressure. For two hours they fought off the tanks and infantry with Bren guns and rifles, and when the Brens' barrels warped through the intense heat they fought with rifles alone. In the early afternoon they withdrew to a perimeter near the centre of the town, and there they prepared grimly to make their last stand. The Welsh Guards, similarly, withdrew into the town and fought their way back from street to street.

At 15.00 dispatch riders brought the word to both Guards battalions that they were to be evacuated immediately. By this time the German artillery was in command of the heights around Boulogne, from which position it directed a steady stream of shellfire at the harbour and the destroyers that were arriving there, two by two, to carry out the process of embarkation. These craft – the destroyers *Vimy*, *Keith*, *Whitshed*, *Vimiera*, *Wild Swan*, *Venomous*, *Venetia* and *Windsor*, with a French destroyer flotilla consisting of the *Cyclone*, *Orage* and *Frondeur* under Capitaine de Portzamparc lending their support – returned the enemy fire spiritedly, and it was heartening for the Guards to see the naval 4·7s blazing away and registering hits on the enemy.

Nevertheless it seemed that the chances of carrying out a successful evacuation were slim, particularly when – just as the embarkation was getting under way at 18.30 – Stukas appeared overhead and subjected the ships to a vicious dive-bombing attack, setting on fire the *Orage*, which later had to be scuttled, putting the *Frondeur* out of action and near-missing the *Whitshed*. The last-named got away with her load of troops, mainly wounded, and as she steamed past the German-occupied Fort de la Crèche she fired a couple of salvoes, causing a big explosion. Other bombs blasted the quays close to where the *Vimy* and *Keith* were berthed, flying splinters causing many casualties and killing the commanders of both warships. The Germans were now close enough to use mortars and heavy machine guns which added their fire to the holocaust. All the while the naval gunners returned the fire as fast as they could, grimy with cordite, soaked through and caked with the mud that erupted from bomb, bursts in the harbour, some of them wounded by the flying metal.

In the middle of the bombardment a cheer suddenly rose from soldiers and sailors alike as six RAF Hurricanes appeared over the harbour, diving through the maze of friendly anti-aircraft bursts to get at the Stukas just as a second wave was making its attack. The Hurricanes broke up the enemy formation and sent four dive-bombers down in flames, bringing some respite.

The destroyers *Keith* and *Vimy* backed out of the embattled harbour, their armament still hammering away, and were replaced by *Vimiera* and *Whitshed*, the latter still having room for more souls These two craft quickly embarked the Welsh Guards battalion and departed, their places being taken by *Wild Swan* and *Venomous*. A third destroyer, *Venetia*, also began her approach to the harbour, but as she reached the entrance she was badly hit and set on fire by a salvo from an enemy battery in the hills. Despite severe damage she backed off and regained the open sea, heavily ablaze and listing, but still firing with all guns that could be brought to bear.

Wild Swan and *Venomous* now proceeded rapidly with the embarkation of the Irish Guards, completing the task shortly after 21.00. During the process almost every German gun in the area was brought to bear on the two destroyers, which fortunately were hull down because of the low tide and their superstructures protected to some extent by installations on the quay. German tanks and infantry

moved on to a parallel dock and also began to pour fire at the
destroyers, which immediately turned their 4·7s on this new threat.
The effect was devastating; shrapnel scythed among the enemy
troops and one tank, receiving a direct hit, was blasted into the air
and turned a complete somersault. A minute later the gunners
spotted a machine gun firing from the upper storey of an hotel, and
blasted away the building's entire top floor.

On the bullet-swept quay the Guardsmen never wavered. 'It says
a great deal for the discipline of the troops,' wrote their commanding
officer later, 'that no move of any sort was made towards the
destroyers until I gave the order, and then the move was carried out
lowly and efficiently.' This comment was substantiated by a naval
officer: 'The courage and the bearing of the Guardsmen were
magnificent, even under a tornado of fire with casualties occurring
every second. They were as steady as though on parade and stood
like rocks, without giving a damn for anything.'[3]

Both *Wild Swan* and *Venomous* were clear of the harbour by 21.30.
An hour later the destroyer *Windsor* arrived and lifted off some six
hundred troops, including a small number of wounded. The last
warship to arrive was the *Vimiera*, which departed shortly before
daybreak with no fewer than 1,400 soldiers and civilians on board.
Many of the civilians were Jews and Poles, who because of the
special risks they would run under German occupation were permitted to embark once the destroyer had taken on her quota of
troops. The *Vimiera's* load included most of the remnants of
Lieutenant-Colonel Dean's Pioneers, who had fought a gallant
series of rearguard actions before reaching the harbour, where they
defended the access routes.

Some isolated groups fought on, even after the last ships had gone
and the early morning sun peered blood-red through the pall of
smoke that rose from the fires of Boulogne. In the Ville Haute,
General Lanquetot's troops successfully resisted all attempts to
dislodge them until, at 10.00, the Germans delivered an ultimatum:
if the French did not surrender immediately the town would be
destroyed. Lanquetot felt compelled to accede to the enemy's
demand in order to save civilian lives, and raised the white
flag.

As the Germans entered the harbour area they encountered still more resistance from the ruined Gare Maritime railway station, where about five hundred troops – what was left of a Welsh Guards company, three hundred pioneers and one hundred Frenchmen – had taken refuge under the command of a Welsh Guards officer, Major Windsor Lewis. Despite heavy shelling from enemy tanks Lewis's force held out until 13.00 on 25 May, and only surrendered when stocks of food and ammunition were exhausted. With that, Boulogne passed completely into German hands.

Meanwhile on the evening of 22 May Guderian had at last managed to secure the release of his 10th Armoured Division, which had been held in reserve on von Kleist's orders following the Allied counter-attack at Arras. He now decided to send the 10th towards Calais to relieve the 1st Panzer Division, which by this time was very close to the port. The capture of Calais was not considered urgent and Guderian felt confident that this task would be well within the means of 10th Panzer, heavily supported by the Luftwaffe. Dunkirk – the sole remaining port through which the Allied armies in the north could be supplied or evacuated – was of far greater importance, and on the night of 22/23 May Guderian ordered 1st Panzer to pivot eastwards towards this new objective in a two-pronged drive along the Bourbourgville and Gravelines roads. The armour had to fight its way through some strong resistance and it was attacked on several occasions by both the RAF and the French Air Force, but on the twenty-fourth the tanks reached the Aa canal between Holque and the coast and secured bridgeheads across it at Holque, St Pierre-Brouck, St Nicholas and Bourbourgville.

Guderian also ordered the ss 'Leibstandarte Adolf Hitler' Division, which had just been placed under his command, to advance on Watten in support of 1st Panzer, while 2nd Panzer at Boulogne was to send all the troops it could spare to reinforce the ss. The following day the heavy artillery that had been used in the capture of Boulogne was also to move up. By nightfall on the twenty-fourth General Reinhardt's XLI Army Corps had secured a strong bridgehead over the Aa at St Omer and everything seemed set for Guderian's final drive on Dunkirk, dangling like a ripe plum only a dozen miles up the coast from his panzers.

Then, suddenly, everything changed. Guderian wrote later:

> On this day [the twenty-fourth] the Supreme Command inter-
> vened in the operations in progress, with results which were to
> have a most disastrous influence on the whole future course of the
> war. *Hitler ordered the left wing to stop on the Aa.* It was forbidden to
> cross that stream. We were not informed of the reason for this . . .
> We were utterly speechless. But since we were not informed of the
> reasons for this order, it was difficult to argue against it. The
> panzer divisions were therefore instructed: 'Hold the line of the
> canal. Make use of the period of rest for general recuperation.'4

Over the years no single incident to emerge from the six-weeks'
Battle of France has caused more controversy than this famous
'*Halt Befehl*' – order to halt. According to General Halder, chief of
the German general staff, the order was issued directly by Hitler,
who was alarmed that his panzers might get into difficulties in the
terrain before Dunkirk: flat, marshy ground crossed by a network
of canals. By this act, Halder claimed, Hitler left open a great gap
that would enable the British Expeditionary Force to extricate
itself from the trap. Other, far wilder suggestions were subsequently
put forward to account for Hitler's action, one such being that the
Führer deliberately left the British with a way out – a 'golden
bridge', as one of his generals colourfully termed it – in the belief
that such a move would enhance the prospects of future peace
negotiations with the British Government.

All these suppositions, however, including Halder's, are based on
the erroneous idea that the '*Halt Befehl*' originated with Hitler; in
fact this was not so. The war diary of Army Group A, which was
preserved intact throughout the war, clearly states that the order
originated with the army group commander, von Rundstedt; it was
merely *confirmed* by Hitler.

It was, after all, a logical step to take, and quite apart from the
fact that the panzers did need to rest and replenish before undertaking a further offensive (although they had taken part in little
serious fighting since the breakthrough on the Meuse von Kleist's
armoured divisions had come a long way in a very short time, and
many of the tanks urgently required maintenance) the halt order

complied fully with the textbook of strategy that the Germans had employed during the campaign so far.

This strategy involved a double blow designed to cut off the Allied armies in the north – the left hook swung by Army Group A and the right by Army Group B. The punch of Army Group A, driving across Belgium and northern France, carried the most weight, for the whole success of the plan depended on its armoured spearhead reaching the sea as quickly as possible. Once the armour had reached the Channel coast, eliminated Boulogne and Calais, consolidated its position and opened the way for von Rundstedt's infantry formations to expand the corridor it had created, it had achieved its primary goal; the anvil against which von Bock's Army Group B was to pound the trapped Allied armies had been forged. Von Rundstedt saw no reason to exceed his brief and commit his armour in an over-hasty rush towards Dunkirk at this point.

Besides, enemy air activity appeared to be on the increase and the Luftwaffe had still not caught up with the speed of the armoured advance. The dive-bombers of Fliegerkorps VIII, which operated in conjunction with the armour, had moved to bases in north-east France, but even so the Channel coast represented the limit of their range. On the twenty-fourth a few flights of Stuka-geschwader 2 (StG 2) and the Messerschmitt 109s of No. 1 Gruppe, Jagdgeschwader 27, were moved up to St Pol, but the support column carrying their fuel and ammunition was held up and the aircraft were unable to operate effectively.[5]

Nevertheless it seems probable that the opposition of some German commanders in the field – Guderian in particular – to the halt order might have persuaded Rundstedt to change his mind had it not been for Hitler's support. There is no doubt that Hitler was worried by the prospect of employing the tanks in the terrain around Dunkirk without proper reconnaissance and planning; moreover he wished to conserve the armour for the next stage of the campaign – Plan Red, the offensive against the French armies in the south. There was, however, another factor that influenced his decision greatly.

Late on 23 May Reichsmarschall Hermann Göring, the Luftwaffe C-in-C, received the latest situation reports from the front and studied them in the special train that served as his mobile headquarters, which was then in the Eifel mountains near the Luxembourg border. As he read, it became apparent to Göring that the Allied armies in the north were doomed; the panzers were investing Boulogne and Calais, leaving only Dunkirk as an avenue of retreat, and in fact Guderian's armour on the Aa canal was about thirty miles closer to that port than was the bulk of the still hard-fighting British Expeditionary Force.

Göring seemed determined that the Luftwaffe should be in at the kill. More than that: he clearly wished his airmen to have the lion's share of the glory. His chief of staff, General Schmid, who was present in the train, told later how Göring suddenly thumped the table and bellowed: 'This is a special job for the Luftwaffe![6] Within minutes he was on the telephone to Hitler, expounding on the suitability of the air force for eliminating the encircled armies and urging the Führer to order the leading armoured units to draw back in order to allow a clear target area for the bombers. Hitler did not immediately agree, but Göring's boast was certainly at the forefront of his mind when he visited Rundstedt's headquarters in Charleville on the morning of the twenty-fourth and gave his blessing to the halt order. It is probable that neither Hitler nor his subordinates sensed any real urgency in crushing the trapped armies. Not counting the Belgians, who were virtually done for anyway, the French and British between them had close on half a million men in the trap; what chance could they have of pulling off any kind of spectacular rescue operation, with the jaws of the German nutcracker closing relentlessly and the Luftwaffe standing by to shatter their only lifeline?

Meanwhile the 10th Panzer Division had been closing in steadily on Calais, conscious that the ancient port would prove a tougher nut to crack than Boulogne. The terrain around Calais was more on the side of the defenders, the town being surrounded by marshy land with a network of dykes running across it, and the nearest high ground was two miles away to the west. The town itself was stoutly protected by strong ramparts and ditches covering an eight-mile perimeter, on which there were eleven strongpoints at strategic intervals. In fact the port of Calais could be divided into two

distinct areas, the new town and the old; the latter was surrounded
by a sweeping moat of water that broadened out into the docks at
its eastern extremity.

The man on whose shoulders fell the responsibility of organizing
the Calais defences was Colonel R.T. Holland, the assistant adjutant
general, who had been sent to the port to make arrangements for
evacuation. The British forces at his disposal initially comprised a
single platoon of infantry from the 6th Argyll and Sutherland
Highlanders, together with detachments of one searchlight and one
anti-aircraft regiment which had set up their positions at two forts
outside the main perimeter. There was also a French garrison manning the Citadel, the fortress that guarded the west flank of the old
town, and a few coastal gun batteries manned by French sailors.

Early on 22 May reinforcements arrived in the shape of the 3rd
Royal Tank Regiment, with twenty-seven cruiser tanks armed with
two-pounder guns. It was not until noon on 23 May that the last of
these vehicles was offloaded in the harbour, and as they moved off
to their laager position at Coquelles, two miles west of Calais,
Holland learned that their commander – Lieutenant-Colonel Keller
– had been instructed by GHQ to take part in the defence of St Omer
and the Canal Line, and not to launch an attack on the flank of the
10th Panzer Division as had been expected.

Meanwhile in England the 30th Brigade had also received orders
to embark for Calais. This brigade, which had originally been formed
to take part in the Norwegian campaign, consisted of the 2nd
Battalion the King's Royal Rifle Corps (60th Rifles) and the
1st Battalion the Rifle Brigade – both motorized units of the 1st
Armoured Division, to which the 3rd RTR also belonged – and the
1st Battalion Queen Victoria's Rifles, a territorial unit affiliated to
the KRRC. The brigade was under the command of Brigadier Claude
Nicholson, an experienced cavalry officer who, at the age of forty-
two, was rather younger than most officers of similar rank.

The Queen Victoria's Rifles were the first to embark, having been
close to the coast in Kent when the order was received. They arrived
in the afternoon of the twenty-second and were immediately sent
out to block all six main roads into Calais, with the task of turning
back the refugees that were streaming towards the port. It was a

difficult and heartbreaking task, and it says much for the diplomacy
and tact of the young soldiers that they carried it out with the minimum of antagonism on either side.

The transports carrying the main body of the brigade did not
arrive at Calais until the early afternoon of Thursday 23 May, the
troops having embarked at Southampton after moving down from
East Anglia. The convoy had then moved round the south coast to
Dover, where Nicholson had gone ashore briefly to confer with Vice-
Admiral Sir Bertram Ramsay, the flag officer commanding Dover,
and Sir Douglas Brownrigg, who had recently arrived from Boulogne.
After some consultation, it was agreed that Nicholson's force should
sail for Calais and from there move at once to the relief of Boulogne,
a decision that was confirmed by a telephone call to the War Office.

On reaching Calais, however, Nicholson quickly decided that his
first priority was to organize a defence of the port with the forces at
his disposal. Not only that; he had to put a stop to the chaos that
was rapidly building up. Already the quays were congested with
military personnel and civilian refugees, mingled with piles of stores
and equipment and wreckage resulted from sporadic attacks already
carried out by the Luftwaffe. Besides, in the middle of the afternoon
he learned that units of the 3 RTR – having set off for St Omer –
had run into a strong force of panzers and received a severe mauling,
leaving twelve of their cruiser tanks in flames; it was fast becoming
clear that the enemy now commanded all the principal exits from
Calais, and in strength. This gloomy realization was strengthened
when, at 16.00, enemy tanks were seen near the outskirts of the
town, and an hour later the first German shells dropped into the
harbour area, causing further delays in the unloading of Nicholson's
troops and their equipment.

That same evening, Nicholson received fresh instructions from
the War Office. Instead of proceeding to Boulogne, he was now to
force a way through to Dunkirk with a convoy of desperately-
needed rations for the BEF. These rations, together with 7,000
gallons of petrol, had been unloaded at Calais during the past
forty-eight hours. Nicholson accordingly made arrangements with
Lieutenant-Colonel Keller of 3 RTR to push out a force along the
Dunkirk road early the next morning, as soon as sufficient transport

had been offloaded to carry detachments of the Rifle Brigade to escort the supply convoy.

During the night four tanks of 3 RTR set out to make a reconnaissance, followed by a platoon of the Rifle Brigade. In the darkness the tanks drove past laagered German armour without being detected and eventually reached Gravelines, where they joined up with other British troops. The tank commander decided to stay there, realizing the futility of any attempt to get back to Calais. The infantry platoon meanwhile advanced seven miles up the Gravelines road and suddenly found themselves surrounded by Germans. With enemy activity going on all around, the platoon commander coolly reported his findings by radio, then prudently pulled out. He and his men regained Calais safely.

At 22.00 on 23 May, while the above reconnaissance was getting under way, the destroyer HMS *Verity* arrived at Calais and disembarked Major-General A.G.L. McNaughton, whose 1st Canadian Division was now stationed in England. McNaughton had been sent over by the CIGS to see if it was feasible to keep open the BEF's lines of communication through either Calais or Dunkirk. After a short survey he left by sea for Dunkirk; it had not taken him long to make up his mind about the future of Calais, and his coded message to the War Office resulted in an urgent signal to Nicholson from Major-General R.H. Dewing, the director of operations. Arriving at 03.00 on the twenty-fourth, it stated: 'Evacuation decided in principle. When you have finished unloading your two MT ships commence embarkation of all personnel except fighting personnel who will remain to cover final evacuation.' This signal, which was sent on Dewing's own initiative, was to have repercussions in high quarters, as will be seen later.

Despite the evacuation order, Nicholson decided to go ahead with the attempt to push through to Dunkirk, and at first light on the twenty-fourth five tanks of 3 RTR, supported by a company of the Rifle Brigade, set out through the eastern suburbs of Calais to clear the route. They had not gone two miles before they were stopped by a roadblock and heavy anti-tank fire, which compelled the armour to withdraw. Soon afterwards the troops encountered heavy mortar and artillery fire as they tried to make a flanking attack on the

German positions, and since they had only their rifles with which to retaliate they too were compelled to pull back to the defensive perimeter set up the previous day. Other units also began to trickle back to the perimeter under heavy enemy pressure. At 05.00 a strong German attack from the south-west broke through the outposts of the Queen Victoria's Rifles, and although the latter fought back hard and claimed the destruction of several enemy light tanks their position soon became untenable and they came back to lend strength to the 60th Rifles and the 1st Rifle Brigade, being more or less equally divided between the two.

The enemy launched their preliminary attack in strength from the south-west, preceded by heavy shellfire from tanks and 150-mm guns that made several breaches in the perimeter wall. Several enemy tanks were knocked out by the gunners of the 229th Anti-Tank Battery, but the assaulting German infantry – two rifle regiments – gained a foothold on the perimeter in a number of spots, and although counter-attacks mopped up some of the enemy penetrations those that remained placed the 60th Rifles in a dangerous position. Brigadier Nicholson consequently ordered a withdrawal, instructing the 60th to take up new positions in the old town behind its watery moat; the Rifle Brigade in turn pulled back to form a new front behind the Marck canal, with the Calais canal on their right and the perimeter canal on their left. By this time the situation was becoming desperate; there was no supporting artillery, only two remaining anti-tank guns, and a complete lack of demolition charges to blow up the canal bridges. Every man knew that once the evacuation started, it would be virtually impossible to hold back the flood of German armour that would pour across those bridges into the harbour area.

Meanwhile, behind the scenes, high-level decisions were being taken that would very soon change the whole situation. The first was General Weygand's decision, early on the twenty-fourth, to appoint General Fagalde of the French xvi Corps to command all military forces in the Channel ports; Fagalde's first directive in his new capacity was to forbid the evacuation of Calais and to place the French troops there under the command of Brigadier Nicholson. This decision was upheld by Churchill, who on the twenty-fourth sent a message to General Ismay of the War Cabinet Secretariat which read:

> Vice-Chief of the Naval Staff informs me that an order was sent at 2 a.m. to Calais saying that evacuation was decided on in principle, but this is surely madness. The only effect of evacuating Calais would be to transfer the forces now blocking it to Dunkirk. Calais must be held for many reasons, but specially to hold the enemy on its front. The Admiralty say they are preparing twenty-four naval 12-pounders, which with S.A.P. [semi-armour-piercing shells] will pierce any tank. Some of these will be ready this evening.[7]

The first Brigadier Nicholson knew of these pronouncements affecting the future of his command came in the early hours of 25 May, when the destroyer HMS *Wolfhound*, which had been standing offshore and bombarding enemy positions inland, crept into Calais harbour and disembarked Vice-Admiral Sir James Somerville, commanding the small force of warships that had been sent to lend its support to the defenders. Somerville carried the following War Office order addressed to Nicholson:

> In spite of policy of evacuation given you this morning fact that British forces in your area now under Fagalde who has ordered no repeat no evacuation means that you must comply for sake of Allied Solidarity. Your role is therefore to hold on, harbour being at present of no importance to B.E.F. Brigade Group 48 Div started marching to your assistance this morning. No reinforcements but ammunition being sent by sea. Should this fail RAF will drop ammunition. You will select best position and fight on.

The message was, to say the least, worded in a most unfortunate manner, with its demand that Nicholson should sacrifice his men to hold a useless objective. The only glimmer of hope or sense it contained was in its promise of ammunition – which Nicholson desperately needed and which Admiral Somerville promised to try and supply – and in the possibility of relief by units of the 48th Division, although this was a slim chance indeed. (In fact, the 48th Division's 145 Brigade, then in the Kassel-Hazebrouck area, had been standing

c

by to march to Calais for some time – but within hours their orders would be cancelled and they would once again become part of the BEF's defensive line.)

Churchill did not like the tone of the War Office order, either, as was shown by the text of his minute to the Secretary of State for War and the CIGS later that day:

> Pray find out who was the officer responsible for sending the order to evacuate Calais yesterday, and by whom this very luke-warm telegram I saw this morning was drafted, in which mention is made of 'for the sake of Allied Solidarity'. This is not the way to encourage men to fight to the end. Are you sure there is no streak of defeatist opinion in the General Staff?[8]

And, later, to the CIGS:

> Something like this should be said to the Brigadier defending Calais: Defence of Calais to the utmost is of the highest impor-tance to our country and our Army now. First, it occupies a large part of the enemy's armoured forces, and keeps them from attacking our line of communications. Secondly, it preserves a sally-port from which portions of the British Army may make their way home. Lord Gort has already sent troops to your aid, and the Navy will do all possible to keep you supplied. The eyes of the Empire are upon the defence of Calais, and His Majesty's Government are confident that you and your gallant regiment will perform an exploit worthy of the British name.[9]

The text of this message was sent to Nicholson at 14.00 on the twenty-fifth. By the time he received it, the order dispatching the 48th Division's brigade to Calais had been cancelled several hours earlier, and the only supplies to have reached him by sea consisted of a small amount of mortar and small arms ammunition.

At sunrise on the twenty-fifth Calais was the scene of desperate fighting, with strong enemy attacks against the Rifle Brigade's positions on the south of the perimeter in the wake of a fierce artillery barrage. The brigade had only a handful of scout cars, light tanks and Bren carriers to support it, for most of the 3rd RTR's tanks had been destroyed – many of them deliberately when the earlier order to evacuate was received. What those tanks might have achieved now did not bear contemplating. Nevertheless when the enemy infantry came storming over the canals through the dust and smoke of their own shells they encountered withering small-arms fire and recoiled after suffering fearful losses at the hands of troops who were probably the finest marksmen in any army. For several hours they held their own, but in the end the weight of enemy numbers began to have a telling effect and the brigade's line was pierced at several points, forcing the British troops to withdraw to a new position between two dock basins. During the withdrawal action Lieutenant-Colonel C. B. A. Hoskyns, commanding the 1st Rifle Brigade, was mortally wounded, and the brigade lost five officers and two platoon sergeant-majors killed in the space of an hour.

Meanwhile the 60th Rifles – whose main task was to cover the three bridges that linked the old and new towns of Calais – had also been subjected to a formidable artillery barrage, directed by a German observation post in the town hall on the other side of the waterway. Behind the Rifles' right flank was the Citadel, the old fortress into which Brigadier Nicholson had now moved his headquarters and which was occupied by a garrison of two hundred Frenchmen and the Royal Marine Detachment, sharing a pair of 75-mm guns between them. The task of the old town's defenders was made incredibly complicated by the presence of masses of refugees, including about a thousand unarmed French and Belgian soldiers, all desperately seeking refuge from the rain of shells.

Suddenly, in mid-afternoon, the curtain of high explosive lifted and at 15.00 a German lieutenant approached the 60th's positions, accompanied by a French captain and a Belgian soldier. The German arrogantly demanded the garrison's surrender, failing which, he pointed out, the defenders would be pulverized.

The brigadier's reply, which was recorded in the war diary of the 10th Panzer Division, was short and to the point: 'The answer is no, as it is the British Army's duty to fight as well as it is the German's.'

During the rest of the afternoon the Germans kept up a steady and accurate mortar barrage on the British positions, causing many casualties and setting fire to a number of buildings until the whole of the 60th's front was obscured by smoke. The British replied with their only two 3-inch mortars, deriving scant comfort from the steady drumroll of naval gunfire they could hear out to sea as Admiral Somerville's destroyers hammered away at the German gun positions west of the town. Then, at 18.30, the enemy laid down a terrific blanket of artillery fire on the 60th's sector. It lasted for half an hour, and when it lifted the enemy infantry, led by tanks. attempted to storm the three bridges. On the first two bridges the infantry were forced to retreat when their supporting tanks were knocked out, but they managed to get across the third bridge and overran some of the 60th's forward positions. The 60th rallied and counter-attacked, and the enemy were dislodged after some vicious close-range fighting. Another attack, on the left flank, was also broken up by the joint action of the 60th and the 1st Rifle Brigade,

Shortly before dusk the Germans showered the British positions with leaflets, once again demanding surrender, but there was no further major assault that night and the battered defenders took the opportunity to tend their wounds and swallow a little food and water. During the night small craft of the Royal Navy evacuated some wounded and brought ashore some ammunition.

At daybreak on the twenty-sixth the bloodied, exhausted troops stood to and prepared to face what must surely be the last act of their ordeal. At 07.00 the Germans opened up with another crippling barrage, and behind it two separate infantry assaults developed along the coastal flanks. The first, from the west, pushed towards the Gare Maritime, while the other became involved in heavy fighting around a strongpoint west of the Citadel held by British and French troops. For a time both prongs of the German advance became bogged down in the face of bitter resistance, but the odds were overwhelming and the inevitable breakthrough came at 08.30. By 09.00 the defensive perimeter had shrunk to a tight ring around the Citadel – and it was now that the Luftwaffe appeared in strength over Calais.

Although the harbour of Calais had been subjected to limited attacks by Luftwaffe medium bombers at intervals since 19 May, it was only on the twenty-fifth that strong formations of Junkers 87 Stuka dive-bombers began operating in the area, and even then their principal targets were the Allied warships out at sea rather than the town itself.

The Luftwaffe unit that carried out the first heavy dive-bombing attack off Calais on the twenty-fifth was Stuka-geschwader 2 (StG 2) which had moved up to an advanced base at Guise, east of St Quentin, under the command of Major Oskar Dinort, who had led the Geschwader through the *blitzkrieg* on Poland and who had achieved fame as a competition pilot in pre-war Germany. Now, while the 10th Panzer Division pounded away at the stubborn defenders of the town, Dinort led two *Gruppen* of StG 2 – about forty Stukas – against Admiral Somerville's naval squadron, consisting of the British cruisers *Arethusa* and *Galatea*, the destroyers *Wessex*, *Vimiera*, *Wolfhound*, *Verity*, *Grafton*, *Greyhound* and the Polish *Burza*, which had been either taking part in the evacuation or employing their naval guns against targets on shore.

It was the first time that the Stukas had been called upon to attack warships, and as yet no firm technique had been worked out for dive-bombing such small, elusive targets. Dinort knew that it would be a question of trial and error; a dress rehearsal for the bigger contest that would soon be fought further along the coast, at Dunkirk.

Dinort screwed up his eyes; with the reflection of the early morning sun on the sea, and the considerable haze, it was difficult to see anything. Over on the left, a mushroom of smoke rose through the mist; at its foot lay Calais.

Suddenly, a group of ships came into sight. Over the radio, Dinort ordered his two *Gruppe* commanders, Hauptmann Hitrschold and Hauptmann Brückers, to select their own targets and led his own section of three Stukas in a dive from 12,000 feet. He picked out a destroyer and placed it squarely in his sight, only to see it drift out again as it took evasive action. He eased out of the dive slightly, captured the warship once more – then lost it again as it turned the other way. The sea was racing up to meet him now and in desperation he kicked the rudder bar, releasing his bomb as the grey hull of the destroyer swung through his sight for the last time. As he pulled out of his dive and raced away through a maze of anti-aircraft bursts, he looked back to see his bomb explode in a geyser of spray a hundred yards from its target.

Everywhere, Dinort's Stuka pilots were having the same

experience; it was clear that attacks on warships manoeuvring at high
speed was going to call for a finer degree of expertise than anything
the Stukas had encountered so far. Nevertheless some of their bombs
found a target; in this and subsequent attacks off Calais they sank
the destroyer *Wessex* and damaged both the *Vimiera* and *Burza*.[10]

As Dinort and his pilots set course for home, half a dozen sleek
aircraft swept through their formation, their hammering machine-
guns leaving grey smoke trails across the sky. Theirs was not the
familiar, hump-backed silhouette of the Hawker Hurricanes which
up to now had been the Luftwaffe's main RAF adversary in the
skies of France. From now on, the warning '*Achtung* – Spitfire!'
would feature prominently in the Luftwaffe's vocabulary. On this
occasion the British fighters – probably short of fuel – vanished as
suddenly as they had appeared, sparing the slow dive-bombers,
but their presence over Calais carried the grim warning that the
French Channel coast was well within the range of the RAF's home-
based fighter squadrons. Already, over the past twenty-four hours,
eight Stukas from other units had fallen victim to the Spitfires in a
series of minor engagements over the coast.

On the morning of 26 May, General Wolfram von Richthofen of
VIII Fliegerkorps – whose command, which included most of the
Stuka squadrons in the west, was responsible for providing close
support for the German ground forces – ordered his dive-bomber
units to carry out an all-out attack on the last bastion in Calais, the
Citadel, in conjunction with an assault by Guderian's troops. At
08.40 the first wave of bombers, the Stukas of StG 77 under Major
Graf Schönborn, made rendezvous over St Pol with sixty Messerschmitt 109 fighters of JG 27 and set course for their objective. The
attack began at 09.30 and lasted for an hour, the dive-bombers of
StG 2 following StG 77 and unloading their bombs into the massive
pall of smoke and dust that now hung over the Citadel and harbour.
Determined attempts by small groups of Spitfires to break up the
attack were frustrated by the Messerschmitts, which stuck close to
the bombers until the British fighters started their attack and then
engaged them in a series of whirling dogfights.

After the dive-bombers, the German artillery opened up and
pounded the Citadel for ninety minutes. Then, at noon, a massive

attack developed against the bridges held by the 60th Rifles, the German infantry dashing forward behind a creeping mortar barrage. One by one, despite heroic resistance, the 60th's forward positions were overwhelmed and their commander, Lieutenant-Colonel Euan Miller, ordered the survivors to pull back and form a new perimeter in conjunction with the Rifle Brigade, still fighting in the docks area.

The Citadel was now completely isolated, and at 15.00 enemy troops supported by tanks broke in from the south. Half an hour later Brigadier Nicholson, his defences completely overwhelmed, was forced to surrender. Sporadic fighting continued until 17.00 as the Germans mopped up isolated pockets of resistance. The last to surrender were the battered survivors of a company of the Queen Victoria's Rifles, who were cornered in a schoolhouse in the harbour and shelled into submission by tanks and mortars.

Miraculously about two hundred of the defenders of Calais managed to escape the trap – thanks largely to the efforts of the crews of two Royal Navy yachts, the *Conidaw* and *Gulzar*. The latter actually rescued nearly fifty men from under the very noses of the Germans in the small hours of the twenty-seventh, creeping in to where the soldiers had been spotted sheltering under the remains of a pier and getting them away safely.

In all, the Germans took 20,000 prisoners, 3,500 of them British. Of their sacrifice, Churchill later wrote: 'Calais was the crux. Many other causes might have prevented the deliverance of Dunkirk, but it is certain that the three days gained by the defence of Calais enabled the Gravelines waterline to be held, and that without this, even in spite of Hitler's vacillations and Rundstedt's orders, all would have been cut off and lost.'[11] Yet how valid was this assessment? German documents revealed since the war, and Guderian's personal testimony, have shown that the capture of Calais was a secondary task, and there is no escaping the fact that even with the 10th Panzer Division committed there Guderian was able to throw three divisions – 1st Panzer, 20th Motorized and SS – against the Canal Line, with 2nd Panzer coming up fast in support. And although the defenders of Calais inflicted such losses on the 10th Panzer's two infantry regiments that they took no further part in the campaign in the north, it is considered with some justification in many quarters that the two rifle battalions sent to Calais, and the 3rd RTR, might have been more profitably employed in the defence of the Canal Line on the approach to Dunkirk and should have been shipped to France through the latter port.

All that, however, is academic. The fact remains that two battalions of first-class fighting men and one battalion of armour were lost; and it is difficult to set the material cost of the sacrifice against the propaganda value which, on the face of it, appears to have been the most compelling factor to emerge from their stirring last stand. Unfortunately the views of the one man well qualified to comment – Brigadier Nicholson – would never be known, for he died in prison camp.

Ironically the final decision not to relieve the garrison at Calais was not taken until the evening of 26 May. At 21.00 Churchill despatched the following signal to its commander: 'Every hour you continue to exist is of the greatest help to the BEF. Government has therefore decided you must continue to fight. Have greatest possible admiration for your splendid stand. Evacuation will not (repeat not) take place.'[12] The message never reached Nicholson, for he and his men were already marching into captivity. The British Government was not aware of his surrender until the following day.

The final irony of all: at dawn on the twenty-seventh, twenty-one Westland Lysander army co-operation aircraft of the RAF dropped water and ammunition into Calais. Three were shot down, and all the supplies fell into German hands.

4 Dunkirk: the Last Lifeline

On 23 May, with the battle for Boulogne raging and the enemy poised for the assault on Calais, the Allied commanders in the north realized with sudden apprehension (although their respective governments had not yet woken up to the fact) that only two ports remained on the Channel coast through which the BEF, the French and the Belgian Armies could receive supplies: Ostend and Dunkirk. The first was considered briefly, then rejected mainly on the grounds that it would involve a longer sea crossing from England and that any RAF fighter squadrons charged with protecting supply ships would be operating at the limit of their range. Consequently it was Dunkirk that became the focal point, and it was clear that no time must be lost in stretching the port's facilities to their fullest capacity.

It was fortunate indeed that the Allied armies had Dunkirk at their back. The third largest port in France, Dunkirk's capacity far outstripped that of any other port on the Channel coast, having seven deep-water basins, four dry docks and no less than five miles of quays. Surrounding it was a flat expanse of marsh which could be flooded as a defensive measure, and, like Calais, it possessed a series of old fortifications to both seaward and landward, all of which were capable of withstanding a formidable weight of high explosive. The most powerful of all these fortifications, known as Bastion 32, commanded the docks area; it housed the headquarters of Admiral Abrial, who commanded all naval and land forces on a sector of the French coastline stretching from the Belgian frontier to the mouth of the Coussnon, near Mont St Michel, and as such was responsible for the defence of Dunkirk itself.

Apart from air attacks, which so far had been only sporadic, the enemy threat to Dunkirk did not seem immediate. The nearest enemy units were fifteen miles away to the west, at St Omer, and had not

yet reached the Aa canal; the possibility of a speedy breakthrough
by the panzers in this sector receded as the twenty-third wore on.
In addition to the Anglo-French units already facing the enemy
across the Aa, reinforcements were promised in the shape of the
French xvi Corps under General Fagalde, who on the twenty-third
was ordered to move his headquarters and one of his divisions –
which, under Belgian orders, had been responsible for the defence
of the line between Terneuzen and Zeebrugge – to the River Aa and
take up new positions between Gravelines and St Omer, protecting
the rear of the Belgian Army, leaving his other division in the
Bruges area. On the evening of the twenty-third, however, Fagalde
learned that the Germans had already reached the Aa at St Omer
and accordingly decided to send his 68th Division only as far as the
Yser, which it reached that same evening. Early the next day the
68th pushed further forward to occupy a line along the Mardyck
canal, midway between Dunkirk and the Aa.

It was on the morning of the twenty-fourth that Fagalde received
a telegram from Weygand, appointing him to command all Allied
ground forces in the area of the Channel ports, under the overall
authority of Admiral Abrial. He immediately went to Dunkirk, to
confer with Abrial and make an on-the-spot appraisal of the defences there. These, he found, consisted of the 272nd Demi-Brigade
(three battalions of reserve troops from the garrison of the Flanders
Fortified Sector), two training battalions, three labour battalions
composed mainly of veteran soldiers from the 1914–18 War, five
infantry battalions (the remnants of the shattered 21st Infantry
Division which the Germans had wiped out near Boulogne), six
batteries of 75-mm guns and five of 155s, and two anti-tank
batteries.

Early on the twenty-fourth Fagalde met General McNaughton
of the 1st Canadian Division, newly arrived in Dunkirk from his
whirlwind inspection tour of Calais. Fagalde took McNaughton's
visit as an indication that a Canadian brigade might soon arrive to
bolster the Dunkirk defences, but the Canadians were destined to
play no part. In fact, on his return to England McNaughton reported to the CIGS that the need in Dunkirk was for organization,
not reinforcement; the area was sufficiently congested.

There was more than an element of truth in McNaughton's comments, as Brigadier R.H.R. Parminter, the deputy quartermaster general, was finding out, having arrived in Dunkirk on the twenty-third after taking four hours to cover the twenty-seven miles between GHQ at Hazebrouck and the port. Parminter's task was to organize the unloading and distribution of supplies for the BEF. Air raids had already caused some considerable disruption in the docks area, where the lack of organization was marked; no one seemed able to give or take orders. Nevertheless under Parminter's direction 530 tons of rations and ammunition were offloaded on the twenty-fourth and sent out for distribution by road and rail. Although this total represented only half the requirement of the BEF it was no mean achievement, for the civilian dockers and pioneers working in the docks were already suffering from severe strain brought about by excessive hours and enemy action. The latter had already caused the breakdown of the town's water supply, and Parminter set about organizing several emergency water dumps in the area; in anticipation of the flood of troops that would soon be arriving 80,000 gallons of water were stockpiled in cans at intervals along the beach. Many a soldier, suffering the torments of thirst, would have cause to bless the efforts of the DQMG and his men.

So far there had been no liaison between Fagalde and Lord Gort on the steps to be taken to implement the defence of Dunkirk. On the twenty-fourth Gort, on his own initiative, briefed Major-General A.F.A.N. Thorne of 48th (South Midland) Division to go to Dunkirk with his divisional headquarters and the 144th Brigade under Brigadier J. Hamilton and organize a defence; the first Thorne knew of the presence of Fagalde's forces in the area was when he arrived in Dunkirk the following morning. After conferring with Fagalde, Thorne agreed to place the 144th Brigade at Wormhoudt, on the left of the French 68th Division, and to organize the defence of Bergues, where a strategic strongpoint commanded the western end of the Bergues–Furnes canal, the principal water obstacle on the approach to Dunkirk. The task of defending Bergues was assigned to 'Usherforce', a composite unit including the 6th Green Howards, the 1st and 3rd Super Heavy Batteries RA, and the 52nd Heavy Regiment. They had already been in action on the Aa canal under their commander, Colonel C.M. Usher. The ancient town of Bergues proved to be an excellent defensive position, standing on a hill and surrounded by a strong wall and moat. There were three bridges across this moat and Usher lost no time in disposing his men to defend them, placing a company backed up by 25-pounders and 2-pounders at each one. The town also had a garrison of French troops and was the headquarters of General Barthelemey, commanding one of the fortified sectors.

So, on the morning of Sunday 26 May, the first link of the Allied perimeter around Dunkirk was forged; but it still had to extend as far as Nieuport to the east, and finding troops to man it in the early stages was not going to be easy. There was also very little time, for it was on the twenty-sixth that Gort received firm instructions from the British War Cabinet to pull his forces back to the coast, a complete reversal of the Government's attitude so far, brought about by the sudden news that Gort had been forced to divert the 5th and 50th Divisions from their projected attack in conjunction with the French First Army to plug the gap created by the disintegration of the Belgian forces.

The final decision to evacuate the BEF was taken in a meeting of the War Cabinet at 09.00 on 26 May, following a series of emergency meetings between the chiefs of staff and service ministers that had gone on virtually throughout the night. Even as this decision was being taken, Gort had been in conference with General Blanchard, newly confirmed in his appointment as commander of Army Group One, discussing the formation of what Blanchard called 'a bridgehead covering Dunkirk in depth . . . to be held with no thought of retreat'. Blanchard's bridgehead involved a withdrawal back to the line of the river Lys, with both the French and British Armies pulling back to the Deule on the night of the twenty-seventh and completing the rest of the withdrawal twenty-four hours later. The tottering Belgian Army was 'to make all possible effort' while this withdrawal was in progress.

When Gort returned to his own HQ, he found a telegram from Anthony Eden awaiting him. It informed him that there now appeared to be no possibility of a French offensive from the south, and went on:

Should this prove to be the case you will be faced with a situation in which the safety of BEF will be predominant consideration. In such conditions only course open to you may be to fight your way back to west where all beaches and ports east of Gravelines will be used for embarkation. Navy would provide fleet of ships and small boats and RAF would give full support. As withdrawal may have to begin very early preliminary plans should be urgently prepared.

The tone of Gort's reply was pessimistic. 'I must not conceal from you,' he cabled, 'that a great part of the BEF and its equipment will be lost.'

Meanwhile, on the twenty-fifth, the French War Cabinet had been in session in Paris. Much of the discussion centred not on the plight of the armies in the north, but on the future conduct of the campaign in the south when the Germans struck in that direction. Weygand told Reynaud that he had discussed with General George, the possibility of shortening the defensive line and retreating south of the Seine, but this would mean either abandoning the troops in the Maginot Line or – a course which most Frenchmen would consider to be more serious – abandoning Paris. Now, for the first times there was serious high-level talk of negotiating a separate peace with the Germans. Weygand insisted that the British should be consulted immediately, but Pétain pointed out that since France had fielded eighty divisions to the British ten, France had every right to initiate peace talks. The meeting closed with a resolution that if the French Government was forced to vacate Paris it would establish itself at Bordeaux. Meanwhile, Reynaud informed his ministers that he was going to London the next day (the twenty-sixth) to have talks with Churchill and sound out the British prime minister's reaction to what had just been discussed.

It turned out to be an unproductive meeting. Reynaud, in conference with Churchill, Lord Halifax (the foreign secretary), Eden, Chamberlain and Attlee, killed once and for all any hope of a French attack from the south and talked at some length on the possibility that the French might be compelled to withdraw from the fighting. Churchill informed him that the policy was to evacuate the British

Expeditionary Force, and requested him to issue corresponding orders. The British premier also pointed out bluntly that it would not be easy for the French, depleted as they were, to negotiate terms with the enemy. On that note Reynaud departed, a very unhappy man.

Immediately after this meeting, Churchill instructed Eden to send another telegram to Lord Gort, confirming his previous message and informing Gort that the French had abandoned all hope of striking from the south. 'In these circumstances,' the text went on, 'no course open to you but to fall back upon the coast in accordance terms my telegram . . . M. Reynaud communicating General Weygand and latter will no doubt issue orders in this sense forthwith. You are now authorized to operate towards coast forthwith in conjunction with French and Belgian Armies.'

Gort's reaction to this directive was to call an immediate conference of his subordinate commanders at 19.00 on 26 May. Together they worked out details of the withdrawal to the Lys, the preliminary phase of which was to begin that night; and now, for the first time, the BEF's senior commanders learned that the British Government had authorized a full-scale evacuation. In the wake of this not altogether unexpected news, Gort instructed Sir Ronald Adam, the GOC III Corps, to go to Dunkirk and make preparations for the exodus, as well as organizing the defensive perimeter. His staff was to consist of Lieutenant-General Lindsell, the quartermaster general, Major-General Pakenham-Walsh, the chief engineer, and a number of other senior officers such as Brigadier Parminter, who were already at work in the port.

While this conference was in progress, some stages of the Allied retreat had already begun. The bulk of the French First Army started its withdrawal before nightfall on the twenty-sixth, with the divisions of IV and V Corps pulling back from the dangerous pocket they occupied south of the Scarpe. These two corps had been subjected to intense pressure on both flanks of the salient, and no supplies had reached them since the twentieth. Their quartermasters had been forced to forage for food in the surrounding towns and countryside and somehow they had kept the men fed. Most serious of all was the ammunition situation; supplies of artillery shells were practically exhausted.

For both corps, the retreat to the Lys involved a move westward
across the Deule canal, between its junction with the La Bassée canal
and Lille. There were only four crossings over the Deule, and by
the evening of the twenty-sixth the German II Corps had already
reached the La Bassée canal, menacing the French left, and indeed
a small bridgehead across it had been established by units of
Rommel's Seventh Panzer Division. Nevertheless General Aymes's
IV Corps managed to extricate itself without too much trouble under
cover of darkness, regrouping around Seclin to the north-west in
preparation for the final move to the Lys on the night of the twenty-
seventh to eighth.

General Altmayer's V Corps, on the other hand, experienced a
good deal more difficulty. Two of its divisions were directly threatened by a heavy German attack that developed towards Carvin,
which the retreating IV Corps troops could see burning in the far
distance. As V Corps withdrew up the Seclin road, passing to the
east of Douai, it came under heavy artillery fire from the west, and
from first light on the twenty-seventh it was subjected to almost continual Luftwaffe attacks. To make matters worse, some units took
the wrong road and became hopelessly entangled with their colleagues of IV Corps, who were trying to get across the Deule. The
result was total confusion, which would soon give way to disaster.

The other First Army formation, General de la Laurencie's III
Corps, withdrew in good order, its left flank covered by the British
I Corps at Bourghelles. On de la Laurencie's right, the British 4th
and 42nd Divisions of Lieutenant-General Alan Brooke's II Corps
also withdrew to the Lys between Armentières and Comines on the
night of the twenty-seventh to eighth; I Corps did the same, leaving
a rearguard on the Deule north of Lille. By mid-morning on the
twenty-eighth de la Laurencie had got four-fifths of his men across
the Lys – all in fact except some units of his 1st Division, which
formed the rearguard. Trapped by the jaws of 5th and 7th Panzer,
this remnant was forced to turn about and take refuge in Lille itself.

That the French III Corps – or most of it – completed its withdrawal without encountering serious problems was a tribute to the
dashing and able de la Laurencie, an officer beloved by the men
who served under him. If only, in those dark hours, France had

possessed more generals of his calibre and power of leadership, men
with the ability to make a decision and see it through to the bitter
end! One historian wrote of him:

> In the midst of this chaos of retreat, in which misinformation and
> rumour, as well as attacks by enemy aircraft, led to bewilderment,
> indecision and despair, at once heroic and absurd, in which the
> prospect of leaving France affected men with terrors more shat-
> tering than the expectation of death, wounds or captivity, the
> figure of General de la Laurencie of III Corps stands out as con-
> spicuously as Kemmel Hill on the Flanders Plain.[1]

On the day the retreat began, de la Laurencie had received orders
that his regiments were to burn their colours. 'Why this act of despair?' he wrote in his diary. 'We are not yet on our knees, and the
gate at Dunkirk is still open. My men trust their officers; they have
ammunition; they *can* and *will* fight. They cannot do that without
colours. I shall not carry out the order, and the regiments will march
past with their colours on 30 May.[2]

Such a man was General Fournel de la Laurencie, whose fortunes
from now on were to be inextricably and proudly mingled with the
'perfidious English' many of his colleagues affected to distrust.

Meanwhile the creation of the perimeter around Dunkirk went
ahead. Sir Ronald Adam's plan was to lay out the British part of the
perimeter in three corps sectors. Adam's own III Corps would assume
responsibility for the defence of the Dunkirk sector itself, with
Lieutenant-General Michael Barker's I Corps on its left and Alan
Brooke's II Corps holding the extreme eastern sector past the France–
Belgian frontier as far as Nieuport. III Corps would be evacuated
first, followed by II Corps and lastly I Corps, which would provide
the rearguard.

Adam was worried about the state of General Fagalde's forces,
which were to provide the defensive shield on the western flank of
the perimeter on the line Dunkirk–Gravelines–Watten–Cassel–
Steenworde. Although von Rundstedt's halt order had prevented
the panzer groups from striking across the Aa against the French,
units of the Leibstandarte Adolf Hitler SS Division had crossed
over and were engaging the 68th Division at both Watten and

Gravelines, inflicting heavy casualties on the French 137th Regiment at Gravelines and gaining some ground at Watten. In most places, however, the French line held, and the situation remained fairly stable until the morning of 27 May, when, following the lifting of the '*Halt Befehl*', Guderian's XIX Panzer Corps threw its weight across the Aa against the already battered 137th Regiment, the attack spearheaded by 2nd Panzer. That afternoon the tanks broke through between Bourbourg and Capelle-Brouck, compelling the French 68th Division to fall back to a line between Drincham and Wormhoudt.

At 07.00 on the twenty-seventh, Admiral Abrial called a meeting in Cassel of the senior officers responsible for the defence of Dunkirk. The principal figures present were Sir Ronald Adam, Generals Fagalde, Blanchard and Prioux, and an emissary from General Weygand, General Koeltz, who had reached Dunkirk via London and Dover only that morning. Koeltz made it clear that Weygand had issued no instructions covering an evacuation of the French forces in the north; instead, the generalissimo regarded the Dunkirk bridgehead as a permanent bastion from which the struggle should continue. Koeltz went on to propose, on behalf of Weygand, that every effort should be made to relieve Calais; no one in Dunkirk yet knew that Calais had fallen. The discussion then turned to the arrangements for the joint defence of the Dunkirk bridgehead; it was rudely interrupted by a German artillery barrage and the delegates went their separate ways.

Koeltz went off with General Prioux, the new commander of the First Army, to the latter's HQ at Steenwerck. After further discussion he moved on to the Belgian headquarters near Bruges, where he had a stormy encounter with the C-in-C, General van Overstraeten. Both Koeltz and General Champon, the senior French liaison officer with the Belgian Army, were certain that the Belgians were on the point of surrendering. Koeltz passed on this impression to Admiral Abrial whom he sought out in Dunkirk later, while *en route* to find Gort's HQ; Abrial confirmed that the Belgian intention was indeed to capitulate, and that a delegation would be sent to the Germans that evening.

Lord Gort had already received a similar indication that morning in the form of a message from Admiral Keyes. King Leopold, Keyes said, was seriously concerned about the morale of his troops after four days of continual air attack and warned that the time was rapidly approaching when he could no longer rely on them to fight. He would therefore be obliged to surrender to forestall a disaster.

This message reached Gort just after he had moved to a new command post at Houtkerque, six miles north-west of Poperinghe. Faced with the grim prospect of a Belgian collapse, with all its attendant dangers to the left flank of the BEF, Gort immediately set off together with General Pownall to try and find Blanchard with a view to reaching agreement on the next stage of the withdrawal. The two British officers reached Dunkirk that evening, picking their way with difficulty through streets choked with the debris of enemy air attacks, and eventually arrived at Admiral Abrial's headquarters in Bastion 32 at about 23.00. Koeltz was there; he informed a dismayed Gort that the Belgians had begun surrender negotiations with the enemy at 19.30 and that King Leopold was sueing for an unconditional surrender to take effect at midnight. Gort returned to his command post, arriving at 03.00 after a nightmare journey over the congested roads; the need to meet Blanchard was more pressing than ever, but Blanchard was nowhere to be found.

In fact Blanchard had set off earlier that day to find his headquarters, which was in the process of moving, although no one had told him to where. Eventually, during his wanderings, it was Blanchard who found Gort at 11.00 in the morning of the twenty-eighth. Gort had just received a telegram from Anthony Eden, authorizing him to evacuate the maximum force possible, and he asked Blanchard if he intended to comply by ordering a full French withdrawal into the Dunkirk bridgehead. But Blanchard was adamant; his forces would hold their present positions and would take part in no evacuation. Both Gort and Pownall pleaded with him to change his mind, but the commander of Army Group One remained inflexible. Finally, he asked Gort whether he still intended to withdraw the BEF into the bridgehead, knowing that the French would not take similar steps. Gort replied that his plans remained unaltered. The BEF commander pointed out that although it would take the

Germans some time to exploit the gap that had been filled until now by the Belgians, the Allied line from Gravelines to the Lys was under heavy pressure and might collapse at any moment. The Allies, he said, must fall back to the line Ypres–Poperinghe–Cassel during the coming night. 'To wait till tomorrow was to give *two* days to the Germans to get behind us, an act of madness. We thought it unlikely that we could get even thirty per cent of our forces away.'[3]

In the middle of the argument, a French staff officer arrived with the news that General Prioux's forces, now assembled between Béthune and Lille, were too exhausted to withdraw any further, That settled matters as far as Blanchard was concerned. 'I was,' Gort wrote later, 'completely unable to move him.'[4]

The collapse of the Belgians created new problems to add weight to those already faced by Sir Ronald Adam in his efforts to form the Dunkirk perimeter. He was desperately short of men; General Thorne's six infantry battalions at Bergues were fully committed to the battle against the divisions of the German XIV Corps, which had just relieved Guderian's XIX and which had been attacking the Bergues sector with renewed vigour since the lifting of the halt order and Thorne had no troops to spare. Adam consequently was forced to scrape together whatever troops were immediately available, while sending urgent requests to the BEF corps commanders to re-ease detachments for perimeter defence duties. With these scratch forces Adam hoped to be able to hold the perimeter until the arrival of the main body of the BEF; now, with the disintegration of the Belgians on the left flank, there was a grave danger that the Germans would reach Dunkirk before the British. Adam, ably assisted by Brigadier E. F. Lawson, did what he could; while Lawson positioned the various artillery units that had already been sent back to cover every bridge along the perimeter as far as Furnes, Adam set out to round up any troops he could find and use them to plug the more dangerous gaps. After that it was a question of waiting for the embattled divisions to arrive, with their all-important weapons and ammunition, to form a stronger defensive line prior to embarkation.

General Alexander's 1st Division had already been squeezed out of the centre of the line on the Lys and ordered to fall back directly on Dunkirk to man the perimeter defences. The order came as a

surprise to officers and men alike, as the history of the Coldstream
Guards records:

> We sat down on chairs making a circle round the room and
> waited. The Commanding Officer looked up and, after a pause,
> said: 'We are to march 55 miles back to the coast' – he paused
> again and looked around at us. Our hearts sank. Fifty-five miles
> seemed a bit too much. Then he went on – 'and embark for
> England!' Immediate sensation. No one had expected this. We
> had had vague ideas of falling back as the armies of 1914 had
> fallen back until, somehow, sometime, we too should stand and
> fight our victorious battle of the Marne. But this! There was a
> sudden loosening of the tension we had been living under so long.
> We felt a surge of contentment beneath our anxiety about the
> war news in general and our own immediate prospects in parti-
> cular. Then we thought again of the 55 miles and wondered.[5]

They were not the only ones to wonder. Everywhere, on that
morning of 28 May, the news was bad for the Allies. In Lille the
French IV and V Corps had been surrounded and were being systematically cut to pieces by the enemy; the garrison would finally surrender on 31 May after forty-eight hours of valiant but fruitless
resistance, being permitted to march out with colours flying by the
victors. Only a few of the defenders managed to escape, some
reaching Dunkirk.

Elsewhere the whole of the BEF and what was left of the French
First Army was under fierce pressure. Time, now, was the vital
factor: and on 28 May time seemed to be on the side of the enemy.

5 'Dynamo'

'The Admiralty have made an order requiring all owners of self-propelled pleasure craft between thirty and one hundred feet in length to send any further particulars of them to the Admiralty within fourteen days from today, if they have not already been offered or requisitioned.'

That, really, was how it all began: with that laconic order issued by some far-sighted and unknown naval officer in the Admiralty and read out to the nation after the nine o'clock news on Tuesday 14 May 1940. The Battle of Flanders was four days old, and although the Germans were breaking through at Sedan and in the Ardennes, although the Dutch Army in the north was shattered, the British Expeditionary Force had not yet made serious contact with the enemy and there was no thought of retreat in the minds of either the British field commanders or the Government; yet somewhere in the corridors of Whitehall a naval staff officer whose name is not on record had envisaged the dark days that lay ahead and, sensing that the sea might become the only avenue of escape for an embattled army, had acted on his premonition.

The response was immediate and overwhelming. From all round the shores of the United Kingdom, from harbours and holiday resorts, from companies and individuals, the required information poured in to the Admiralty. Within days naval clerks had succeeded in compiling a bulky register giving the name, details and location of almost every small craft that lay in the ports, estuaries and rivers of the British Isles: a shadow fleet which, if the circumstances warranted, would be ready to answer the Navy's call.

Five days later, on 19 May, the prospect of massive evacuation as the only means of saving the BEF was fast becoming nightmare reality. On that day the task of operational planning for a possible evacuation was assigned to Admiral Sir Bertram Ramsay, the flag officer commanding Dover. Together with Admiral Sir Reginald Drax, the c-in-c Nore, Ramsay had hitherto been responsible for the naval units – principally destroyers detached from Scapa Flow – which had been providing a kind of shuttle service for naval and military personnel to Ijmuiden, the Hook of Holland, Flushing and Antwerp. With the Dutch collapse these craft had been involved in evacuating servicemen and vips, including the Dutch Royal Family, in clearing useful shipping from the harbours and in transferring the substantial Dutch reserves of gold and diamonds to England. Attention was then switched to the Belgian ports, and naval parties successfully removed large numbers of merchantmen, barges and tugs from Antwerp. The relatively small destroyer force worked tirelessly, embarking and landing troops, bringing out Allied missions and foreign nationals, and bombarding shore targets as well as providing additional anti-aircraft capability against the Luftwaffe's increasingly furious attacks.[1]

When Admiral Ramsay took inventory on 19 May, the picture that presented itself was depressing enough. Apart from the destroyers, which were fully committed, Ramsay had only thirty-six personnel craft of various types and tonnage at his disposal, based either at Southampton or Dover; hardly sufficient to evacuate from Calais, Boulogne and Dunkirk at the rate of 10,000 men from each port every twenty-four hours, as was envisaged during a meeting of the War Cabinet on the morning of 20 May. During this meeting Churchill advised that, 'as a precautionary measure, the Admiralty should assemble a large number of small vessels in readiness to proceed to ports and inlets on the French coast',[2] thus taking a stage further the registration process begun several days earlier. In the meantime, Ramsay's force was increased by the immediate addition of thirty passenger ferries, twelve naval drifters and six small coasters, while on 22 May the Admiralty ordered forty Dutch schuits which had come to Britain on Holland's collapse to be requisitioned and manned by naval crews.

Even at a time when Boulogne and Calais were still in Allied hands, it was clear that any major pickup would have to be from Dunkirk; and Ramsay, who knew those waters intimately from

service during the First World War, was well aware of the difficulties likely to be caused by the geography of the port and its surrounding terrain, quite apart from any interference by the enemy.
For centuries, this stretch of coast had been noted for its treachery;
for twenty-five miles, the sea-bed was littered with the wrecks of
ships, the rusting hulks of twentieth-century freighters and warships
nestling beside the rotting timbers of long-dead galleons. The
beaches east of Dunkirk, stretching for sixteen miles beyond Nieuport to the mouth of the river Yser, formed the longest continuous
stretch of sand in the whole of Europe. They were remarkable for
their uniformity, sloping down gradually into the sea along their
entire length; some three-quarters of a mile from low-water mark
there was the deep-water channel of the Rade de Dunkerque, about
half a mile wide and between forty and fifty feet deep, with wave
of sandbanks to seaward.

The depth of the beaches was also a notable factor. The sands
proper were bounded on the landward side by brick sea-walls, beyond which lay a broad expanse of dunes dotted with clusters of
rough sea-grass and interlaced with drainage channels; here and
there poplars and windmills stood out starkly against the skyline.
Taking the area of the dunes into account, the overall width of the
beaches was, on average, one mile. It was small wonder that in the
days of peace the area had been immensely popular with holiday-
makers; the main holiday resort had been Malo les Bains to the east
of Dunkirk, famous for its casino and kursaal. Further to the east
was a small resort, Bray Dunes, also with a casino, and still further
along the beach lay the village of La Panne, where King Albert of
Belgium had established his headquarters during the First World
War and which, before that, had been a favourite rendezvous for
artists from all over Europe. None of these places had a pier or jetty,
or indeed any facility that might assist embarkation.

Although the vast expanse of dunes would prove ideal for the
assembly of large numbers of troops, and control centres to handle
them could be readily established at Malo les Bains, Bray Dunes and
La Panne, the nature of the beaches themselves would make evacuation a slow and arduous task; yet, as Ramsay was well aware, it
was from the beaches that the biggest lift would have to be made.

Because of strong tidal currents sweeping past the entrance, and a fairly narrow deep water approach, Dunkirk was never an easy harbour to enter at the best of times; the flotsam of war would now make the task doubly difficult, especially since most pickup operations would have to be carried out at night to avoid the worst of the enemy's air attacks and the naval crews would have no peacetime navigation beacons to guide them.

To make matters worse, there was no possibility of using the main harbour, with its seven dock basins; this had already been blocked by air attack on 20 May, and if it had not been for the action of Admiral Abrial, who had ordered several merchantmen and French naval craft out to sea as soon as the attacks began, the blockage would certainly have been much worse. As it was, only two main embarkation points were left in Dunkirk itself; a jetty to the west of the harbour and the Jetée de l'Est, or east mole, a strong wooden structure thrusting out north-north-west into the sea from the Promenade de la Digue, a 900-yard stone causeway bounding the canal mouth on the north side. Although 1,400 yards long the mole itself was extremely narrow, measuring about five feet across for most of its length. It was to defy every attempt by the Luftwaffe and the German artillery to destroy it, and in the event most of the troops who embarked via Dunkirk harbour passed along it.

It was clear that the operation was going to be a job for small craft – boats capable of running a ferry service from the beaches to ships offshore, and ships with a shallow enough draught to enable them to negotiate the obstacle-ridden waters in and around Dunkirk harbour. Destroyers were vital to Ramsay's plans; although far from ideal as troopships, they could take their quota of men and their speed and manœuvrability would make them difficult targets to hit. Moreover their firepower would prove an invaluable asset, particularly in the anti-aircraft role. The problem was that in May 1940 destroyers were fast becoming worth more than their weight in gold; of the 220 on the Royal Navy's inventory at that time, the majority were in the Mediterranean or the Far East, and many of those serving with the Home Fleet were heavily committed in the Norwegian campaign. The withdrawal of destroyers and, to a lesser extent, cruisers from the Home Fleet for service with the Nore and

Dover Commands was a serious step, at a time when the protection of Atlantic shipping routes was fast becoming vital to the survival of Britain, but it was a risk that had to be taken. Fortunately, although the British did not know it at the time, the losses suffered by the German Navy off Norway had been extensive enough to prevent any forays into the Atlantic by enemy surface vessels for some time to come.[3]

After conferring with Admiral Sir Charles Forbes, the c-in-c Home Fleet, Ramsay took stock. He could count on the services of some forty destroyers, although it would be a week before some of them could be released from their stations. Meanwhile those that were available were placed on readiness, although their captains were not yet briefed on the task that lay ahead of them. The task of requisitioning merchant ships went ahead smoothly; by nightfall on 26 May Ramsay would have a hundred and thirty at his disposal: steam packets, cross-channel ferries, coasters and the Dutch schuits, the flat-bottomed barges whose shallow draught would make them invaluable for close-in work.

Around him the dapper fifty-seven-year-old Ramsay assembled a first-rate staff. There was Captain William Tennant, who would have command of the operation on shore at Dunkirk with twelve naval officers and a hundred and fifty ratings under him; Commander Archibald Day, who as hydrographer had the job of working out the cross-channel routes to be followed by the evacuation fleet; Commander James Stopford, Ramsay's flag officer, who would be at the hub of all communications; and others, all of them specialists in their own field, all of them working as a team to control either end of the lifeline that stretched across the English Channel.

Meanwhile in support of the naval operation the biggest movements programme in the history of British transport was rapidly being organized all over southern England. It was only days since, following the news of the German offensive on 10 May, the British Government had broadcast:

The invasion of Holland and Belgium has created a situation in which it is imperative that the people of this country should forgo their Whitsuntide holiday, should remain at work so far as it is practicable, and should avoid all unnecessary travel. The Government has cancelled the Whitsuntide holiday and the King's Birthday holiday for all civil servants and workers in industrial establishments. Additional holiday services which the railway companies and other transport authorities were proposing to run are being cancelled or severely restricted.[4]

On 20 May, with posters advertising the delights of continental holidays by rail still looking down wryly from the hoardings of stations all over the country, the Railway Executive Committee received its orders from the Government. They were simple enough on paper: namely to move the British and Allied troops from the Channel ports to various assembly points as fast as the Royal Navy and its impressed civilian craft could ferry them across. It was plain, however, that the execution of these orders would present huge problems, and the first of these was apparent even now: there was no way of planning ahead, for it was impossible to know how many troops would be arriving, or where and when they would be coming ashore. There was no information on which to work, and no time to prepare and issue written instructions. Everything had to be done by telephone, with railway staff taking split-second decisions as the situation developed.

The burden of the operation was clearly going to fall on the Southern Railway, since most of the ports involved came within this company's territory, and a joint military and civil control centre was established at Redhill in Surrey. The first task was to form a pool of trains, and an urgent request for help went out to the regions. Within three days 186 trains had been assembled, of which 55 came from the Southern, 40 from the Great Western, 44 from the LMS and 47 from the LNER. Each train consisted of ten coaches, a number that could easily be handled by any locomotive.

As a prelude to the evacuation proper – and an immensely valuable one – fifty-five special troop trains were laid on between 20 May and midnight on the twenty-sixth to bring a total of 24,108 soldiers away from the Channel ports to assembly points inland; these were mostly non-combatants and wounded, whose evacuation had already been given priority. It proved a very useful exercise and progressed fairly smoothly; any snags that appeared were meticulously noted and ironed out before the really hectic days arrived.

While this operation was in progress, railway staff laboured to work out routes for the expected flood of traffic. Because of congestion problems it was decided to bypass London altogether, which meant that the cross-country routes selected would have to handle an intensity of traffic for which they had never been designed. One factor was in the planners' favour: the railways would not be called upon to handle heavy equipment. Only men would be coming back, and they would be travelling light.

Dover was selected as the principal railhead since its port facilities were more extensive than those of other cross-channel stations like Folkestone. Also the presence there of the Naval and Military Commands would make the task of close liaison a lot simpler. The fact that Dover was relatively exposed and close to the French coast, with the consequent danger of air attack, was a risk that had to be taken. Railway and military officials shuddered to think what would happen if the Luftwaffe bombed the tunnels along the coastal section between Dover and Folkestone, or the junction at Redhill, where the troop trains would diverge to their destinations in many parts of the country.

Estimates on how many troops could be lifted from the beaches varied wildly, although it was generally thought that between 30,000 and 45,000 could be brought away in the two days or so that would be available before the enemy closed the net. Speed was the essential factor, and for this reason it was planned to use the shortest sea crossing between Dunkirk and Dover – the thirty-nine-mile Route z. Besides this, however, Ramsay's hydrographer had also set up two alternative routes: Route y, an eighty-seven-mile dogleg that crossed from Dover to the Kwinte Buoy off Ostend before veering to approach Dunkirk from the east, and a fifty-five-mile-long Route x, which crossed the Ruytingen Bank and joined the deep-water channel halfway between Dunkirk and Gravelines. It was as well that these two alternates were available, for by 26 May the Germans had reached Gravelines and had seized the French coastal gun batteries there, menacing all shipping on the short Route z.

As 26 May drew to a close, the Admiralty dared wait no longer.

Every hour's delay from now on would mean the sacrifice of men as the jaws of the German vice tightened. At 18.57 hours on that day, the signal went out: 'Operation Dynamo is to commence.' It was a singularly appropriate code-name, and had been thought up by someone on Ramsay's staff because the operations room at Dover Castle had once housed electrical plant. The room was now a power-house of a different kind, and in the days to come it would be taxed to the utmost of its capacity.

The ships that were to spearhead Dynamo – the elderly Isle of Man steam packets *Mona's Isle* and *King Orry* – were already at sea. They berthed at Dunkirk shortly after dark and at once began taking on troops. The *Mona's Isle* was the first to leave, at dawn on the twenty-seventh, carrying 1,420 soldiers. As she retraced her path along Route z she was straddled by enemy shellfire, and a few minutes later low-flying Messerschmitts raked her decks with cannon and machine-gun fire. By the time she reached Dover, twenty-three of her passengers were dead and sixty wounded.

Meanwhile five more transports had made an abortive attempt to reach Dunkirk early that morning. They ran into the heavy shells from the Gravelines batteries. The motor vessel *Sequacity* was hit and sank within minutes; the remainder, unable to break through the fearsome curtain of water hurled up by the shells, turned away and came back to Dover empty.

It was clear that it was only a question of time before Route z would have to be closed, which meant using the longer routes – and then, with the armada of ships exposed for hours on the long haul, it would be the Luftwaffe's turn. For the bulk of the BEF, still fighting its way back to the perimeter, the chances of survival now seemed slender indeed.

6 Fighting Retreat

By the morning of 26 May, as we have seen, the rapid collapse of the Belgian Army had opened up a dangerous gap on the left of General Brooke's II Corps, where nothing now stood in the path of the three German divisions advancing through Belgium except a solitary British brigade, the 143rd of 48th Division, which had been hastily pushed into the breach to hold a 10,000-yard front along the Ypres–Comines canal. The danger that the enemy divisions would reach the coast before the bulk of the BEF was now a real and fearsome possibility, and it was to stave it off that General Franklyn was briefed to march north with the 5th and 50th Divisions following the collapse of the projected Anglo-French counter-offensive and hold the Ypres–Comines Line for as long as possible.

As the divisions moved northward – with the 5th in the lead by a considerable distance – Franklyn knew that it would be touch and go whether they arrived in the line before the enemy spearheads struck at the tenuous defences of 143rd Brigade. He issued his orders while the divisions were still on the march; 143rd Brigade was to close in to its right and reduce the frontage to be defended to 5,000 yards, leaving the remaining 5,000 yards to the 13th and 17th Brigades of 5th Division. The 13th Brigade would be responsible for defending the 3,000-yard centre sector of the line, while 17th Brigade would hold the 2,000 yards on the extreme left.

Franklyn had a considerable advantage; he was familiar with the terrain to be defended, having fought over it in 1916. Setting up his HQ in Ploegsteert Château, he set out at dawn on 26 May to make a first-hand reconnaissance and to confer with Brigadier Muirhead of 143rd Brigade, which was settling into its new positions after completing the closing manoeuvre to the right. Shortly afterwards the leading elements of 13th and 17th Brigades began to arrive;

they were greeted by heavy mortar fire from advance units of the German Sixth Army, which had just reached the other side of the canal.

Franklyn's reconnaissance of the ground did little to reassure him All along the 5th Division's front, which extended from a bend in the canal north of Hollebeke to Zillebeke, a village three miles south-east of Ypres, the nature of the terrain compelled the British positions to be sited for the most part on forward slopes in full view of the enemy and open to heavy and accurate mortar and shellfire. The canal itself was of no real use as an anti-tank obstacle, being completely dry; it had long been disused and contained only some mud and weeds. To add to the defenders' problems, a railway line on a raised embankment ran parallel to the canal on the opposite bank, providing excellent cover for the enemy. Nevertheless the canal formed the only barrier in an otherwise featureless countryside, and Franklyn had to make the best of it. There was one bright spot in a generally unfavourable situation: General Brooke had managed to secure the whole of the heavy and medium artillery of 1 Corps, and this was now placed under Franklyn's command together with two regiments of field artillery. Further support had also been promised from the French 1st Light Armoured Division, but when Brigadier Stopford of 17th Brigade went to Zillebeke in search of them he found only a handful of tanks, and these were getting ready to move out to Ypres. It was therefore clear that 17th Brigade would have to hold the Zillebeke sector alone until the arrival of reinforcements from 50th Division. Selecting his positions carefully, Stopford placed the 6th Seaforth Highlanders on the left of the brigade, along the railway line, and the 2nd Royal Scots Fusiliers on the right, holding the 2nd Northamptons in reserve in an area of thickly wooded country on the west bank of the canal. On 17th Brigade's right, Brigadier Dempsey's 13th Brigade, with the 2nd Royal Iniskillings on the left, the 2nd Cameronians on the right – linking up with the 17th Royal Warwicks of 143rd Brigade – and the 2nd Wiltshires in reserve, holding the high ground half a mile east of the St Eloi–Warneton road, extended as far as the village of Houthem (not to be confused with Houthem on the Dunkirk perimeter).

The German assault was not long in coming. The enemy's plan

envisaged an attack by the 18th, 31st and 61st Divisions of von Reichenau's Sixth Army with the primary objective of taking Kemmel and Poperinghe. The first major assault developed on the early morning of 27 May against Comines, on 143rd Brigade's front, and the Germans succeeded in penetrating among some of the widely-dispersed British positions. A few of these were completely surrounded, but the defenders hung on grimly and throughout that day there was a confused mixture of friendly and enemy troops all along 143rd Brigade's sector. The 1/7th and 8th Royal Warwicks suffered particularly heavily, withering before a rain of mortar bombs and deadly streams of Spandau machine-gun fire. The brigade's position would have quickly become untenable had the Germans been able to use their artillery, but the intermingling of friend and foe prevented this.

The British artillery, on the other hand, was able to keep up a brisk fire on the concentrations of enemy troops which could be seen moving beyond the railway line. Realizing that he would have no air observation facilities, Franklyn had lost no time in setting up a network of excellent observation posts which were able to direct the artillery with considerable accuracy. To some extent targets had to be selected by guesswork, but Franklyn had so much artillery at his disposal that whole areas could be blanketed.

Although 143rd Brigade continued to cling on stubbornly throughout the afternoon of the twenty-seventh, an enemy attack against Houthem, another between the 2nd Cameronians and the 2nd Royal Iniskillings and a third on Hollebeke put the neighbouring 13th Brigade in a dangerous position by early afternoon. Brigadier (later General Sir Miles) Dempsey accordingly ordered his forward battalions to pull back to the high ground along the Eloi–Warneton road, where the 2nd Wiltshires were already in place. The withdrawal was difficult, being harrassed by continual shellfire and enemy patrols.

Further to the north, 17th Brigade had also been under heavy attack since 10.00 hours; in this sector relentless enemy pressure threw back the 6th Seaforth Highlanders from their positions along the railway line and almost surrounded the 2nd Royal Scots Fusiliers. By 13.00 hours both battalions had pulled back to the south of the

2nd Northampton reserve position, which soon also found itself under attack.

Meanwhile the 50th Division column had been moving up to the Ypres area with all possible speed, passing through places where every name resounded with history; Armentières, Neuve Eglise, Kemmel. Every few miles there was a 1914–18 cemetery, slumbering in the May sunshine while a new war seethed all around. The division's passage was not easy, for the roads were choked with transport of every description. The sight of mile upon mile of road-way lined with vehicles all trying to move in opposite directions, as was the case around Armentières on that Sunday afternoon of 26 May, was little short of terrifying. Because of this congestion, it was not until the evening of the twenty-seventh that the division's leading element, 150th Brigade, began to filter into the line at Zillebeke, the remainder of the division following during the night to take up positions in and around Ypres.

General Brooke of II Corps, in the meantime, had been making determined efforts to secure other units to strengthen the British line. From the 1st Infantry Division he drew the 3rd Grenadier Guards, the 2nd North Staffords and the 2nd Sherwood Foresters; from the 4th Division came the 10th and 11th Infantry Brigades, together with the division's Royal Engineers, and GHQ provided the 13th/18th Hussars. With these fresh units Franklyn planned to launch a series of counter-attacks before nightfall to alleviate the pressure on all three brigade fronts and particularly on the left flank, where the situation was serious. He also made an impromptu arrangement with 4th Division to the effect that some of the division's troops, who had been sent across the Lys to cover the flank of the 4th's withdrawal, should mount an attack along the banks of the river up to Comines. The units involved were the 6th Black Watch and the 7th and 59th Field Companies Royal Engineers, supported by some light tanks of the 13th/18th Hussars. They jumped off at 19.00 hours on the twenty-seventh and after some heavy fighting succeeded in driving the enemy back to the line of the river Kortekeer, inflicting substantial casualties on them.

This limited success prompted Franklyn to mount a bigger counter-attack on the right flank of the defensive line later that evening, using the 3rd Grenadier Guards and the 2nd North Staffords. Franklyn was well aware of the risks involved; the attack would have to be made in the twilight over unknown ground, always a hazardous undertaking. Nevertheless the demand was urgent and Franklyn believed it a justifiable risk, as did the two battalion commanders involved: Major Alan Adair of the Grenadiers and Lieutenant-Colonel Butterworth of the North Staffords.

The North Staffords were the first to cross the start line at 21.00, followed by the Grenadiers twenty minutes later. The two battalions advanced separately in the dusk; there was no contact between them and, indeed, there had been no time to work out anything but a sketchy plan for co-ordination. Surprisingly enough the advance went better than anyone had anticipated. Moving along either side of the Messines road on the left, the North Staffords encountered only light opposition for the first mile, and this mainly from groups of Germans who had infiltrated. As they pressed on, however, the troops met increasingly heavy mortar and small-arms fire. Just before midnight the spearhead of the battalion reached the Kortekeer, where it relieved some hard-pressed Royal Warwicks of 143rd Brigade, and at this point Butterworth decided to consolidate the ground he had won.

The Grenadiers, meanwhile, had moved up towards Comines on the left of the railway line that led to the town. After advancing for half an hour, meeting only slight opposition from isolated enemy groups, they heard sounds of battle ahead and increased their pace. As they topped a slight rise they saw a confusion of figures in the distance, moving in the glare of burning farm buildings; it was the Black Watch and Royal Engineers, fighting hard at the limit of their advance. Among them, like crawling beetles, the light tanks of the 13th/18th Hussars darted streams of glittering tracer at the enemy positions. The Grenadiers quickly joined up with the others and charged with the bayonet, driving out the remaining Germans. The cost to the British had been high, but by midnight most of the enemy had been cleared from the west bank of the canal and the threatened right flank secured.

During the night the 11th Brigade of 4th Division arrived in the line and was positioned behind the central sector of Wytschaete

D

Ridge, which had been the scene of bitter fighting during the earlier war. Some time later units of General Montgomery's 3rd Division also began to arrive in the battle area, passing behind the British front and moving into position on the left of 50th Division, extending the frontage along the Yser canal to the north of Ypres. The 3rd Division's move was highly complicated by congestion on the roads, and for the sake of rapid movement the divisional artillery was ordered to disable and abandon its medium guns. It was now that the high standard of training among Montgomery's men paid dividends; the move was successfully completed in conditions of pitch darkness and pouring rain, with both British and German artillery shells screeching overhead, and the division's 8th and 9th Brigades were established in the line by 10.00 on 28 May.

Franklyn had planned to make a counter-attack with the help of the 4th Division's 10th Brigade on the morning of 28 May, but before this could be carried out the German 18th Division launched a heavy assault on the sector of the line held by the Grenadiers and North Staffords, and although both battalions managed to hold on they suffered more casualties than they had sustained during the counter-attack on the previous evening. Heavy attacks also fell on Brigadier Dempsey's 13th Brigade, but the British held on here with great determination and gave the enemy a hard beating. A subsequent counter-attack by the 10th Brigade sealed off the holes torn by the infiltration of the German attackers, and by nightfall on the 28th the British line was fairly secure once more.

At this point, however, all officers of company commander level learned that the evacuation of the British Expeditionary Force had begun. Only now was it fully realized to what extent the salvation of the BEF had depended on the gallant two-day defence of the Ypres–Comines Line; it was also clear that, following the hammer-blow of the Belgian Army's surrender, the line would rapidly become untenable as the enemy speared round its left flank. At 22.00 hours on the twenty-eighth orders were accordingly issued for the units in the line to begin a gradual withdrawal, with the 3rd and 50th Divisions swinging back north-westwards from the Yser canal and Ypres to form a new line between Poperinghe and Noordschote, blowing bridges over the Yser as they went. This was carried out only just in time; minutes after the last bridge had been blown a mass of German motorized infantry was seen pouring into Dixmude, on the other side of the Yser. Had they captured the bridges intact they would have been in a position to thrust straight on to Nieuport on the coast, threatening the Dunkirk bridgehead from the north-east.

Further south, along the line of the Ypres–Comines canal itself, the 5th Division was desperately hard-pressed throughout the twenty-eighth. Of 17th Brigade, the Northamptons were over-whelmed after a bitter four-hour battle, only one company managing to make its escape, while the Royal Scots Fusiliers were virtually annihilated. A counter-attack by the 2nd Duke of Cornwall's Light Infantry of 10th Brigade temporarily saved the situation on the right flank of the Royal Scots, the regiment's carrier platoon raiding St Eloi and killing some seventy Germans, and in the respite gained by this operation two battalions of the 10th Brigade, the 2nd Bed-fords and the 1/6th East Surreys, were able to plug the dangerous gap. Although too late to save the 17th Brigade, the 10th's action brought some relief to the 13th, which managed to beat off suc-cessive attacks until the enemy's efforts dwindled away under a fierce downpour of rain in the late afternoon.

The withdrawal began at dusk, the battered, exhausted battalions falling back towards Poperinghe over roads littered with debris. Here, while the 5th Division moved on its way towards the Dunkirk perimeter, halting on the river Yser five miles behind the battle-front, the units that had come down from Ypres and the canal be-yond set up the final rearguard position. On either side of Poperinghe stood 150th Brigade of 50th Division, with 151st Brigade falling back into line with them on their left, while 9th Brigade of the 3rd Divi-sion also swung back to join the left of the 151st. At the end of the line the 8th Brigade of 3rd Division was positioned between Noord-schote on the left and Steenstraat, on the Yser canal, on the right.

The Steenstraat position – in other words the right flank of 8th Brigade – was held by the 4th Royal Berkshire, and it was on this battalion that the full fury of the renewed German attack broke at dawn on 29 May. The German 30th Infantry Division struck hard at the British positions under cover of a heavy artillery barrage, forcing the Berkshires to make for higher ground to the rear. This short and bloody action is vividly recalled by Private Mons Trussler, of the 4th Battalion:[1]

In the early hours of the 29th the section I was in was ordered back to a farmhouse on a small hill. Things were rather quiet at first, but about 3 am we came under shellfire that grew more intense as time went by, and at dawn the enemy were within small-arms range. Soon afterwards we were told to go down to the forward positions to help strengthen the line. As we left the farmhouse the enemy started belting us with the most accurate mortar fire I have ever seen. There were six of us, and the bombs were actually falling among us as we ran. It was impossible to take more than one or two strides before a fresh bomb sent us face down in the dirt. I saw one man with his hand sliced clean off. They mortared us all the way down the slope until we reached the breastworks at the bottom; they had been built during the 1914–18 War and formed our main defences. Our arrival was greeted by an enemy observation plane, which dropped a smoke marker almost on our heads – the signal for more mortar fire.

Not long afterwards a stream of chaps came along from B Company, or what was left of them; they said that the Germans had overrun No. 1 Platoon and that now there was nothing to prevent them breaking through *en masse*. Our officers, Captain Rylands and Lieutenant Partridge, conferred and decided to pull us out to the higher ground, as we had no chance of holding our present positions.

As we started to move out the Germans let go at us with everything they had – artillery, mortars, Spandaus. The concentration of fire was terrific. The only way to reach the high ground was through a group of cottages straddling the road a couple of hundred yards away; the fields around were lined with fine-mesh wire fences and we would have been picked off easily as we tried to get over them. So we doubled off down the road, about two hundred of us I suppose, all making for one house in particular which seemed to have a large garden; we intended to work our way through it from front to rear.

Just as we reached the house down came the mortar bombs, right in among us. I was well to the rear, and as I crept closer I could see a group of men struggling to get through the garden gate. Smoke and flames were everywhere and the ground shuddered with explosions. I looked up again, and suddenly it seemed that everyone else had gone and that I was alone: a terrifying feeling. Then, as I crawled nearer the gate, I saw a man lying in a pool of water. He had been badly hit in the back. I got him out of the water and laid him by the side of the road. He didn't want me to leave him and clung to me as hard as he could. There was nothing I could do, and my fear of being taken prisoner was strong. In the end, muttering something about going to get help, I left the poor chap and threw myself under cover on the other side of the road.

I inched along on this side until I was opposite the garden gate, then dashed across the road again and through into the garden. There was a fearful mess all around the gate; men had been killed ten times over, their bodies ripped apart by the mortar bombs. I went into the garden; there wasn't a soul in sight and I had no idea where they had gone, so I thought I would just keep going in a straight line beyond the house and hope for the best.

After going a short way I came upon a soldier who was terribly wounded in the waist area. The legs of his trousers were soaked in blood; there wasn't a patch of khaki to be seen. I asked him which way the others had gone; he showed me and off I went. Away on the hill ahead I could see a lot of smoke and shellbursts, and I guessed that was where our chaps would be. A few moments later I spotted a line of lorries, looking just like toys as they moved along the road that wound up the hillside. A terrible panic seized me; I thought Christ, they're going off without me, and I started to run. Although I was pretty well exhausted the running caused me no effort at all. It seemed as though my legs didn't belong to me.

After a while I staggered into a little hamlet near the foot of the hill, where to my relief I came across two of my mates, Tom Calow and Johnny Kemble. There was a fearful barrage in progress; it was absolutely pouring with mortar bombs and those terrible shrapnel shells. Compared with that the bullets didn't amount to much really; nobody took much notice of them. We made our way along a ditch to a farm where Company HQ had been set up. Most of the chaps who were left had assembled there. We were reformed to make a counter-attack. There didn't seem to be much point in it really, but we set off just the same, advancing down to the valley until we came out on to a track where we took cover among some trees. My friend Tom had gone to the top of the hill with Lieutenant 'Ginger' Partridge, our 2 i/c; some time later he came running back with two bullets in his side. He was a little tough sort of kid, but he was sweating quite a bit and I advised him to take off his equipment and make his way back to HQ before he became too weak. He pushed his way into a cornfield and that was the last I ever saw of him.

We were unable to continue the advance, for the enemy had gained some high ground on either side and we were caught in a crossfire. There was no alternative but to pull out. Our advance had brought us down to where the soldier lay with the blood-stained trousers, and we brought him out with us. Our only avenue of escape lay along a ditch that bordered the track. It was broken at intervals by gateways where other tracks led into the fields on either side. The leading group of men reached the first of these openings, raised themselves out of the ditch and started to make their way across. It looked as though they were going to make it when suddenly the Spandaus opened up and cut them to ribbons.

I could see men still trying to run across among all that murderous fire, but I stayed where I was until things quietened down a bit and then I crawled over, sheltering behind the bodies of the poor devils who lay in the gateway. I got back into the ditch, which was full of crawling men. It was very shallow and the Spandaus were pecking away at us all the time; as soon as you raised your head you drew a burst of fire, and every time a man was hit in front of you, you had to crawl over the top of him, which made you still more vulnerable. There were about six gateways, with tracks traversing the ditch, and every time you came to one you had to get up and take a flying leap to the other side. Every opening had

those hellish machine guns trained on it. When it came to my turn
I made a terrific leap, aiming to land a few yards along the ditch;
land short, and the odds were that you would come down on top
of someone, in which case the machine guns would have you.

I crawled on up the ditch, together with the other survivors.
Suddenly, I was almost sick. In front of my face lay a man's liver,
still steaming. I eased myself over it carefully and went on. It
must have taken us three hours to crawl along that ditch. In the
end I reached the last gateway, and prepared to make my usual
flying leap. Perhaps I was over-confident; perhaps I didn't move
fast enough. At any rate, as I jumped a Spandau got me in the
leg. I landed heavily, swearing hard – not so much because of the
pain, but because I thought my leg was broken. I found that I
could still move it, however, so things didn't seem quite so bad.

Those of us that were left eventually got back to the farm and
Lieutenant Partridge led us back to our transport, which was
waiting some way further back. The enemy shellfire was not so
intense now, because it was dusk and the valley was filled with
drifting smoke from the barrage they had been putting up all day.
It helped to screen us from the enemy guns.

We boarded the lorries and went away into the night. Lots of
times as we drove on, we heard the cries of wounded men, beg-
ging us to stop. But there was no stopping; nobody was really
interested in the wounded. It was the fit men who mattered now.
And so, filthy, exhausted and bloodstained, we made our way
back towards Furnes on the Dunkirk perimeter.[2]

While the British divisions in the north-east leapfrogged back towards Dunkirk before the offensive of the German Sixth Army, the
divisions holding the southern wall of the corridor had been subjected to a ferocious onslaught by the armour and infantry of von
Kleist's and Hoth's Panzer Groups. The fury of the German attack
here fell on Major-General Irwin's 2nd Division, holding a twenty-
mile front along the La Bassée canal. Throughout Sunday 26 May
the division was subjected to heavy artillery fire and infantry attacks;
then, on the morning of the twenty-seventh, the British line was
assaulted by the 3rd, 4th and 7th Panzer Divisions, together with

part of the 5th, supported by the ss Verfugungs and ss Totenkopf Divisions. Before noon that day the British 6th Brigade – comprising the 2nd Durham Light Infantry, the 1st Royal Welch Fusiliers and the 1st Royal Berkshire – had been overrun and practically wiped out; the British positions were sited in open country, ideal for tank operations, and since most of the 2nd Division's anti-tank guns had been sent back for the defence of Dunkirk perimeter the panzers encountered nothing more damaging than Brens and rifles.

While the remains of the 6th Brigade escaped into the Forest of Nieppe before the swarming tanks, the 4th Brigade on their immediate left had also been hard hit. By daybreak on the 27th the 2nd Royal Norfolk, in the centre, had been decimated in an attempt to check an enemy breakthrough between themselves and the 1st Royal Scots, while over on the left the 8th Lancashire Fusiliers were faced with an enemy bridgehead between their position at Béthune and the canal. The main assault against 4th Brigade was preceded early that morning by a fierce artillery barrage, in the wake of which units of XLI and XVI Panzer Corps moved in to the attack. With great daring, three Junkers 52 transport aircraft touched down on Merville airfield, on the very edge of the British positions, disgorged their troops and took off again before any serious fire was directed against them. While the airborne force and other units fought for possession of Merville, 4th Panzer and the ss Totenkopf Division set about the systematic destruction of the 4th Brigade. The 8th Lancashire Fusiliers were surrounded and mopped up after a bitter fight that lasted until mid-afternoon, while the Royal Norfolks were steadily hemmed in by tanks and infantry at Le Paradis. By 16.30 all that remained of them were about ninety men under the command of Major Ryder, the acting battalion CO, holding out desperately in some farm buildings; in the end, with hardly any ammunition left and the buildings on fire, Ryder made up his mind to surrender.

As he appeared in the doorway with a white flag, accompanied by a small group of men, a machine gun opened up and they were mown down. Then the firing ceased and the remainder were ordered out of the building with their hands up. All of them, fit and wounded – the latter including Major Ryder, who had survived the first burst

– were rounded up and herded into a paddock, accompanied by kicks and blows. There, with utter cold-blooded ruthlessness, they were raked by two machine guns. Afterwards ss troops moved among the bloodstained bodies, finishing off the wounded with revolver shots and bayonet thrusts. Miraculously two men survived, both terribly wounded, and feigned death until the ss had moved on. They were cared for by the farmer's wife and later taken prisoner by ordinary Wehrmacht troops. The stories they subsequently told led, after the war, to the execution as a war criminal of the ss company commander involved, Lieutenant-Colonel Fritz Knoechlein. In fact the incident caused repercussions among the German General Staff, and von Reichenau, commanding Sixth Army, was asked to supply an explanation. Before an investigation could be held, however, the ss Totenkopf Division passed from his command and nothing more was done. Besides, it soon became unhealthy, even in high-ranking German Army circles, to question the motives of the ss.

On the right of the Royal Norfolks, the 1st Royal Scots had also been progressively reduced to the equivalent of little more than a company. They too were compelled to surrender and were actually being lined up to be shot by the ss when a senior staff officer of the Wehrmacht, who happened to be passing by, saw what was going on and put a stop to it. So the remnants of the Royal Scots marched into captivity.

On the extreme left of 2nd Division's line, the 5th Brigade, with the 2nd Dorset, 7th Worcestershire and 1st Cameron Highlanders in position from right to left, were subjected to heavy shellfire and probing attacks on the evening of the twenty-sixth, when a company of the Worcesters was overrun. The next morning Rommel's 7th Panzer Division set about enlarging the German bridgehead; a company of the Camerons launched a spirited counter-attack, supported by six Somua tanks of the French 1st Light Armoured Division, but after some initial success this was shrivelled up by superior enemy firepower and the Allied force was compelled to retreat, having suffered severe losses. Rommel quickly poured his armour into the bridgehead and on the afternoon of the twenty-seventh launched a massive attack on the British position with tanks and infantry, forming a giant steamroller that ground slowly forward in impeccable order to drive a wedge between the 2nd Division and the French v Corps, over on the left.

Meanwhile on the right of 2nd Division the 44th (Home Counties) Division under Major-General E.A. Osborne had been able to consolidate its positions. Two days earlier, on the twenty-fourth, the division had received orders to advance to the canal line in the southwest as part of a co-ordinated move with 2nd and 48th Divisions. Although these orders were issued at 10.00 it was not until 17.00 that the move began, because of problems in obtaining petrol and the fact that one of the 44th's brigades, the 131st, was still *en route* from its previous location. This brigade, in fact, had been heavily bombed the previous afternoon and many of its vehicles destroyed.

Over the next twenty-four hours the division's other brigades, the 132nd and 133rd, moved up to occupy the Forest of Nieppe and the Caestre areas respectively, the right flank of the 132nd curving back north-east of Hazebrouck to link up with the 133rd. On 26 May, to consider a possible advance between Hazebrouck and Cassel, General Osborne carried out a reconnaissance with Brigadiers Whitty and Norman and subsequently arranged for 132nd Brigade to carry out an attack that night and occupy Ebblinghem. Later it became obvious that a German assault was developing towards Caestre with tanks and infantry, but the belated arrival of 131st Brigade nevertheless made it possible for 133rd Brigade to concentrate between Caestre and Eecke while 131st Brigade occupied the line from Caestre to Vieux Berquin, where it was in contact with the French 1st Light Mechanized Division. By nightfall on the twenty-sixth 131st, 132nd and 133rd Brigades were all in line, but enemy activity was on the increase and as a result the projected advance towards Ebblinghem had to be cancelled.

During the night of 26 May Major-General Wason, newly appointed to command III Corps, arrived at 44th Division HQ and briefed Major-General Osborne on the plans for withdrawal to Dunkirk. These envisaged a withdrawal by the French First Army west of the line Armentières–Poperinghe, with I and II British Corps withdrawing on the right. The 2nd and 44th Divisions were to form flank guard against the advancing enemy tanks and infantry, and were subsequently to withdraw along the roads allotted to the

French. The 44th Division was to maintain contact with the French
v Corps on its right.

During this meeting, it was agreed that elements of 44th Division
would attempt to advance to the railway line between Hazebrouck
and Cassel and hold the Germans there; this move was to be carried
out on the authority of Major-General Wason, who was to return to
divisional HQ that day. Throughout the twenty-seventh Major-
General Osborne remained in his command post, in telephone contact with his brigade commanders; at frequent intervals he was
visited by French staff officers, all of whom appeared determined
to make certain that the flank guard formed by 44th Division was
holding fast and also to emphasize that the division was now under
French command – a statement which Osborne accepted politely,
albeit with considerable reserve. Nevertheless he felt justified in
asking the French for some tank support for the projected advance
to the railway, which was to be carried out at dawn on the twenty-
eighth; this was promised, but subsequently altered to the alternative
of using the tanks either to support the advance or the defences at
Cassel, which was in considerable danger during the night of 27 May.
Since Cassel was the important point, the idea of the advance to the
railway was dismissed; it would have been impossible to carry it out
without armoured support.

During the night of the twenty-seventh to eighth, contact was lost
with the French v Corps, which had given way before the onslaught
of Rommel's 7th Panzer on the left of the 2nd Division. In the early
hours of the twenty-eighth General Osborne got in touch with HQ
2nd Division, and after consultation with General Irwin it was
agreed that the 2nd Division had done all it could. Its battered
remnants were to move north towards Dunkirk the following day,
handing over the responsibility for the rearguard to the French.

At the same time General Osborne decided to move his divisional
HQ to the Mont des Cats, sending his sappers on ahead to prepare
fortifications. By this time the position of both the 44th and 48th
Divisions was precarious in the extreme, and had the panzer divisions been able to get into full stride on the morning of the twenty-
eighth they would doubtless have made considerable progress.
Fortunately it rained heavily throughout the night and the boggy

ground hampered the tanks' movements. As a result, when the enemy assault was renewed at dawn its weight was directed against infantry objectives, principally Hazebrouck and the Forest of Nieppe. After hammering Hazebrouck with artillery fire the Germans assaulted the town and 44th Division's positions on either side of it, pushing armour across the Hazebrouck canal. This move placed the 1st, 4th and 5th Battalions of the Queen's Own Royal West Kent Regiment (comprising 132nd Brigade) in grave danger, and the British troops were compelled to escape the trap by a series of fighting withdrawals.

General Osborne had still received no instructions about withdrawing, other than the order he had earlier received to act in co-ordination with the French. Early on the twenty-eighth he accordingly went to Steenwerck, HQ French First Army, where he found, both General Prioux and General Aymes, commanding IV Corps. Prioux had by this time decided to withdraw no further, although he had authorized de la Laurencie's III Corps to do so, and expressed alarm at Osborne's proposals for the 44th Division's withdrawal. Osborne pointed out that as yet he had withdrawn only his HQ and assured the French that the flank guard position was holding firm, requesting a company of French tanks to assist 133rd Brigade at Caestre. A dozen or so tanks did eventually put in an appearance later that morning and were of considerable assistance, although 133rd Brigade reported that they did not fight very actively. There was also another group of French tanks north-east of Flêtre, but they remained passive even when 44th Division's HQ units and ambulances were being attacked by enemy armour in that vicinity.[3]

In the afternoon of the twenty-eighth Osborne visited General de la Laurencie of III Corps, who told him that the corps would begin its withdrawal to Dunkirk that night. Osborne's first inclination was to order 44th Division to make a similar move, but since his engineers were preparing intermediate defences on the Mont des Cats to the north-east he decided to concentrate in this area, even though it meant deviating from the direct route to Dunkirk. Elements of the battered 2nd Division had already bypassed the Mont and were now in position at Watou, six miles beyond it.

Meanwhile the right of the British line was in peril. At Socx, detachments of Usherforce had been heavily attacked and compelled to fall back on Bergues, creating a dangerous gap between Bergues and Wylder. Had the German armour exploited more rapidly in this direction, it could have carved through the BEF's line of retreat; as it was the enemy halted only two miles beyond Socx, enabling the gap to be plugged by a hastily-assembled force comprising the 1st Fife and Forfar Yeomanry, the 1st Welsh Guards and the 6th Green Howards.

On the left of Usherforce General Thorne's 48th Division had seen some heavy fighting, particularly around the key position of Wormhoudt, which was defended by the 2nd Battalion the Royal Warwickshire Regiment and the 8th Battalion the Worcestershire Regiment. The British positions were subjected to heavy artillery fire, and at 10.00 the enemy tanks and infantry moved up. Several tanks were knocked out by the British 2-pounders, but the Germans continued to advance steadily and by late afternoon they had overwhelmed most of the Royal Warwicks, about a hundred of whom surrendered to the ss Adolf Hitler Regiment. Eighty of the British prisoners were shot or bayoneted by their captors, adding to the list of ss war crimes to be reckoned after the war.

Wormhoudt fell that evening, the surviving defenders fighting their way out of the closing trap with rifle, grenade and bayonet and withdrawing towards Bambecque, on the river Yser. It was now impossible to hold Cassel, along the road to the south, and General Thorne accordingly issued orders for the withdrawal of 145th Brigade. Because of blockages and German wireless jamming, however, these orders did not reach 145th Brigade's commander, Brigadier the Hon. N.F. Somerset, until the early morning of 29 May, and he decided to wait until nightfall before attempting a breakout.

To the east of Cassel, meanwhile, 44th Division was completing its withdrawal to the Mont des Cats. One man's view of the withdrawal is provided by Robert W. Lee, at that time a General Staff clerk in 44th Division, who was one of the first to pull back to the Mont from the division's former HQ at Ecole de Steentje:

The first party left after 5am [Tuesday 28 May]. After they had gone we burned a mass of papers and I had the feeling that we

were not going to get through. SSM Phillips sent out a message that
we were to make for Dunkirk. Our party left at ten – consisting of
SSM Phillips, Wood, Fisher and myself – in office truck. At Flêtre
we came under shelling from tanks and had to take cover in a
ditch. We turned back and were again shelled. Flêtre had been
bombed after we had passed through. Spent afternoon in torren-
tial rain at 131 Brigade HQ. During the evening ditched the truck
and smashed up everything else that might have been of use to the
enemy.

Wednesday 29 May. In the night we marched to the Mont des
Cats, Major Parker and SSM Phillips leading. Met our advance
party when we arrived on the Mont at 3 am. Had a short sleep in
a café. With the arrival of daylight the enemy spotted the concentration of men on the Mont and we were subjected to a heavy
dive-bombing attack, shelling and machine-gun fire.[4]

The air attack, which began at 06.00, was carried out by some
sixty Stukas, which caused about a hundred casualties. Since his men
were in no condition to meet the ground assault that was clearly in
the offing, having no artillery support and only two 2-pounder anti-
tank guns, Osborne decided to continue the withdrawal to Dunkirk
at 10.00 on the twenty-ninth. So, splitting up into small parties, the
44th Division abandoned the Mont and streamed down the road
towards Poperinghe, where the 50th Division held the line. All
around was a scene of utter devastation, the roads clogged with
abandoned or burning transport, guns and equipment, and debris
of every kind. Exhausted as they were, the troops of the 44th hardly
noticed it; ahead of them, on the far horizon, an ink-smudge of smoke
beckoned them. Beneath it lay Dunkirk, with its promise of salvation.

Further north the 48th Division continued to take a pounding,
along with its attached units. At Vyfweg and West Cappel the Welsh
Guards put up a spirited resistance, but the Germans eventually
succeeded in breaking through and advancing on Rattekot, where
defences had been set up by the Fife and Forfar Yeomanry and the
6th Green Howards. The hamlet was heavily shelled and tanks were
sent against it, although their supporting infantry was still held up
by the Welsh Guards. Some of the tanks overran the forward

defences, and the position looked grim until a pair of 18-pounders of
the 5th Regiment Royal Horse Artillery opened up and drove them
away with some highly accurate fire. At Bambecque on the Yser,
the 8th Worcesters were fiercely attacked and by nightfall on the
twenty-ninth their remnant was surrounded, with enemy forces at
Oost Cappel and Rexpoede to their rear. Both these objectives were
defended by the 127th Brigade of 42nd Division, whose 1st Highland
Light Infantry and 4th East Lancashire were involved in bitter hand-
to-hand fighting, the troops engaging tanks with grenades.

At nightfall on the twenty-ninth Brigadier Somerset of the 48th
Division's 145th Brigade at last attempted the breakout from be-
leaguered Cassel, which by now was completely isolated. Leading
the exodus, the 4th Ox and Bucks quickly encountered enemy
infantry, who were dispersed with a bayonet charge, but daybreak
found the battalion surrounded by more infantry and tanks near
Watou and they were compelled to surrender, along with Brigadier
Somerset. Of the remainder of the brigade, the 2nd Battalion the
Gloucestershire Regiment was trapped in a wood by enemy tanks
and also forced to surrender, only one officer and thirteen men getting away. Bringing up the rear, the East Riding Yeomanry ran into
a minefield and most of their transport went up in smoke.

During the night of the twenty-ninth to thirtieth the 3rd and 50th
Divisions, on the left of the line, pulled back across the Yser, their
movement shielded by the 5th Division. As soon as the 3rd and 50th
were clear the 5th and 42nd Divisions joined the general retreat
towards the Dunkirk bridgehead. The final withdrawal across the
Yser was not accomplished without loss, the heaviest being suffered
by the battered 3rd Division. One company of the 50th Division's
8th Durham Light Infantry was also cut off.

On the south-west flank, the failure of nine German divisions,
six of them armoured, to break through the hastily improvised
defences of the 42nd, 44th and 48th Divisions had been almost
unbelievable. Had they succeeded in doing so, two-thirds of the
BEF –not to mention de la Laurencie's III Corps – would have found
themselves encircled. The easiest method for the Germans to have
achieved this object would have been to exploit the gap between
Cassel and Hazebrouck, instead of concentrating on the reduction

of Cassel itself; but this would have meant exposing their flanks, and since the shock of the British counter-attack at Arras a week earlier this was a move the enemy would not risk.

So the fighting retreat of the BEF moved towards its conclusion, as the weary troops trudged back over the reeking, littered roads towards Dunkirk. Of that retreat, General Osborne of 44th Division later observed:

> The speed with which the Germans brought up their trench mortars and infantry guns gave us a great deal of trouble. Reviewing various stories, it was obvious that many medium and light German tanks were knocked out by our 18-pounders and anti-tank guns of both natures. German light tanks were not as good as French light tanks; the former knew it and withdrew at any threat of attack.
>
> BUT — YOU CANNOT FIGHT TANKS WITHOUT TANKS![5]

7 The Perimeter

Along the narrow roads, strafed and dive-bombed, tortured by thirst and the pangs of hunger, the khaki columns streamed back towards Dunkirk. Ahead of them, trailing its sombre cloak across the May sky by day and providing a lurid beacon by night, was the funeral pyre of the town; behind them the rumble of battle as the rearguard actions continued; and on all sides reeking debris and corpses.

Despite the confusion, despite the exhaustion, despite the agony of blistered, lacerated feet and the burden of equipment that weighed like lead, despite the uncertainty and the fear, most units – whether of company strength or split up into small parties – maintained a high degree of cohesion. For many that last nightmare trudge back to the perimeter is remembered dimly, through a haze of fatigue; others recall it with great clarity, as though they had reached a point beyond fatigue where the mind's power of observation was stimulated to its fullest capacity. One such is ex-LAC Ken Anderson, who was part of a seven-strong RAF meteorological team attached to the 2nd Survey Regiment, Royal Artillery.

On Sunday 26 May, following the German breakthrough on the Belgian front north of Menin, the regiment, which was then near Armentières, was ordered to move back immediately to Fleurbaix, some way to the south. Anderson remembers vividly the subsequent march back to the perimeter:

The sun shines; the sky is a cloudless blue. The Luftwaffe is everywhere, smashing everything that moves. We are surrounded by field guns, and we share with the gunners ninety minutes of dive-bombing Stukas: the terror weapon. Helpless, we cower in the ditches and pray. Hedge-hopping fighters machine-gun us – spurts

of dust in the road – whoosh of flame and smoke from stricken
vehicles. Noise. Smoke. Flame. Why are we here? How did we
reach this place? We know that the Boche has cut our routes to
south and west and is assaulting also from the north and east, but
we do not accept these facts because we do not want to accept them.
As a unit we are now valueless except as individuals with rifles –
any time now we may find a desperate use for these. The day wears
slowly on; we wait for we know not what. We are very frightened.

Then, at 17.00 hours, orders! Smash all equipment, burn all
secret documents. Make for the coast and report to the Navy!
Never in British history has that phrase seemed so important; to
our young ears it means salvation – if only we can make the coast.
We set off in the warm, sunny afternoon back to Armentières,
through Comines and on to Messines Ridge, where we are held
up by a squadron of Belgian cavalry. Incredible to see horse
soldiers! On along the hot dusty road towards Ypres, turning off
for Poperinghe.

It was here, with myself and LAC Harry Targett in the cab of
our vehicle – which we had nicknamed 'La Vache Espagnole' –
that we had a narrow escape. Targett, for no reason he could ever
offer, suddenly shouted: 'Stop the bloody truck!' I braked hard,
and as we crunched to a stop a small bomb exploded on the *pavé*
only yards ahead, severely damaging the cottages on either side.
We were covered in dust but unharmed, and our Fordson tender
unscratched. From the interior came a howl of abuse, particularly
from Corporal George Rudram who had been shaving and who
was now covered in suds and blood. The protests died away, however, when we drove slowly past the smoking bomb crater.

We pushed on, throwing all wrecked instruments, clothing, the
ashes of documents, gas cylinders – anything that could be abandoned – into the roadside ditches. On across the 1914–18 battle-
fields into which our fathers poured their blood, holding against
the same enemy; bitter thoughts. Targett and I gorged ourselves
on looted asparagus; the others refused to be tempted, hating the
stuff. Shortly before midnight we arrived in Hoogstade, where
all small vehicles were wrecked and abandoned and we devoured
our last scraps of food. After an hour or so we all crammed into

the larger vehicles and set off through the night for Bulscamp. It was a night of fatigue and frustration, with tired drivers cursing and each of us wrapped in his own private cocoon of fear, doubt, and thoughts of home.

We reached Bulscamp late in the morning of the twenty-eighth and were issued with messy coloured water which the cooks called tea. Now the ordeal really began, for we were ordered to split up into parties of twenty-five and make a forced march to Teteghem, east of Dunkirk. Laden with small arms, ammunition and the kit of some officer – severe doubts cast on his parentage – our party set out for the sea. There was little doubt about the point we were making for; away to the north-east rose a vast plume of smoke. Our leader was an attached officer of the French Military Mission, armed with a map torn from a school atlas. This gentleman succeeded twice in leading us astray, but on both occasions units of the RAOC and RASC turned us back from the direction in which we were heading – which would have brought us into contact with the enemy – and set us on the right road. A captain of the RASC was gravely suspicious and suggested that we take steps to eliminate him, this being no time for squeamishness; we managed to ditch him further along the road.

At Teteghem, we were allowed thirty minutes' rest and some food – two 12-ounce tins of bully beef between the twenty-five of us, plus two hardtack biscuits per man. On these scant provisions, exhausted in mind and body, torn between despair and hope, we renewed our march to the outskirts of Dunkirk and made our way through the rubble to the sand dunes beyond. Against the darkening sky the flames of the burning town were reflected in the sullen canals and waterways, silhouetting other marching groups. We passed a battery of destroyed anti-aircraft guns, their barrels split open and curled back like sticks of celery. Over everything hung the towering pall of black smoke from the burning oil tanks, stretching across the eastern horizon. Forward we stumbled, a cursing, motley crew, calling upon our ebbing physical and mental strength to push one foot in front of the other, some of us with boots that squelched blood. So we came to the dunes, where we halted, to fall and sleep in the sand and the coarse grass.[1]

The collapse of the Belgian Army, meanwhile, had placed the extreme left of Sir Ronald Adam's makeshift perimeter in extreme jeopardy; at Nieuport, the sector held by the 4th Division was being menaced by the German 208th and 256th Divisions, while their 56th Division confronted the British 3rd Division at Furnes. On the morning of the twenty-eighth the 53rd Medium Regiment Royal Artillery, which had put its guns out of action after supporting the 3rd Division's withdrawal, was ordered to proceed to Nieuport with all speed. The regimental commander, Lieutenant-Colonel Brazier, arrived with twenty-five officers and two hundred men to find that the 12th Lancers had just fought a violent engagement with German motor-cycle troops, who had come down the road from Ostend mingling with the ever-present stream of refugees. Brazier, who had been made responsible for the defence of Nieuport, immediately set about organizing the forces at his disposal. In addition to the men of his own 53rd Regiment, these consisted of 147 officers and men of the 11 Corps Ammunition Field Park, RASC, 1 Corps Field Survey Company RE, 127 men of the 1st Heavy Anti-Aircraft Regiment, thirty troops of the 2nd Medium Regiment and twenty Grenadier Guardsmen, who had been detached from the 7th Grenadiers at Furnes.

Brazier's main worry concerned the bridges in the Nieuport sector, which were to have been blown by the Engineers of the 4th Division. The biggest problem was presented by the main road bridge that spanned the canal and the mouth of the river Yser; although this had been made ready for demolition all the firing leads were on the opposite bank, and when the 12th Lancers suddenly withdrew across the bridge in the face of growing enemy strength during the afternoon it proved impossible to blow the structure. By early evening on the twenty-eighth, as Brazier hastily plugged the last gaps in the Nieuport defences, advance units of the German 256th Division were well placed to cover the bridge with mortars and machine guns. When the 4th Division's 7th Field Company RE – which had taken part so gallantly in the defence at Ypres-Comines – finally arrived at 20.00 hours a seven-man detachment at once attempted to rush across the bridge and detonate charges, but they were picked off by the murderous Spandaus.

During the night of the twenty-eighth the enemy began to shell

Nieuport with 150-mm guns and to make probing attacks on the RASC, holding the right of the line. Brazier's anxiety increased; his task was to hold the Nieuport sector until the arrival of its designated defenders, the 4th Division's 12th Brigade, but according to his latest information they were only just in the process of leaving the river Lys and it would be well into the next day before they arrived. In the meantime, if the Germans decided to launch a strong assault across the troublesome bridge, there might be little he could do to stop them. His anxiety was relieved a little during the small hours of the twenty-ninth with the arrival of the 4th Division's 22nd Field Regiment, complete with two dozen 25-pounders, but it was still a tense situation. In fact, unknown to Brazier, the bulk of the German 256th Division – which had to cover a forty-mile distance from a point east of Bruges to Nieuport – had been held up by the 60th Division of General Fagalde's XVI Corps. This division, which had been attached to the Belgian Army, was holding a line along the canal de Dérivation, with its left flank on the sea at Zeebrugge, at the time of the Belgian collapse; the whole of its artillery had been lent to the Belgians and consequently lost.

In the evening of 27 May General Champon, the French liaison officer at Belgian HQ, realizing that the Belgian capitulation was imminent, issued orders for the troops of the 60th Division to embark in Belgian lorries and fall back to the Yser. The movement did not get under way until the following morning, and the slow-moving columns suffered heavily from the attentions of the Luftwaffe. In the early hours of the twenty-ninth, still short of Nieuport, the German 256th Division caught up with the confused mass of French troops and surrounded most of the 270th Infantry Regiment, which surrendered soon afterwards. The 60th's other regiment, the 241st, managed to reach the coast more or less intact and eventually reassembled at Bray Dunes, east of Dunkirk.

The disaster that overwhelmed the 60th Division brought a measure of respite for Brazier's defenders of Nieuport. Meanwhile the 4th Division's 12th Brigade (Brigadier Hawkesworth), having left the Lys at 21.00 on the twenty-eighth, had been moving throughout the night, their withdrawal covered by the 6th Black Watch. At 05.00 on the twenty-ninth they passed through Poperinghe, and five hours later Lieutenant-Colonel Allen of the 2nd Royal Fusiliers, the leading battalion, got through to Nieuport and made an on-the-spot assessment of the situation. It was serious; the Germans had moved up reinforcements during the early morning and Brazier's RASC troops on the right flank were beginning to crumble under the withering and continual Spandau and mortar fire. Although the approaches to the town were swept by bullets and shellfire, Allen at once decided to commit a company of his Fusiliers; these, supported by Bren carriers, threw the enemy back and held them until the arrival of the main body of the Fusiliers at dusk on the twenty-ninth, closely followed by the 1st Battalion the South Lancashire Regiment. Between them these two battalions secured the town and the canal banks, relieving Brazier's hard-pressed forces.

Shortly afterwards units of the 10th Brigade also began to arrive in the Nieuport sector, the men tired out after their hard fighting in support of the 5th Division at Wytschaete on the twenty-eighth. Two battalions of the 10th Brigade, the 1/6th East Surrey and the 2nd Duke of Cornwall's Light Infantry, entered the line on the right of 12th Brigade during the evening of the 29th, and a little later the 11th Brigade also fell in on the right of the 10th, extending the 4th Division's frontage westward towards Furnes.

Furnes lay in the sector of the perimeter allotted to Montgomery's 3rd Division, and the defence of the town itself was assigned to the 7th Guards Brigade (Brigadier J.A.C. Whitaker). By the time the leading unit, the 2nd Grenadier Guards, reached the town in the evening of the twenty-ninth after a ten-mile forced march the town was already being infiltrated by troops of the German 56th Division, who subjected the Grenadiers to a considerable amount of sniper fire and killed their CO together with two company commanders. The remainder of the 3rd Division, alongside the 50th Division, was still fighting a rearguard action to the south at this time; both had orders to withdraw during the night of the twenty-ninth to thirtieth and take over the defence of the perimeter west of Furnes.

Still further west General Alexander's 1st Division also began to move into the perimeter line in the Hondeschoote sector in the early hours of 29 May. Since being ordered back to the perimeter, Alexander's troops – who had seen little fighting, with the exception of the three battalions which were attached to Franklyn's 5th Division – had endured a series of gruelling marches over roads cluttered with the debris from bombing, by pathetic trails of refugees and by units of other divisions using the wrong routes. During most of the division's two-day withdrawal it rained, which – although uncomfortable for the men – at least brought them some respite from air attack. The congestion grew as the division approached the perimeter, destroying its vehicles at Hondeschoote. Alexander later wrote:

> I myself reached the beaches on a pushbike after abandoning my car some miles back, because the roads were hopelessly blocked by French, Belgian and British soldiers. The car was set alight in order that the Germans should not have the enjoyment of my personal belongings or the use of the vehicle itself. Thus my sole remaining possessions for the remainder of the battle were my revolver, my field glasses, and my brief case.[2]

The first unit of Alexander's division to take up position on the perimeter was the 1st Duke of Wellington's, which dug in around a bridge commanding the Hondeschoote–Bray Dunes road. Exhausted men of the badly mauled 2nd and 44th Divisions passed through their lines during the day, handing over a considerable number of small arms, notably Brens, to the defenders. At noon on the twenty-ninth the 2nd Coldstream Guards moved into position on the right of the Duke of Wellington's two-mile front, while Brigadier Hudson's 2nd Brigade moved into reserve near Bray Dunes.

The remnants of General de la Laurencie's French III Corps also reached the Dunkirk perimeter during 29 May. They comprised two regiments, each with two battalions, of the 12th Division, together with three artillery batteries; two and a half battalions of the 32nd Division; the artillery and reconnaissance group of the 1st Division, but no infantry; the 92nd Reconnaissance Group of the 2nd North African (which was trapped in Lille); and two squadrons of tanks from the Cavalry Corps. De la Laurencie immediately reported to British GHQ at La Panne and demanded that his troops be allowed to take their stand on the perimeter; he was authorized to take up positions east of Bray Dunes, along the Belgian frontier, behind the sector held by the 4th and 3rd Divisions.[3]

Units continued to come into the perimeter, more or less in good order, during the night of the twenty-ninth to thirtieth. On the left of the line the 3rd Division's 8th Brigade passed through Furnes and relieved the 11th Brigade, which now passed into reserve, while the 50th Division moved into the line from Furnes to Houthem between the 7th Guards and the 1st Division, enabling what was left of the 5th Division to pull back to an assembly area near the beach. Like most of the other divisions, the 50th destroyed its transport as it came up to the perimeter. Often the task was far from easy. Ken Carter, a driver with 150th Brigade, recalls:

> There wasn't a great deal we could do except try and put a pick-axe through the radiator or the petrol tank, smash the distributor and that kind of thing – destroy the batteries and generally do as much damage as possible. We broke all records to get the job done, and it's the only time in my life I have felt like a vandal. Nevertheless, I know that a lot of the stuff we left behind was more or less intact.[4]

By the morning of 30 May, therefore, the defensive perimeter from Nieuport to the right of the 1st Division was firming up nicely in the sectors assigned to I and II Corps. It was in the sector assigned to III Corps, in the area of Dunkirk town itself, that the problems arose, for neither the battered 44th nor 48th Division was in any fit state to make a contribution to the defences here. The only troops immediately available to Major-General Wason, the corps commander were two battalions of the 46th Division, drawn from the BEF's lines of communication and sadly undertrained, and a few companies of the 2nd Division. In the early hours of the thirtieth the 126th Brigade of 42nd Division was diverted from the division's general movement towards the beaches through the rear of the 1st Division in order to fill the gap between the 1st and 46th Divisions all these forces now coming under the command of I Corps.

The British right now rested on the ancient town of Bergues, which was the only position still remaining forward of the Bergues–Furnes canal and which was still doggedly defended by the mixed garrison under Colonel C.M. Usher. Despite continual enemy bombing and shellfire the defenders held firm, their ranks swollen

during these last days by many British and French volunteers.
'Usherforce' was finally relieved on 30 May by the 1st Battalion the
Loyal Regiment (2nd Brigade, 1st Division), who arrived under
fire at about 20.00 after a five-hour march from Bray Dunes. Not all
of 'Usherforce' withdrew from Bergues; a company of the 2nd Royal
Warwicks, some Welsh Guards and other miscellaneous troops
remained to carry on the defence alongside the Loyals and the
garrison of two hundred Frenchmen.

Stretching like a shield to the west of Dunkirk, between Bergues
and Mardyck and completing the twenty-five-mile length of the
perimeter, there still remained the well-entrenched troops of the
French 68th Division, in good fighting order and with considerable
artillery support. The French in this sector were confronted by the
German 208th and 225th Infantry Regiments and by the 9th Panzer
Division, with its supporting infantry, Guderian's XIX Panzer Corps
and part of the XLI Motorized Corps having withdrawn on the
twenty-ninth to refit for the next stage of the campaign, the drive
southwards across the Somme. It was against the French that the
only major enemy attack on the right of the defences developed
during the thirtieth; launched by 9th Panzer, it fell on the French
137th Infantry Regiment on the Haute–Colme canal, east of Bergues,
and lasted all afternoon before the enemy withdrew. Elsewhere
along the line there were more attacks on Nieuport, where the Royal
Fusiliers, the South Lancashires and the East Surreys held on
grimly; and on Furnes, where the sadly depleted 4th Royal Berkshire of 3rd Division came in for more punishment and were forced
to give ground until the 1st Coldstream Guards counter-attacked
on their right and engaged the enemy in savage fighting that lasted
throughout the hours of darkness.

As dawn broke on 31 May, the haggard, grimy defenders of the
perimeter waited for the massive assault that was bound to come.
On the other side of the waterline ten German divisions were assembled to deliver the final blow. No one on the perimeter knew
how, or when, or even if, they would be withdrawn to the beaches
for evacuation, Yet somehow every man knew that the thirty-first
would be the decisive day.

8 The Beaches

By nightfall on 27 May, with the bulk of the BEF heavily engaged in its fighting withdrawal to the Dunkirk perimeter, the concentrations of Allied troops in Dunkirk and along the beaches to the east of the town were already creating serious problems of control. The task of co-ordination that forced Captain William Tennant and his small band of naval officers, who had arrived only hours earlier, was enormous; they found little of the discipline that would mark the later arrival of the fighting units. Dunkirk was under almost continual air attack, and every cellar and place of refuge in the town was crammed with human flotsam; French troops in the main, but with a considerable number of personnel from British rear units who were awaiting embarkation or who had simply arrived in Dunkirk as refugees, having lost touch with their units. There were deserters, too, submerging themselves in the anonymity of confusion.

All these men, who had no further part to play in the battle, had to be got away from Dunkirk before the front-line troops began to arrive *en masse*; the resulting confusion, otherwise, would be appalling. However, there were as yet no small craft to assist in the embarkation, despite Tennant's desperate pleas for them, and as a result the lifting of troops from Dunkirk and the beaches on the twenty-seventh was a fearfully slow process, particularly as the effectiveness of the German-controlled coastal gun batteries at Gravelines frustrated attempts by merchant vessels to reach the port by the designated short route. Most of the work on the twenty-seventh was carried out by destroyers' whalers, which ran a shuttle service from the beaches to the warships waiting offshore.

Many of these craft were filled with wounded, who were streaming back to the beaches in increasing numbers and whose care presented a major problem. Nevertheless RAMC and Allied medical personnel who had been detailed to supervise the care and evacuation of the injured in the beach areas found, to their surprise and delight, that the available medical facilities were often far more complete than they had anticipated. The hotel on the promenade at La Panne, which had been fitted out as a military hospital by the Belgian authorities and which was taken over by the RAMC early on the twenty-seventh, was a good example. One of the RAMC personnel who moved in was Corporal W. McWilliam, who provides this detailed description of the facilities and the often-forgotten work of himself and his colleagues:

On the ground floor, just inside the hall, we found the lounge being converted into a casualty reception area, and the operating theatre adjoined this. The fittings were all up to date, with a shadowless lamp fixed over the operating table and a number of glass-topped trolleys. Next door, the ballroom was divided into two wards, one large and one small, with single wooden beds spaced out over the available area. On the second floor was the dispensary, and our two sergeant dispensers were very pleased with the stock of measures, bottles, scales and pill and ointment boxes by the dozen. With such a plentiful stock of medical supplies we felt truly ready to receive all casualties.

The next day was spent adding more equipment and cleaning the wards. During the night Dunkirk was bombed, and in the morning we saw volumes of smoke rising skywards. Casualties began to arrive by ambulance, many of them badly wounded in head, back and limbs. Some limbs were past surgical repair and were amputated in the theatre. Anyone in severe pain was injected with a $\frac{1}{4}$-grain dose of morphia. All the casualties were evacuated by motor ambulance convoy (MAC) in the evenings, to be shipped home to 'Blighty'.

Each day we received many more wounded. One man I remember had been hit in the face by a bullet, which smashed his lower jaw badly. He was incapable of eating, of course; all he could do, with great difficulty, was take fluids by way of a feeder, and he soon got to the stage where he could not even swallow. We washed his mouth with cold water regularly, but he died the next day. We were kept extremely busy dressing stumps of amputated limbs and packing gauze soaked in eusol (an antiseptic chlorate of lime solution) into wounds. Outside on the beaches were anti-aircraft guns, and every time they fired the whole building shook. At one time, a terrific barrage shattered the windows; fortunately the glass blew outwards, saving the patients from injury. We had several air raids during the day, and the noise from Bofors, Brens and machine guns was terrifying.

As the days went by, so many casualties came in that we had to put some of them two to a bed. Patients were also lying on stretchers in the corridors and hall. Every evening we were cleared of casualties by the MAC, but we quickly filled up again during the night. We were supposed to go off duty at 8pm, when the night staff came on, but we usually worked past 10pm as there were so many casualties to be dealt with. We were always dog-tired afterwards and never had any difficulty in sleeping, despite the noise of gunfire.

One night, as we were preparing for bed, we noticed many ships anchored just off the shore, with an escort of destroyers further out to sea. In the morning the beaches were packed with troops awaiting embarkation. During the remainder of the week troops were continually lifted from the beaches, and at last the rumour spread that we too would soon be going home. It seemed too good to be true – but then the day came when, having evacuated all our casualties, we received orders to move out. We were just packing our gear when Jerry dropped a stick of bombs across the beach, killing and wounding many men. A number were injured around the hotel when the remaining windows blew out, scattering glass over the road below.

When the noise had died down, two of us set off down the beach in search of wounded, carrying a door which we planned to use as an improvised stretcher. We walked slowly along among the scattered remains of men who had been blown to pieces, searching for the living among the multitude of dead, and came upon a man half buried in a sand hill. He was breathing feebly, with blood coming from ears, nose and mouth, which indicated a fracture at the base of the skull. An ammunition truck was burning nearby, so we lost no time in digging him out and carrying him back to the hospital. Unfortunately, he proved to be dead on arrival.

Having evacuated our latest batch of casualties we finally moved off from the hospital at 6pm on Friday 31 May, leaving behind an officer and eight men to look after the remaining wounded. We marched off down the beach in single file, past the debris of war: lorries of every description, stores, arms, ammunition, the wreckage of aircraft – and the bodies of our comrades. Behind us, shells screeched into La Panne, and we saw one explode on the rear of the building we had just left. In front of us Dunkirk was ablaze, and we could see shells dropping into the sea close to the ships. Halfway along the beach we were machine-gunned from the air, and took refuge in a concrete shelter. Packed inside like sardines we heard a bomb drop, and a puff of sand blew in through a small window. When the noise had subsided we resumed our trek towards the ships.'

One of the men who passed through the hospital at La Panne during these last bitter days was Len Trussler of the 4th Royal Berkshire, who had his leg wound dressed there while his battalion fought in the perimeter defences at Furnes. He had arrived at Furnes with a truckload of men whose exhaustion was extreme:

We hadn't been there long when an officer came along and crawled into the lorry, wanting to know how many men there were with rifles. Nobody answered him. 'Come on,' he said, 'Senior NCOs!' Still nobody moved. He got a torch and shone it into the face of a sergeant, then on the face of each man in turn. After a long pause he nodded, as though in sympathy, and left. It wasn't cowardice on their part, when they didn't answer; it was just the fact that human beings can have just about enough. If you are hungry, exhausted and shell-shocked you just don't want any more.

That was where I left them, and that was where they made their last stand. I went down to the hospital at La Panne, with the huge Red Cross flag flying over it. Until now I had never really believed all the stories about Dunkirk, and evacuation; but now that I saw the sea I began to have an inkling that they might be true after all. I asked a chap in the first aid station whether he knew anything about it, but he just laughed. Anyway, the next morning – 31 May – we were evacuated, the stretcher cases crammed into ambulances and the rest on foot, and away we went towards Dunkirk. We crossed the Belgian border into France and arrived at No. 12 Casualty Clearing Station, which was in a big château; German patrols had been reported in the area and we had to wait there for two hours before setting off ont he last lap. As we passed along the sea-front we scanned the beaches; there wasn't a soul in sight. What struck me was the acre upon acre of abandoned lorries and equipment; there were piles of mail bags, all ripped open with their contents strewn for miles down the road. I couldn't help thinking of the boys those letters would never reach.

We came to the outskirts of Dunkirk, and that was as far as the ambulances were supposed to go; from then on we had to make our way on foot. I had no boots on and the streets were full of broken glass. Seeing my predicament, the ambulance driver took pity on me and told me to get back into the vehicle, together with several other wounded. As we drove slowly through the rubble the enemy began to shell Dunkirk, and debris showered down on the ambulance.[2]

It is virtually impossible to obtain a consistent impression of the conditions on the beaches; some units and individuals had an easy passage to their designated embarkation areas, others experienced the full fury of enemy action. Much depended on the time of day and the prevailing weather conditions, and it should be remembered that the primary objectives of both the Luftwaffe and the German artillery were the harbour installations of Dunkirk and the ships lying offshore, not the expanse of beach itself. The enemy effort against the beaches was essentially sporadic and of a secondary nature to the main targets. Nevertheless those unfortunate enough to be caught on the beaches during a strafe retain vivid memories of its unpleasantness. LAC Ken Anderson was one of them:

Here in the sand we grovelled, with the burning town as back-cloth, the flash of guns and bursting bombs as light and sound effects. Cold, hungry and despondent, we were sure we had been forgotten and deserted. With the first light of dawn the Luftwaffe and Wehrmacht began, again, to hurl exploding horror at this sandy shore and at the ships, yachts, and all the other vessels of that noble company. For us there was a gruelling twelve-kilometre march along the loose sand to La Panne, there to burrow like rabbits in the dunes – to march into the sea up to our necks only to march out again, a hellish diversion to be repeated again and again.[3]

For others, the sojourn on the beaches was characterized by a deep sense of unreality, underlined by the waiting that seemed to go on for ever. Captain N.D.G. James, of the 68th Field Battery RA:

It was dark when we reached the sandhills and we were very tired. The day before, or it might have been the day before that, guncotton and detonators had been issued with orders to blow up the guns. Since then the purpose of our existence had changed. We were no longer a fighting force but simply a unit moving back towards the coast.

Behind the sandhills lay the sea and beyond the sea – England. This seemed incredible and wholly beyond one's comprehension, but lack of sleep dulls the senses and blunts the ability to comprehend. We lay down where we stood and we slept where we lay down; I found I was on the edge of a trench and dropped into it. I awoke in a grey still dawn to the sound of a voice reciting French. Looking over the lip of the trench I saw a French burial party at work a few yards away and realized my trench was a grave. I got out and walked away.

An hour later the order came for us to move down to the beach, and we made our way over the sand hills. It was now quite light, and, as we came to the edge of the dunes, we saw the beach spread out before us, stretching away on either side. As far as we could see it was black with men. They were in groups, in broken lines and circles; sitting, lying and standing – all of them waiting. Just in front of us someone had tried to build a jetty of lorries. They were placed head to tail, two abreast, and stretched out into the sea. A few men were clambering along them, but otherwise no one seemed to be interested.

We sat down in the sand and waited. Offshore were ships and boats of various shapes and sizes from destroyers downwards; some were moving and others were apparently at anchor. By this time the sun had risen and revealed the clear blue sky of an early summer morning, and with the sun came the Stukas. They approached from behind us, spread out according to their fancy and proceeded to bomb what they liked. Some chose the ships, others the beaches and a few the sea. As far as we could observe they were good at missing, and they went as quickly as they had come.

Near the end of the jetty of lorries stood a small group, in the centre of which was a brigadier who, according to rumour, was in charge of the evacuation. He did nothing because, one suspected, there was nothing he could do. One gathered that there were no plans for getting the men off the beach, and our only orders were to wait where we were.[4]

The waiting and uncertainty were made no easier by the gnawing hunger and thirst experienced by most of the troops assembled on the beaches. The void in a man's stomach, the agony of a caked throat transcended the fear of bomb and shell, and the search for food and drink became an obsession. Jack Duffy, of the 52nd Heavy Regiment RA, recalls that:

It was every man for himself. On the Wednesday [29 May] we were still on the beaches, and most of us hadn't eaten for days. Gunner Townsend spotted what looked like a grocer's van parked on the beach and went to it in search of food. On opening the rear doors he found a heap of dead soldiers, piled one on top of the other. We eventually found some very hard Army biscuits, which relieved our hunger a little.[5]

For Ken Carter, of the 4th Green Howards, the highlight of his stay on the beaches came when someone miraculously produced a huge tin of damsons; Carter and four others huddled in a foxhole and shared it out. 'God only knows where it came from; we didn't care. We just sat there and munched and munched, feeling the sweetness trickle down our throats, almost passing out with ecstasy.'

Like Carter, the troops in the sandhills awaiting their turn to go down to the beach proper for embarkation became very attached to their foxholes as the hours – sometimes days – went by. In these shallow holes, clawed from the loose sand with bare hands or anything else available, the men curled like children in their mother's womb, often feeling a ridiculous sense of security from the bullets and flying shrapnel. 'You sort of scraped yourself a little hole and stayed there, and if anything happened you just stuck your head down. One minute you could see heads and shoulders dotted all over the dunes; the next, when shells or aircraft came over, there wouldn't be a soul in sight. Everybody just disappeared below ground level.'

Nevertheless, although the sand did provide some measure of protection from the enemy gunfire and bombing, there was plenty of evidence of the fearful toll that was being taken. During the latter stages of the evacuation the whole shoreline was awash with corpses, some terribly burned and mutilated, others without a mark on them, killed by the concussion of exploding bombs as they waded out to the rescue craft. Sergeant A. Bruce, of the 7th Field Company RE, noted harrowing sights as he trekked along the beach towards La Panne:

As we trudged on we passed horses, their stomachs ripped apart and entrails scattered all over the place. Men were lying there in grotesque attitudes of death, eyes and mouths wide open; it was hard to believe that they had ever been human beings. I could not help thinking, as I half fell, half walked through that wet sand, of the funeral those boys would have had at home, with tenderness and flowers; yet here they lay where they had died, like dogs that had been run over in the street.[6]

Wednesday 29 May was the day on which the concentration of troops on the beaches and dunes reached truly massive proportions. Apart from the fact that the attentions of the Luftwaffe and German artillery had by this time made Dunkirk harbour unusable, this was the day on which the bulk of the 2nd and 44th Divisions arrived on the beaches, and these men – together with substantial numbers from other formations such as the Royal Artillery and Royal Engineers, as well as a mass of French troops – caused a lot of congestion, particularly in the area of Malo-les-Bains. The British units managed to maintain cohesion, being split up into parties of fifty to await evacuation, but the milling French troops presented a problem. Admiral Abrial had as yet received no instructions to evacuate them, but many were nevertheless determined to leave and harassed the British embarkation officers almost to breaking-point.

It was fortunate for the dark mass of men on the beaches that on 30 May the weather took a hand. The day began grey and overcast, with a veil of mist and smoke hanging over the beaches. Although a stiff breeze made the loading of small boats at the water's edge difficult work, the weather conditions persisted throughout the day and the Luftwaffe's effort was reduced to sporadic attacks. Embarkation was able to proceed with little molestation, although the swell made it a slow process. It was, however, greatly assisted by the jetty of lorries at Bray Dunes, built on the orders of General Alexander; thousands of troops passed over this improvised bridge to the waiting small craft.

30 May also saw a command reshuffle as the evacuation moved towards its final phase. General Brooke of II Corps departed for England, handing over command of the corps to Montgomery. Command of the latter's 3rd Division now devolved on Brigadier K.A.N. Anderson of 11th Brigade (4th Division), who in turn was replaced by Colonel Brian Horrocks, General Sir Ronald Adam also left, his task at Dunkirk now at an end.

General Pownall, Lord Gort's chief of staff, had left for home the previous day, but Gort himself appeared determined to stay with his troops until the last and share whatever fate might befall them. Gort personally believed that the shrinking perimeter around Dunkirk could not continue to hold out for longer than forty-eight hours more, and the issue now at stake was to try and rescue as many Britons as possible during those two days or to fight on longer for 'the sake of Allied solidarity' – a phrase that had already shown itself to be meaningless. On the morning of the thirtieth, from his HQ at La Panne, he asked the War Office for instructions, but it was from Churchill that the reply came several hours later:

Continue to defend the present position to the utmost in order to cover maximum evacuation now proceeding well. Report every three hours through La Panne. If we can still communicate we shall send you an order to return to England with such officers as you may choose at the moment when we deem your command so reduced that it can be handed over to a Corps Commander. You should nominate this Commander now. If communications are broken you are to hand over and return as specified when your effective fighting force does not exceed the equivalent of three divisions. This is in accordance with correct military procedure, and no personal discretion is left to you in the matter. On political grounds it would be a needless triumph to the enemy to capture you when only a small force remained under your orders. The Corps Commander chosen by you should be ordered to carry on the defence in conjunction with the French, and evacuation whether from Dunkirk or the beaches, but when in his judgement no further organized evacuation is possible and no further proportionate damage can be inflicted on the enemy he is authorized in consultation with the senior French Commander to capitulate formally to avoid useless slaughter.[7]

As night fell on 30 May, therefore, the overall sentiment was one of hopelessness for the troops of I Corps, who were to be entrusted with the final perimeter defence while II Corps evacuated their sector and embarked. It was envisaged that the evacuation would have to be completed by the morning of 1 June, and the assumption was that 60,000 men could be lifted off before that deadline; the majority, it was thought, of those who remained. The hopelessness would no doubt have intensified had it been realized, amid all the confusion, that there were at least twice as many troops inside the Dunkirk perimeter, not counting the French.

Moreover there still remained one big question mark: the weather. As darkness fell on 30 May, the cloud cover that had hung like a protective shield over the Dunkirk beaches showed signs of breaking up. If the improvement continued the Luftwaffe would be back in force at dawn, throwing all its resources into a final bid to smash the operation. In the air, as well as on the ground, it was clear that the thirty-first would be a day on which the evacuation would float or founder.

9　The Air Battle

At the outset of the German offensive in the west, on 10 May 1940, the Luftwaffe air fleets responsible for supporting the land campaign – Luftflotten 2 and 3, commanded by Generals Albert Kesselring and Hugo Sperrle – possessed a total of 2,750 combat aircraft of all types. This total, which included 1,120 bombers, 324 dive-bombers and 1,264 fighters, was split up among six air corps: Fliegerkorps 1 and IV, which were responsible for air operations over Holland and Belgium, II and V, supporting the offensive in north-east France, one Special Duties Fliegerkorps responsible for airborne operations, and finally Fliegerkorps VIII, which included most of the Stuka dive-bomber squadrons on the western front and which was commanded by Lieutenant-General Wolfram Baron von Richthofen, a cousin of the famous air ace of the earlier war.

By 24 May, at the end of two weeks of fighting, the Luftwaffe had achieved almost total air supremacy in the north, except along the Channel coast, which was in range of the RAF's home-based fighter squadrons. Inland the battered French and British air squadrons which had opposed the German assault so valiantly had withdrawn their remnants south of the Somme, leaving the Luftwaffe as mistress of the sky. Nevertheless the cost to the Luftwaffe so far had been high, and its combat squadrons – now operating at the extreme limit of their range as they followed the Panzers' headlong dash to the sea – were desperately in need of a rest.

It was therefore hardly surprising that the news of the high-level decision to leave the destruction of Dunkirk and the British Expeditionary Force to the Luftwaffe was received with incredulity by both air and ground commanders. Kesselring, c-in-c Luftflotte 2, objected that such a task was completely beyond the strength of his depleted forces – yet it was Göring who had the last word, having boastfully committed himself to the Führer. The Luftwaffe alone would be responsible for the destruction of the Dunkirk pocket.

Quite apart from the question of depletion, there was no possibility of the Luftwaffe's bomber squadrons launching an immediate full-scale onslaught on Dunkirk, for they still had heavy operational commitments elsewhere. When von Richthofen, the commander of Fliegerkorps VIII, visited von Kleist's command post on the morning of 24 May, the day on which the armoured divisions were ordered to halt on the Aa canal, he found an atmosphere of tension verging on hostility. General von Kluge, the Fourth Army commander, was there together with his corps commanders Guderian and Reinhardt. Sarcastically, he asked Richthofen if the Luftwaffe had succeeded in taking Dunkirk from the air yet. Embarrassed, Richthofen had to admit that his Stuka squadrons had not even attacked the port; they were still too far back, and the demands of the Army for close-support aircraft meant that they were split up all along the front.[1] It would be some time before they could be assembled to make a concentrated attack on Dunkirk, and even then the success of such an attack would depend on strong fighter escort; the Channel ports were too close to the home-based squadrons of RAF Fighter Command for comfort. The twin-engined bomber squadrons were even more poorly situated; a few had moved to bases in Holland but most were still in Germany, and it was a fairly long haul to the Channel. Later, on returning to his headquarters at Proisy, Richthofen voiced his misgivings over the telephone to the Lufwaffe chief of general staff, Hans Jeschonnek, who was a personal friend: 'Unless the Panzers can get moving again at once, the English will give us the slip. No one can seriously believe that we alone can stop them from the air.'[2] Yet that, apparently, was what Hitler and Göring had both come to believe, despite all the evidence to the contrary. The order for the Luftwaffe to concentrate its effort on Dunkirk held firm.

On 25 May small numbers of medium bombers drawn from Fliegerkorps I and IV made sporadic attacks on Dunkirk, but Richthofen's Stukas played no part at all; they were still heavily engaged elsewhere, at St Quentin, Boulogne and Calais. It was the same story on the twenty-sixth, when the town and harbour of Dunkirk were again attacked by small formations of Heinkel IIIs and Junkers 88s; on this day the three Stuka wings of Fliegerkorps VIII were operating at maximum effort against Calais, Lille and Amiens.

That night, however, Calais fell, and on the twenty-seventh the Luftwaffe was able to turn its full fury on Dunkirk. The first bomber formations arrived overhead in the darkness before dawn: twenty-five-strong squadrons of Kampfgeschwader (Bomber Wings) 1 and 4, the Heinkels unloading their bombs into the harbour area. At first light they were followed by the Heinkels of KG 54, whose bombs started new conflagrations in the docks and sank the 8,000-ton French freighter *Aden*, berthed by the east mole.

By 07.15 Dunkirk was a blazing shambles, and the harbour had been effectively blocked, compelling the evacuation force to concentrate on lifting troops from the beaches themselves. There was to be no respite. At 07.20 Richthofen's Stukas appeared, screaming down through the smoke at the ships and boats that swarmed offshore. As had been the case at Calais the Stuka pilots found the vessels difficult targets, but several bombs found their mark; among the ships that went down was the French troop transport *Cote d'Azur*. (For details of naval operations off Dunkirk see Chapter 11 'The Narrow Seas'.)

As the Stukas flew away from the carnage, they were replaced by the slim, twin-finned Dornier 17s of KGs 2 and 3, which had flown to the target area from their airfields at Rhine-Main. In impeccable formation they droned over Dunkirk, showering their bombs into the inferno of blazing oil tanks and shattered streets. Nevertheless the Dorniers did not have it all their own way. As the bombers of KG 3's No. 3 Squadron (III/KG 3) turned for home after bombing the oil storage tanks, they were bounced by a squadron of Spitfires. Six Dorniers were shot down in flames and as many more were forced to crash-land with severe battle damage; at one blow, half of III/KG 3's effective strength had been wiped out. III/KG 2 fared little better, as its commanding officer, Major Werner Kreipe, reported: 'The enemy fighters pounced on our tightly knit formation with the fury of maniacs.' On this one day alone, Fliegerkorps II – according to its own war diary – lost twenty-three bombers, with sixty-four aircrew killed and seven wounded. The loss, especially in terms of human life, exceeded that sustained during the preceding ten days – and it took no account of aircraft that managed to stagger back to base with such severe battle damage that they had to be written off. If the troops on the beaches cursed the RAF for its supposed absence, the German bomber crews cursed it too, but for a different reason. They had been made grimly aware of the extent to which Fighter Command was committed over Dunkirk – and this had been only the first day of major air fighting.

British fighter cover over Dunkirk was provided by a total of sixteen first-line squadrons drawn from Air Vice Marshal Keith Park's No. 11 Fighter Group, spread out over its Kentish airfields: Biggin Hill, Manston, Hornchurch, Lympne, Hawkinge and Kenley, to name the principals. This standing cover of sixteen squadrons was frequently rotated, those which suffered a high rate of attrition being sent north for a rest and replaced by fresh units drawn from Nos 12 and 13 Groups, so that in fact thirty-two RAF fighter squadrons in all participated in the nine days of Operation Dynamo. No more than sixteen, however, were committed at any one time, for Air Chief Marshal Sir Hugh Dowding, the c-in-c Fighter Command, knew that the real test would soon come in the skies over southern England and was anxious to preserve what remained of his fighter strength to meet it; losses so far in the Battle of France had been fearfully high – the equivalent of six Hurricane squadrons.

On 27 May – the day on which the Luftwaffe carried out twelve major attacks on Dunkirk, using a total of 300 bombers, flying 550 escort fighter sorties, dropping 15,000 high explosive and 30,000 incendiary bombs – AVM Park's sixteen fighter squadrons, with 287 serviceable aircraft at their disposal, carried out twenty-three patrols over Dunkirk between 05.00 and nightfall; these patrols varied in strength from nine to twenty aircraft. During the course of the day fourteen Spitfires and Hurricanes were lost, but the RAF claimed the destruction of thirty-eight enemy aircraft – including two Messerschmitt 109s and three Heinkel 111s shot down by the Boulton Paul Defiants of No. 264 Squadron, newcomers to the battle. The Defiant was a single-engined fighter with an armament of four ·303 machine guns in a power-operated turret behind the pilot's cockpit; it bore some resemblance head-on to the Hurricane and was frequently mistaken as such by the Luftwaffe pilots during these first encounters, but they soon got the measure of it and during subsequent battles the squadrons using it were decimated. It was finally withdrawn from daylight operations and assigned to the night-fighter role. The British propaganda machine later claimed that the Defiants had destroyed thirty-nine enemy aircraft over Dunkirk, but this was completely untrue.

Although Fighter Command emerged from the battles of the twenty-seventh as the decided victors, some of the squadrons had suffered heavily, many Spitfires and Hurricanes limping back to base riddled with holes. At Hornchurch, for example, No. 54 Squadron ended the day with only six serviceable aircraft; it had to be withdrawn to Catterick in Yorkshire (in No. 13 Group's area) to refit, and its place was taken by No. 41 Squadron.

The combat record of RAF Biggin Hill was typical of an 11 Group fighter station on this hectic day. All three of Biggin's squadrons – No. 610 (Spitfires) and Nos 213 and 242 (Hurricanes) were in action:

On their first sortie the pilots of 610 Squadron, flying in their Spitfires at 18,000 feet, sighted a twin-engined Heinkel 111 bomber some 3,000 feet below. Anxious, in this his first combat, to make certain it was a Hun, Squadron Leader Franks dived down and calmly flew alongside taking a good look: the swastika on the tail, the black crosses on the wings were plain to see. Franks ordered Red Two and Red Three to attack. Flying Officer Smith poured all his ammunition into the Heinkel, only breaking off when the starboard engine was enveloped in flames. Sergeant Medway followed him up with a five-second burst, then the three Spitfires of Yellow Section joined in. Blue Section lined up to speed the Heinkel to its doom, but were called off by Franks. Plunging down out of control, the German pilot managed to fire Very Signals which brought forty Messerschmitt 109s to avenge him. Undismayed by odds of over three to one, the Spitfire pilots went straight in to attack and sent three Messerschmitts spinning down in flames, with another three 'probables'. From this brief but hectic party Flying Officer Medcalf and Sergeant Medway failed to return. Flying back to Gravesend the squadron sighted a big formation of Junkers 87s and 88s. To their fury the pilots could do nothing about them as all their ammunition was spent.

The two Hurricane squadrons operating from Biggin Hill enjoyed a more modest success that day. On a joint patrol over Gravelines they met ten Messerschmitt 109s and shot down two without loss.[3]

The twenty-eighth dawned overcast and the weather grew steadily worse as the day went on, severely hampering Luftwaffe operations and bringing respite to the exhausted men on the beaches and in the rescue fleet. Although German bomber formations attacked both Ostend and Nieuport, very few got through to Dunkirk itself; the low cloud, combined with the pall of smoke and dust, made target identification and accurate bombing impossible. No. 11 Group flew eleven squadron patrols in the Dunkirk sector during the day, with 321 individual fighter sorties. The RAF claimed the destruction of twenty-three enemy aircraft for the loss of thirteen of their own number.

The following morning was even worse from the weather point of view, with pouring rain and a cloud base down to three hundred feet. For nearly thirty-six hours now, the tonnage of bombs that had fallen on Dunkirk had been only a fraction of the envisaged total. Von Richthofen wrote in his diary: 'All levels of the higher command were clamouring today for VIII Fliegerkorps to go again for the ships and boats, on which the English divisions were getting away by the skin of their teeth. We had, however, a ceiling of just over three hundred feet, and as general in command I expressed the view that the enemy's concentrated flak was causing greater loss to our side than we were to his.'

The lower the enemy bombers were forced to fly, in fact, the greater were the chances of success for the anti-aircraft batteries ashore and afloat. The most concentrated barrage came from the warships, for although the 2nd Anti-Aircraft Brigade had been made responsible for the defence of Dunkirk all its 3·7-inch guns had been deliberately put out of action on the evening of the twenty-seventh as the result of an unfortunate miscarriage of orders, leaving only the

Bofors of the 51st Light Anti-Aircraft Regiment to defend the port, and these were only effective up to 4,000 feet.

Towards noon on the twenty-ninth the clouds at last began to disperse, and by 14.00 hours conditions were once more suitable for dive-bombing operations. Forty-five minutes later, Fliegerkorps VIII launched a massive attack with 180 Stukas, which screamed down on the evacuation fleet in three waves and caused a great deal of devastation. They were followed, at 15.30, by powerful bomber formations from Luftflotte 2, among them the Dutch-based Junkers 88s of KG 30 and also the 88s of Lehrgeschwader 1 (Operational Training Wing No. 1) from Düsseldorf. By the end of the day, these concerted attacks had resulted in the sinking of three destroyers and five large passenger vessels, with seven more destroyers damaged. It was the biggest disruptive effort made so far against Operation Dynamo.

During the day the RAF carried out nine patrols, with formations of between twenty-five and forty-four fighters providing cover over the Dunkirk sector. They succeeded in intercepting three out of the five major attacks launched by the Luftwaffe that day, but all the German raids were heavily escorted by fighters and the RAF could not succeed in breaking them up. The score at the end of the day was marginally in the Luftwaffe's favour, with sixteen British fighters shot down against fourteen German aircraft.

During the night the weather deteriorated once more, and 30 May opened with fog and rain. All day long three hundred German bombers and their fighter escorts stood on readiness to fly against Dunkirk at the slightest sign of improvement, but the fog persisted right through to the following morning. It began to clear towards midday, permitting the Luftwaffe to carry out several attacks, but these were restricted to relatively small formations and never reached the intensity of the raids of the twenty-ninth. No. 11 Group, which had flown nine squadron patrols the previous day without making contact with the enemy, carried out eight 'sweeps' over Dunkirk on the thirty-first and destroyed seventeen enemy aircraft. The Luftwaffe, in the course of its three biggest attacks that day, sank one freighter and damaged six destroyers.

Also on the thirty-first, the Blenheim medium bombers of the RAF's No. 2 Group flew several sorties in support of the Allied forces on the Dunkirk perimeter, now sorely pressed by the enemy divisions. The French took part in this effort too; six American-built Vought 156 dive-bombers of the French Naval Air Arm's AB 1 Squadron flew from Cherbourg to Tangmere, in southern England, where they refuelled and bombed up for an attack on Furnes. The mission was carried out successfully, four of the aircraft landing at Cherbourg and the others flying back across the Channel.

More attacks were carried out at dusk on the enemy positions by eighteen Blenheims of 2 Group, joined by Avro Ansons of RAF Coastal Command and by Fairey Albacore biplanes and Blackburn Skua dive-bombers of the Fleet Air Arm. Byt his time the RAF air-fields in the south of England were crammed with a remarkable collection of aircraft, all engaged in air operations over Dunkirk; while the Spitfires and Hurricanes of Fighter Command took on the Luftwaffe high overhead, Avro Anson and Lockheed Hudson reconnaissance-bombers of Coastal Command flew what became known as the 'Sands Patrol', covering the beaches and the rescue craft. Often these slow machines engaged vastly superior enemy formations, the pilots attacking with little regard for their own safety. There was a good deal of improvisation, too; some of the Ansons of No. 501 Squadron, for example, were hastily fitted with machine guns firing out of the side windows, and by this means they accounted for at least three unsuspecting Messerschmitts.

Another example of improvisation was 'Operation Flash', for which two Blackburn Skua target-tugs were flown from their base at Gosport to Detling, near Maidstone. Their task was to fly fixed courses over the Channel after dark, to the north of the evacuation routes, illuminating the sea with flares so that the Anson squadron operating from Detling could spot any enemy naval activity. The pilots were briefed to patrol ten miles offshore between Dunkirk and the Scheldt Estuary, dropping flares one at a time until the whole load of twenty or thirty was used up. Each flare burned for about three and a half minutes and produced 20,000 candlepower – quite sufficient to light up the sea and also the aircraft that dropped it. One of the pilots, Flying Officer D.H. Clarke, described the first mission:

Three bombed-up Ansons led the way to Dunkirk, and I followed

the leader's blue formation lights without difficulty ... Dunkirk was an inferno of fires, surrounded by flashing pin-pricks of light which I assumed were guns hammering ceaselessly at our troops. We turned to port before we reached the land and the leading Anson blinked his formation lights.

'Stream all the wire,' I ordered Phelan over the intercom. When he reported that the 6,000 feet was out, I pulled clear of the Ansons. 'Right! Let go the first flare!'

Half a minute dragged in agony. I pictured the two-foot tube sliding through the darkness down the long wire. When it reached the toggle at the end the jerk would snap the firing pin home and – suddenly the night sky vanished; the faint horizon disappeared. A billion misty droplets of water, almost invisible in the darkness, hurled back the glare of 20,000 candlepower so that I could see nothing outside the cockpit. We were locked in a bowl of brilliant whiteness, and it was as if we had flown inside an electric light bulb – even the instruments showed their black and white daytime faces.

Somehow I managed to keep straight and level. When the first flare died, the enveloping blackness which smothered my eyes was even worse than the glare ... For three quarters of an hour I sweated a blind course up the Belgian and Dutch coast. I never saw a thing – neither land, sea nor Ansons ...

Then I did see something! A vague blur of movement over the silver disc of the spinning airscrew – half seen through concentrated attention on the instruments. What was it: a night fighter?

There was a sudden jolt. For a moment the engine note changed – then it resumed its steady beat.

'Sir! An aircraft's fouled the wire. The flare's gone!' And then the blackness ... once more the green instruments ... I told Phelan to reel in, and he reported that only a few hundred feet of wire were left. Whatever it was I had seen must have flown into the wire and snapped it. With the toggle at the end gone we could light no more flares that night.[4]

Such were the hazards faced by the host of unsung pilots who, day after day, night after night, flew their slow machines across the

Channel to bring whatever aid was possible to the BEF. Meanwhile, high over the beaches, Fighter Command continued to hit the Luftwaffe hard. The morning of 1 June was bright and clear, and the Germans took the opportunity to throw every available aircraft against Dunkirk. At first light a violent attack was launched against the ships by forty Stukas of Fliegerkorps VIII; as they were turning for home twenty-eight Hurricanes arrived and engaged in a fierce dogfight with the Messerschmitt 109s of Colonel Theo Osterkamp's JG 51 and the twin-engined Messerschmitt 110s of Lieutenant-Colonel Huth's ZG 26. Elsewhere along the beaches three Ansons of 501 Squadron engaged nine Messerschmitts with their sideways-firing guns and destroyed two for certain, with two 'probables', while three Hudsons dived into the middle of a Stuka formation as the latter was pulling up from an attack on the ships and shot down three of the dive-bombers.

Fighter Command carried out eight squadron-strength patrols during the course of this day, claiming the destruction of seventy-eight enemy aircraft – a figure that was later officially reduced to forty-three. However, Luftwaffe records admit the loss of nineteen bombers and ten fighters only for 1 June, with a further thirteen damaged; and since the Royal Navy claimed ten aircraft destroyed and the French fighters another ten the actual score must remain in doubt. What is certain is that Fighter Command lost thirty-one aircraft during the air battles of 1 June, and that the Luftwaffe sank four destroyers and ten other craft off the beaches.

Luftwaffe activity over Dunkirk was very much reduced on 2 June, the reason being that the German combat squadrons were held in readiness for a major operation which was to take place on 3 June: a massive air attack on factories and airfields in the Paris area, code-named 'Operation Paula'. There was one major raid on Dunkirk in the course of the day, a hundred and twenty bombers at 08.00; this was intercepted by five squadrons of Spitfires and Hurricanes and broken up, the bombers succeeding in damaging only two ships. However since the bulk of the evacuation was now taking place under cover of darkness the Luftwaffe was turning its attention to targets on shore, and that afternoon Fort Vallières, one of the strongpoints in the suburbs of Dunkirk, was knocked out by a highly

accurate attack delivered by twenty-four Stukas. Dive-bombers also
struck at various points on the perimeter, including Leffrinckoucke,
Teteghem, Uxem, Bergues and Mardyck, which were then attacked
towards evening by Dornier 17s of Luftflotte 2.

On 3 June the Stukas of Fliegerkorps VIII were the only German
bombers operating over Dunkirk; the others were already heavily
engaged in attacking French positions south of the Somme in
preparation for the big German offensive that would soon burst
across the river.

During the nine days of Dunkirk, between 26 May and 3 June
1940, the RAF squadrons committed to the battle over the beaches
and beyond had carried out 171 reconnaissance, 651 bombing and
2,739 fighter sorties. Combat losses for the RAF during those nine
days were 177 aircraft destroyed or severely damaged, including
106 fighters. On 4 June, Fighter Command had suffered such attrition over Dunkirk that its first-line strength was reduced to 331
Spitfires and Hurricanes, with only thirty-six fighters in reserve.

On the other side of the coin, the pilots of Fighter Command
claimed the destruction of 377 enemy aircraft, a figure that was later
officially reduced to 262; the gunners of the Royal Navy claimed
thirty-five more. German records for this period, however, admit a
loss of 240 aircraft of all types along the whole Franco-Belgian front,
of which 132 were lost in the Dunkirk sector; a number that
corresponds roughly with the losses of Fighter Command. The same
kind of ratio was to apply later, during the Battle of Britain.

Nevertheless it should not be forgotten that the ratio of daily
RAF losses over Dunkirk was generally higher than that experienced
during the Battle of Britain a few weeks later – or that for the
majority of the British fighter pilots who took part this was their
first real taste of action, whereas many of their opponents were already
veterans. The RAF pilots were also operating at a disadvantage in
that they were separated from their bases by the Channel – a short
stretch of water that seemed never-ending when struggling with the
controls of a battle-damaged aircraft, as the Germans were also to
find at a later date.

All in all the RAF emerged from the battles over Dunkirk with
credit – despite the bitter criticism of thousands of troops to whom

the sky always seemed to be devoid of British aircraft. Many, however, have a different story to tell; Mons Trussler, for example, recalls seeing a huge formation of RAF fighters circling protectively over Dunkirk, and others remember cheering as they watched the Spitfires and Hurricanes ripping into the enemy formations. Some cheered too soon, like one group who stood and waved as a Lysander flew slowly overhead; the Lysander turned out to be a German Henschel 126 observation aircraft, of similar appearance, which dropped a couple of small bombs on their heads.[5]

Several pilots, their aircraft disabled over Dunkirk, took to their parachutes only to be killed by small-arms fire as they drifted down, for the troops on the beaches often blazed away indiscriminately at friend and foe alike. One German pilot who was fortunate to survive was First Lieutenant Erich von Oelhaven,[6] whose Junkers 88 was shot down in flames by Spitfires on the morning of 2 June. Bullets crackled around him as he floated down, but miraculously he was unharmed. He drifted in over the beach and landed heavily among the dunes. Slightly winded, he released himself from his parachute and got to his feet to find himself confronted by a group of armed British soldiers. The expressions on their weary, haggard faces left him in no doubt what would happen if he tried to run for it; he raised his hands.

During the next few hours, von Oelhaven found out what it was like to be on the receiving end of his own side's bombs and shells. Together with the soldiers who had captured him, he cowered in a shallow foxhole in the dunes while geysers of sand and smoke erupted across the beaches. At dusk, urged on by the barrel of a rifle, he moved with the others down to the water's edge, where a jetty had been built from abandoned army trucks. At its far end was a trawler.

The pilot knew that once he was aboard the ship, he had only two alternatives; to be sunk by the Luftwaffe's bombs – or, if he survived, to face a prison cage in England. If he was going to escape it had to be now, in the next couple of minutes, as the queue of battle-stained soldiers shuffled slowly from truck to truck towards the waiting ship. Cautiously, he looked around; the soldiers nearest to him were almost asleep on their feet.

Gradually, von Oelhaven moved to the edge of the queue. Then, taking a deep breath, he hurled himself into the water. He heard a babble of confused shouting, then the sea closed over his head. He groped his way down the line of trucks, squeezed between two of them and broke surface, gasping for air. A couple of feet above him, boards had been laid as a bridge between the two vehicles. Sand filtered through as a steady stream of soldiers tramped across. Sometimes, for long periods of what must have been an hour or more, the queue halted. The pilot could hear the soldiers talking as they waited patiently for the next boat. Then the steady shuffle of feet would begin again.

The hours of darkness seemed endless. The water that lapped around von Oelhaven was red from the fires of Dunkirk and its foul, oily taste made him retch repeatedly. At first the pilot was able to stand upright, his feet touching the bottom, but as the tide came in he was forced to float in order to keep his face above the surface. At high tide his head was jammed in a tiny pocket of air between the water and the planks.

At dawn all movement on the jetty ceased. In the dunes, the last contingents of troops crouched in their holes and prepared to sweat it out under the hot June sun until nightfall, when it would be safe for them to embark. Meanwhile the Stukas and the German artillery continued to pound the dwindling bridgehead; time after time, the little jetty shuddered as bombs and shells exploded in the sea. Not daring to move from his hiding-place, von Oelhaven was dazed by the concussions that tore through the water.

As the day wore on the pilot became tormented by hunger and thirst. There was a packet of emergency rations in the pocket of his overall, but its protective cover was torn and the contents were a sodden pulp. He tried to force down some of the mess, but his stomach rebelled. His thirst was the worst of all, aggravated by the undrinkable water that was all around him.

Night fell, and the movement of soldiers along the jetty began once more. This time, however, the tramp of feet ceased well before dawn, and von Oelhaven decided to risk moving back along the jetty into shallower water. Worming out of his hiding-place, he waded carefully along the line of trucks until he reached firmer ground. Then he took cover under the planks again. It was an even tighter squeeze than before, but at least he was partly out of the water.

The sun rose on the morning of 4 June. Shelling was still in progress, and von Oelhaven – reasoning that the beaches were still in British hands – decided to stay where he was, at least for the time being. It was close on ten o'clock when he emerged, into an uncanny silence. The beaches were deserted, except for the piles of equipment left behind by the British. All he wanted now was to get out of the water. He floundered through the shallows and collapsed on the sand. The last thing he remembered, before falling into an exhausted sleep, was the feel of the warm sun on his back. It was there, some time later, that German soldiers found him.

For a third of a million allied troops, and one German pilot, the nightmare of Dunkirk was over.

On the morning of 31 May, following Churchill's recall order, Lord Gort travelled from his HQ at La Panne to say farewell to Admiral Abrial in Bastion 32 and to make final arrangements for the joint evacuation of British and French troops in equal numbers, authorization for which had reached him during the night. As his successor, he had decided to appoint the able General Alexander, although this decision had been reached only after much soul-searching, as Montgomery later described:

It is commonly supposed that at this final conference Gort 'nominated' Major-General H.R.L.G. Alexander to command after he himself had left. This is not so; moreover, Alexander himself was not even present at the conference. I will describe what actually happened.

The two Corps Commanders at the conference were Lieutenant-General M.G.H. Barker, 1st Corps, and myself, who had just taken over command of 2nd Corps. Gort's plan was based on the War Office telegram and he ordered that I was to withdraw 2nd Corps the next night, 31st May/1st June, and that the 1st Corps would then be left in final command. He informed Barker that as a last resort he would surrender himself, and what remained of his corps, to the Germans. The conference then broke up. I stayed behind when the others had left and asked Gort if I could have a word with him in private. I then said it was my view that Barker was in an unfit state to be left in final command; what was needed was a calm and clear brain, and that given reasonable luck such a man might well get 1st Corps away, with no need for anyone to surrender. He had such a man in Alexander, who was commanding the 1st Division in Barker's corps. He should send Barker back to England at once, and put Alexander in command of the 1st Corps. I knew Gort very well; so I spoke plainly and insisted that this was the right course to take.[1]

So Alexander took over 1 Corps, which was to assume full responsibility for the final defence of Dunkirk from 18.00 hours on the 31st. Alexander's brief was 'to assist our French allies in the defence of Dunkirk', for which purpose he was to act under the orders of Admiral Abrial unless such orders directly threatened the safety of the British forces. At this stage it was his opinion that the perimeter could not hold longer than 2 June, and that the final evacuations would therefore have to take place on the night of the first to second.

In the meantime Churchill had flown to Paris for a meeting of the Supreme War Council. His statement that 165,000 British and 15,000 French troops had so far been evacuated was received with incredulity by the French and particularly by Weygand, who stormily demanded to know the reason for the British preponderance – forgetting that he had only just authorized Abrial to evacuate any French forces at all. Only the previous day, in an hysterical telephone conversation with the admiral, Weygand had exhorted him to 'hold on at all costs, for God's sake'.[2]

Churchill quickly explained that the disparity in numbers was the direct result of different sets of orders being issued by the respective Allied commands; the French calmed down somewhat and the delegates set about drafting instructions for the joint evacuation of the bridgehead. The first draft, composed by Admiral Darlan, the French Navy C-in-C, read:

1 A bridgehead should be held around Dunkirk.
2 As soon as you are convinced that no more troops outside the bridgehead can make their way to points of embarkation the troops holding the bridgehead shall withdraw, the British embarking first.
3 Once Dunkirk has been completely evacuated of land and naval units, the harbour will be blocked. The British Admiralty shall be responsible for this action.
4 The evacuation of Dunkirk will be carried out under your orders.[3]

Before this instruction was despatched to Admiral Abrial, Churchill insisted on paragraph 2 being amended to read ' . . . the British forces acting as rearguard as long as possible', a rephrasing which was accepted by the French with considerable relief.

This instruction had not yet reached Abrial when Alexander went to see him in the afternoon of the thirty-first, accompanied by Captain Tennant and Lieutenant-Colonel William Morgan, his senior staff officer. It was not a profitable meeting; Abrial was not in favour of evacuation and merely proposed to pull in the Dunkirk perimeter to a line running from Bergues through Uxem to the sea. Alexander was strongly opposed to this idea, which, he stated, would bring enemy artillery within range of the east mole at Dunkirk, from which large numbers of troops were still being lifted. He went on to say that in his view the existing perimeter could not be held longer than 1/2 June, and therefore planned to withdraw his forces that night (31 May–1 June). A lengthy argument ensued during which the French tried hard to persuade Alexander to reverse his decision, but the British general remained adamant. His only concession was to delay the final embarkation by several hours, running into daylight on 1 June, and to make it clear that all evacuation facilities would be shared equally with the French.

Alexander then went off to contact the War Office for confirmation of his decision, and to obtain approval to act contrary to Abrial's orders. After an hour's delay a reply came through from Anthony Eden, and its content left no room for doubt: 'You should withdraw your force as rapidly as possible on a 50–50 basis with the French Army, aiming at completion night 1st–2nd. You should inform the French of this Definite Instruction.' Alexander lost no time in doing so. He returned to Bastion 32 early that evening to advise Abrial of the British Government's decision; when he had finished the Admiral showed him the instruction which he had just received from the Supreme War Council in Paris. Alexander's reaction to its contents was hostile:

Had my Prime Minister been here instead of in Paris he would never have subscribed to these conditions. And I have been in touch with Mr Anthony Eden. He has ordered me to co-operate with the French forces in the fullest measure compatible with the security of the British troops. I consider their existence seriously threatened and I am sticking to my decision to embark tomorrow, 1st June.[4]

Meanwhile, during this fateful day of 31 May, while controversy raged at high level, the Germans had launched their expected attack along the length of the Dunkirk perimeter. Its main weight fell on the line held by II Corps, which was getting ready to pull out, some of the heaviest assaults falling on the sector held by the 4th East Yorks and the 4th and 5th Green Howards of 150th Brigade, on the right of the corps front. Early on the morning of the thirty-first, the 5th Green Howards at Houthem sighted an enemy spotter aircraft overhead – a sure sign of activity on the other side. A few minutes later the Germans opened up a fierce barrage with mortars and artillery, with counter-battery fire directed against the British artillery to the rear. The expected heavy attack came on the Green Howards' left, on the already depleted 6th Durham Light Infantry of 151st Brigade, and the Durhams took a lot of punishment. However, they managed to contain the enemy attempt to break through, and the next assault fell on the Green Howards, shells and mortar bombs causing many casualties.

Among them was Captain Tony Steede, OC C Company, who describes his experience:

My Company had a frontage of 800 yards, which was far too big to hold successfully. More important still, the German side of the canal in front of us was completely wooded, whereas on the Dunkirk side the terrain was completely flat and open. We dug in in sections and there was absolutely no way to camouflage the trenches; the enemy just climbed trees on the other side, spotted every last one of our positions on ground that was as flat as your hand, then brought up their heavy mortars and systematically plastered us. I remember thinking: 'If ever I get out of this bloody lot it'll be a two-man trench for me.'

I was kneeling in one of the trenches when I got as near a direct hit from a mortar bomb as it was possible to get. My batman was on one side of me and my driver on the other; they were both killed outright and I was badly hit in the knee. I came round some time later to find myself in a ditch, where I had been carried by a very brave officer who had been going round with the stretcher parties and who must have rescued me in full view of the Germans.[5]

Another strong enemy thrust came from Bulscamp, where the Germans succeeded in driving a wedge between the 9th DLI and the 1st King's Own Scottish Borderers, on their left. The German advance was halted and the 8th DLI and 3rd Grenadiers rushed in to plug the gap. At Furnes, which was ablaze from end to end, the 1st and 2nd Grenadiers were involved in bitter fighting, but they managed to hold on to part of the town. Throughout the day the British artillery and mortars kept up accurate fire in support of the infantry, although ammunition was in short supply and barely sufficient to last until nightfall.

Troop Sergeant Major C.S. Best, of 1 Troop 67 Anti-Tank Battery, 20th Anti-Tank Regiment RA – whose 2-pounders had been used to good effect during the long withdrawal through Belgium – was in action at Bulscamp with four guns facing the enemy across the canal, two in support of the Grenadiers and two attached to the KOSB, their fire directed from Troop HQ which had been set up in a farmhouse. He recalls:

We were subjected to heavy mortar fire, during which time Major Phillips [the battery commander] arrived at Troop HQ. We both dived behind a beet heap for cover, but unfortunately Major Phillips was killed; we buried him close by. I went to Battery HQ to report his death, and on the way back a KOSB company commander told me that our position had been overrun by the enemy, although his men were driving them back. Not long afterwards he said it was safe to go back to the farm; on arrival I found we had sustained only one casualty, a gunner who had been killed outright by mortar fire.

After this we cut the gun crews down to three men per gun and sent the others back. Sergeant Smith, my troop sergeant, offered to stay so that I could go back; it was a magnificent gesture, for he was a married man with four children. The next day [1 June]

Captain Egerton, who had taken command on Major Phillips'
death, came up and told me to disable the guns and vehicles and
place the men at the disposal of the infantry. We ran up the
engines of the vehicles until they seized, then dismantled our guns
and threw the parts down a well. It seemed a terrible waste.[6]

Elsewhere on II Corps' front a heavy attack fell on battered
Nieuport, with waves of infantry assaulting the canal at first light
under cover of a smoke screen. Minutes after the attack began a light
breeze dispersed the smoke and the defenders took fearful toll of the
enemy with Brens and rapid rifle fire. Nevertheless the Germans
managed to secure a foothold across the canal on either side of
the town, moving forward and threatening to encircle the exhausted
Royal Fusiliers. On the left the enemy were held by a much depleted
company of the 1st South Lancashire, while the 1st East Surrey were
rushed up from divisional reserve to bolster the flank of the 1/6th
East Surrey. Together these battalions drove the Germans back, but
things looked grim that afternoon when large enemy troop movements across the canal indicated that an even bigger attack was in
the offing. Then the miracle happened: at this point eighteen
Blenheims of the RAF's No. 2 Group, supported by six Fleet Air Arm
Albacores, swept across the town and delivered a highly accurate
raid on the enemy, who melted away in the explosions of the sticks
of bombs. The British troops cheered until they were hoarse, some
weeping openly as they caught sight of the roundels on the bombers'
wings.

The order for the withdrawal of II Corps reached the weary units
as darkness fell on 31 May. Throughout the night men silently
evacuated their positions and joined the great throng trudging back
towards La Panne. The march turned out to be longer than most
had anticipated, for at both La Panne and Bray Dunes a concentrated
bombardment by both the Luftwaffe and German artillery had
seriously disrupted the embarkation facilities. There was a long
queue of men at Bray Dunes, waiting patiently to cross the improvised jetty of lorries and take their place in one of the small craft that
hovered nearby, but for most the only alternative was to drag
themselves over the ten miles of beach to the mole at Dunkirk.

At dawn the sands were black with men like crawling columns of ants, many of them asleep on their feet as they staggered on. Some felt a deep sense of dismay and betrayal as the sun rose; they had been told that the Channel was crowded with ships, yet the coming of daylight revealed only an empty sea. The ships would be back at nightfall, but it was hard to reassure exhausted men. Some were too tired to care what became of them, stumbling on blindly and mindlessly on legs that no longer seemed to be part of them. Peter Pring, of the 1/6th South Staffords, remembers:

> We were utterly worn out. I think that if someone had got us all together and ordered us to march off straight towards the Germans we'd have done it; all we wanted was to sleep, and nothing else mattered. We arrived at Dunkirk after dark and flopped down in a field; we had no idea where we were or what we were supposed to do. We were eventually directed through the dunes to the beach where we found utter confusion. We split up in twos and threes, dug ourselves in as deeply as we could and just stayed there, keeping our heads down and hoping for the best. German aircraft continually strafed the beaches from first light onwards, and there were an awful lot of casualties that day.[7]

While the men of II Corps clung to their strip of sand under the blazing sun of Saturday 1 June, other units of the BEF continued to hold on behind the Bergues–Furnes canal. They comprised five brigades: the 139th, to which was added the 1st Battalion the Loyal Regiment from 1st Division and a company of the 2nd Royal Warwicks, and the 138th Brigade, both of 46th Division; the 126th Brigade of 42nd Division; and the 1st Guards and 3rd Infantry Brigades, both of the 1st Division. Facing this force, which in terms of real strength amounted to only six battalions, were the German 14th, 18th, 61st and 254th Divisions, while two more – the 56th and 216th – advanced from the east to engage the French 12th Division on the left of the Allied line, behind which the British 50th Division lay in reserve. To the west of Dunkirk the 9th Panzer Division and its supporting infantry continued to peck away at the French 208th, 225th and 341st Regiments, holding the line from Fort Mardyck on the coast to Spycker.

The first enemy attack against the British line came at 05.00 on
1 June, when the German 14th and 18th Divisions stormed the canal
at Teteghem and Hoymille under cover of heavy shell fire. The weight
of the attack fell on the 1st East Lancashire (126th Brigade) and the
company of Royal Warwicks, who were forced to give ground when
the enemy gained a foothold on the north bank of the canal. Brigadier
R.C. Chichester-Constable, commanding 139th Brigade, at once
ordered the 1st Loyals to evacuate Bergues, which was now in ruins
after its lengthy resistance, and go to the help of the Warwicks.
Leaving Bergues proved to be far from easy, for the troops were
subjected to intense artillery fire on the way out and suffered many
casualties. They subsequently made two counter-attacks against
the Germans on the north bank, sustaining more casualties as they
advanced through a sheet of water two feet deep; the first failed, but
the second succeeded in dislodging some of the enemy from their
newly-won positions and further infiltration was halted.

On the right flank of the East Lancashires, where several forward
positions were overwhelmed, the enemy advance was stopped by a
handful of men under Captain H.M. Ervine-Andrews, who personally killed seventeen Germans with his rifle and twice as many
more with a Bren. Ervine-Andrews and his small group held on to
their position on the straw roof of a barn until late afternoon, en-
during withering small-arms fire and pulling out only when the
building was set on fire. Ervine-Andrews successfully led the eight
survivors back to a reserve position through water that often reached
up to their necks, with bullets churning up spray all around. He was
later awarded a well-deserved Victoria Cross.

Despite their heroic resistance, the East Lancashires and their
neighbouring battalion, the 5th Border Regiment, were slowly
forced back to the reserve positions on the canal des Chats, endanger-
ing the right flank of the 2nd Coldstream Guards. Nevertheless the
latter managed to hold their position on the Bergues canal with
considerable assistance from the 2nd Hampshire and 5th King's
Own. On the extreme left of the line the 1st Duke of Wellington's
and a detachment of the 2nd Sherwood Foresters, thinly spread out
over a front of more than two miles following the withdrawal of
11 Corps, were heavily engaged by units of the German 14th Division.

A threatened breakthrough was stopped in the nick of time with the aid of a company of the 5th King's Own, withering machine-gun fire supplied by the 2nd Cheshire, and the rapid deployment of Bren carriers and a handful of light tanks of the 5th Royal Iniskilling Dragoon Guards.

By last light on 1 June the Germans had made little headway against the defences, their troops finding it hard going across the exposed, sodden terrain. After dark the British received orders to break contact and make their way to Dunkirk and Bray Dunes; to the east the 50th Division also marched down to the beaches, still herding along the four hundred German prisoners captured at Arras ten days earlier. These were lifted off early that night, to face the barbed wire of a POW compound for the next five years.

By 03.00 on 2 June, when embarkations were temporarily suspended with the approach of daylight, some 6,000 British troops remained within the shrinking perimeter, patiently waiting their turn for evacuation. Most were concentrated on Malo, where Alexander had formed a defence with the aid of his few remaining 2-pounders in case enemy armour broke through to the beaches. The guns, however, would not be used in anger again, for on the perimeter the French fought gallantly on.[9]

On the morning of 2 June the Germans seized the bridgehead at Hoymille, which had been held by the 139th Brigade. They were fiercely counter-attacked by three companies of the French 21st Divisional Training Centre; with incredible bravery 550 men charged the enemy across the open, bullet-raked ground, floundering through thigh-deep water. The counter-attack collapsed in a welter of bloody foam, torn apart by the murderous Spandaus, and only sixty-five French soldiers emerged unscathed. On their right, Bergues, now reduced to little more than a pile of smouldering rubble, fell to the enemy at 17.00. At dusk the main line of defence was between Couderkerque and Teteghem, and the leading enemy units were within four miles of Dunkirk. At the other end of the perimeter the Germans made several determined attacks on the defences of General Janssen's 12th Division; all were beaten off with heavy loss, and a spirited counter-attack by the 8th Zouaves and

150th Infantry Regiment took sixty prisoners. Unfortunately Janssen himself was killed in an air raid during the day.

On the west of the line, troops of the ss Grossdeutschland Regiment, supported by Mk III and Mk IV tanks of General Hubicki's 9th Panzer Division, hurled themselves against the defences of the French 68th Division at Spycker. Several tanks were knocked out by the French 75s, their sweating gunners firing over open sights until they were literally crushed under the tracks or mown down by the infantry. The Germans took Spycker, but there the French held them.

Enemy pressure was now strongest against the weak centre of the defensive line, which had been pushed back a mile and a half behind the Bergues–Furnes canal. In the afternoon of the second General Fagalde ordered up reinforcements in the shape of a battalion from the 68th Division and two understrength battalions from the 32nd, supported by whatever armour was available and six groups of 75s. The battalion of the 68th launched a counter-attack from Teteghem, covered by six Somua tanks; they made little progress, but managed to hold on to the ground they had retaken.

Fagalde, conscious of the fact that there was no hope of the evacuation being completed for at least another twenty-four hours, now scraped together every available man – including the Gardes Mobiles from his own HQ – in an effort to hold the line for that length of time. Another counter-attack was launched on the morning of 3 June, this time by a battalion of the 32nd Division; like the effort of the previous day it made little headway, but it held up the Germans for six vital hours.

The 68th Division, meanwhile, had now fallen back to the line of the Bourbourg–Dunkirk canal, holding a five-mile front all morning in the face of determined enemy assaults. Throughout the day the French fought with great courage and determination all along the line, but the rate of attrition they suffered was terrible; when darkness fell on the third, some units, including the 21st Divisional Training Centre and the 1st Battalion of the 137th Infantry Regiment, had been annihilated.

Yet still the line held – although it now consisted of a much reduced perimeter around Dunkirk, with the enemy less than a mile from the port. Had the Germans launched a full-scale attack during the hours of darkness, they would almost certainly have broken through and plunged on into the port mopping up the French forces who still awaited embarkation. But the Germans were every bit as exhausted as the defenders, and the night passed without major incident. Under cover of darkness, on Fagalde's orders, the French troops quietly pulled out of their positions and made for the quays, leaving behind skirmish lines to maintain contact with the enemy. At 02.00 the last of these also withdrew, the grimy, bearded Poilus trudging down to the waiting ships. One or two of the men, the enormity of the disaster looming large in their minds through the fatigue as they stumbled on, stooped down and scooped up a handful of wet earth, stowing it carefully away in a pocket. It would be four years to the month before most of them trod the soil of France again.

11 The Narrow Seas

From the bridge of the destroyer *Wolfhound*, Dunkirk was a terrifying, awe-inspiring sight. The vast column of smoke from the blazing oil storage tanks was the first pointer to the destruction that had already been wrought there by the Luftwaffe, boiling up from its as yet unseen base across the horizon, its top trailing out on the breeze into a great veil through which the afternoon sun shone fitfully as a pale, waxen disc.

On this afternoon of 27 May, as the destroyer creamed through the Channel towards Dunkirk, *Wolfhound*'s crew had already had a taste of the Luftwaffe's fury. For fifteen minutes, with Dover scarcely down over the horizon astern, they had run the gauntlet of a determined attack by von Richthofen's Stukas, zig-zagging wildly as the geysers of foam erupted all around. The Stukas had departed through the maze of anti-aircraft bursts hurled skywards by the embattled destroyer's red-hot guns and now Captain John McCoy once again set course at high speed direct for Dunkirk, conscious that much depended on *Wolfhound*'s safe arrival. For the little ship carried the men whose task it was to organize some order out of the chaos that was even now debouching on Dunkirk and its neighbouring beaches: Captain William Tennant and his small command of naval officers and ratings, through whom the evacuation would be channelled.

As the destroyer churned on, Tennant completed his briefing on the spray-swept deck. Perhaps the hardest task of all would fall to Commander John Clouston, who was to maintain liaison with the ships of the evacuation fleet as they arrived and ensure their loading and departure with the minimum congestion, and to Commander Renfrew Gotto, who was to supervise the departure of troops from Dunkirk harbour itself.

Now, as *Wolfhound* approached Dunkirk, Tennant and his officers began to have some idea of the enormity of the job that lay ahead of them. The pall of smoke assumed frightening proportions as it coiled and billowed into the summer air, and at its foot the whole waterfront seemed to be ablaze. Rivers of flame seethed along the quays from lines of burning warehouses, and as the destroyer approached the harbour a carpet of soot descended on her like black rain.

The *Wolfhound* berthed to the screech and crump of bombs as yet another air raid added to the devastation, which was far greater than Tennant had visualized. The docks, with their five miles of quays, were shattered, the cranes tilted at crazy angles among the piles of rubble. The town's railway system had ceased to exist, the tracks ripped apart and twisted by high-explosive bombs. Beneath the toppled buildings of Dunkirk, a thousand men, women and children lay dead, victims of the first day of severe air attack.

Tennant was greeted on the bomb-shattered quay by Colonel Gerald Whitfield, senior staff assistant to General Sir Douglas Brownrigg, who briefed him on the extent of the damage and the latest battle situation as far as it was known. Having made his assessment, Tennant rapidly issued his orders to his officers, assigning them to their different tasks. Commander Thomas Kerr, one of the naval officers who had crossed the Channel with Tennant in *Wolfhound*, later described his personal impression of the situation in Dunkirk and on the surrounding beaches:

In due course we were marched down through the town to the beach close by and our work began. Such a terrible beach for embarking men because it was practically level and nothing could come in close, not even the boats. We worked without ceasing all the dark hours, restoring order and confidence to the troops. At dawn we withdrew them to the sand dunes for an hour, and afterwards marched them into Dunkirk. We cleared the beach sometime during the afternoon. The Captain in charge, Tennant, reorganized us and said he wanted one officer and party to go to Bray Dunes to embark 5,000 men. There were three of us left and so we cut for it, for it was a poor outlook by the sound of it. Richardson [Commander Hector Richardson] lost, but then said quite rightly that he wanted another officer with him, so he and I set out in a lorry with a party of 15.

It took us some time to reach Bray Dunes because the road was badly cratered and we took the wrong turning once or twice, and it was getting dusk when we finally got our party down to the beach. Then we gave a gasp. Five thousand men? Not a bit of it, there must have been 25,000 at the very least. We asked a destroyer to signal this information direct to the Admiralty, then we got busy. What a terrible night that was, for we had got hold of the odds and ends of an army, not the fighting soldiers. There were hardly any officers, and the few present were useless; but our promise of safety, and the sight of our naval uniforms, restored some order to the rabble. Their faith in the Navy was pathetic; we could only do our best. Some we embarked at Bray Dunes, but the remainder we marched in their thousands to Dunkirk; a difficult task in itself, for the sight of just one little dinghy with a queue of 2,000 men waiting to get into it was enough to make them hesitate on the march.

We were all soaked through, because we couldn't persuade the troops to stand on dry sand rather than in the water; every man was afraid that someone else would get in front of him. Towards morning the weather blew up and embarkation from the beach became impossible, so herding them and marshalling them we marched them towards Dunkirk.[1]

During the twenty-four hours between midnight on 26 May and midnight on the twenty-seventh 3,324 British troops were evacuated from Dunkirk and its neighbouring beaches. Added to this figure were 1,250 wounded and 4,000 Frenchmen, the latter all specialists who could play no part in the defence of Dunkirk and whose evacuation had been ordered by Admiral Abrial. The lifting of troops had been a desperately slow process, and Tennant knew that unless immediate steps were taken to augment the lift the chaos during the next twenty-four hours would become insupportable. The longer the troops had to wait on the beaches, the greater was the likelihood that all semblance of order would break down; and the fighting troops had yet to arrive. Already Tennant and his officers had witnessed the appalling spectacle of drunken soldiers roaming the streets of Dunkirk in armed, unruly mobs, looting and pillaging; he himself had confronted one such mob, at no small personal risk, and disarmed its leader. At this show of authority, the first men had encountered for some time, order was quickly restored – but the worry that the discontent that seethed among the men on the beaches might turn into open revolt if something was not done quickly was constantly at the back of Tennant's mind. At 20.00 hours on the twenty-seventh, after conferring with Admiral Abrial and Brigadier Geoffrey Mansergh, Lieutenant-General Alan Brooke's senior administrative officer, in the underground fortress of Bastion 32, he accordingly instructed his signals officer, Commander Michael Elwood, to signal Admiral Ramsay in Dover that every available craft must immediately be sent to the beaches east of Dunkirk. Otherwise evacuation on the twenty-eighth might become impossible.

The surface forces committed to the evacuation by Ramsay on this, the first major day of the evacuation, had consisted of one anti-aircraft cruiser (HMS *Calcutta*), nine destroyers and four minesweepers, all of which had been ordered to close the beaches and use their small boats to supplement the lifts being carried out by the cross-Channel steamers and drifters. It was not enough; at low tide the destroyers could approach no closer than a mile inshore, which meant that the crews of their whalers faced a twenty-minute pull to the beaches and when they arrived the boats could take on only twenty-five men at the most. By this method loading a destroyer to its maximum capacity of a thousand men could take six hours or more; additional numbers of small craft would help – hence Tennant's signal to Ramsay – but there was the factor of the weather to be considered. The approaches to the beaches were tricky in ideal conditions, and if the wind, at present blowing from the east, veered to the north small-boat operations in the shallows would become extremely hazardous.

The only other alternative was to use the east mole, although it was by no means certain that ships would be able to berth alongside it safely. Nevertheless it was a risk that had to be taken. At 22.30 on the twenty-seventh, a signal was flashed to one of the craft waiting offshore – the personnel vessel *Queen of the Channel* – to come along-side the mole. Cautiously her skipper, Captain W. J. Odell, brought her forward through the darkness at crawling speed until she nudged gently into position against the mole's wooden structure. For the first time Tennant felt a glimmer of hope; where one ship had gone, others could follow, and the mole was long enough to accommodate sixteen vessels at a time.

During the early hours of 28 May, five destroyers bore the brunt of the evacuation from Dunkirk; dispatched hurriedly from Dover and other ports along England's south coast, their captains had not had time to receive any briefing other than the curt order that they were to proceed to Dunkirk to pick up troops. From the bridge of HMS *Wakeful*, which had been about to refuel at Dover when the order to sail for Dunkirk with all speed came through, Commander Ralph Fisher issued orders to clear the mess decks of all furniture while the ship's cooks prepared cocoa, tea and food. Then as an afterthought – and fully conscious of the risk involved – he ordered the crew to jettison the destroyer's six tons of torpedoes and hundred depth charges. By reducing weight in this way the ship would be able to lift off an extra hundred men, and her manœuvrability would be increased if she had to run the gauntlet of the Luftwaffe. So, lightened of her war load, *Wakeful* steamed on for Dunkirk, to berth by the east mole in the darkness before dawn and take on six-hundred men. Thirty minutes later she was on her way homeward once more.

Further up the coast, at Bray Dunes, Captain George Stevens-Guille and his men had been hard at work picking troops from the beach with the destroyer *Codrington*'s whalers when word came through that the east mole was available. Stevens-Guille lost no time in ordering his boats inboard and setting course for the mole, where he quickly took on the rest of his quota and followed *Wakeful* on course for Dover. Other destroyers were not so fortunate: HMS *McKay* became grounded on a sandbank as she felt her way towards the deep-water channel off the beaches, which in turn created problems for HMS *Harvester* following close behind. *Harvester* had been dispatched to Dunkirk so quickly that there had been no time to take on much essential equipment, including charts; her captain, Lieutenant-Commander Mark Thornton, had simply been

ordered to follow *McKay*, and with the latter now stuck fast he had no
alternative but to let his ship drift inshore in the hope that the
tide would carry her into the deepest channel. The plan worked, and
Harvester's boats were soon pulling for the beaches. On board
HMS *Sabre*, Commander Brian Dean was also having his problems; he
had taken on eight hundred troops, but his ship was badly over-
weight and it was touch and go whether she would get over the
shoals safely. While two seamen clung precariously to small plat-
forms slung out from the ship's sides, chanting the depth soundings,
Dean brought the destroyer ahead dead slow. She slipped over the
shoals with inches to spare and headed out into the Channel on the
eighty-seven-mile haul homewards over Route Y.

Meanwhile at Dover Ramsay and his staff were making desperate
efforts to assemble the small craft so badly needed by Tennant. So
far, they had about 100 at their disposal: forty craft which had so far
been registered as a result of the Admiralty's appeal of 14 May, and
another fifty or so boats based in and around Dover. But many, many
more were needed if even a fraction of the BEF was to be snatched
from the beaches. Early on the twenty-eighth, for the first time, the
Royal Navy's motor-torpedo boats took a hand; they were drawn
from the 3rd, 4th and 10th Flotillas based at Felixstowe, and they
had already been employed in evacuating servicemen and civilians
from Holland. Lieutenant Stewart Gould describes the first day's
operations at Dunkirk:

> We left Dover at 06.35 on 28 May and it was not long before we
> came under fire from the guns in Calais and Gravelines. The
> MTBs scattered and eventually reached Dunkirk at 08.30. I took
> MTB 68 under orders and reported to the Senior Naval Officer.
> Destroyers were embarking British troops from the East Pier.
> The town was being bombed and there was a great deal of shelling.
>   MTB 68 was sent back to Dover with a hand message from the
> Senior Naval Officer. We [in MTB 16] anchored close inshore and
> began embarking troops under fire. They were exhausted and
> still carrying full equipment. Few were able to climb on board
> and had to be hauled in through the torpedo stern doors. [The
> early BPB craft launched their torpedoes tail first from the stern.]

Able Seaman Schofield swam voluntarily several hundred yards to save the lives of exhausted men.

We made several trips to and from the beach and transferred over 300 troops to the destroyers. Enemy aircraft attacked and MTB 16's Lewis guns, manned by Able Seaman F. Clark and Telegraphist H.F. McCutcheon, brought down a twin-engined bomber. During one trip inshore we ran aground, damaging the propeller. The centre engine was out of action and the tide was falling. We returned to Commander Maund, who was controlling the evacuation of the beach, and took up duties towing destroyers' whalers. At 21.00 the wind began to freshen and the evacuation continued from Dunkirk itself, to where Maund marched the troops. We left there at 05.50 on 29 May and returned to Dover and Felixstowe for repairs.[2]

The sight of the MTBs – and of other small craft which began to arrive off the beaches during the afternoon of the twenty-eighth – heartened the troops considerably, even though towards the end of the day a growing swell meant that the burden of the evacuation had to fall on Dunkirk's east mole, towards which the columns of fatigued men now tramped. Despite all the problems, 17,804 men were landed in England before midnight on the twenty-eighth – double the previous day's total, thanks to the use of the mole and to the prevailing low cloud and drizzle which thwarted Kesselring's Kampfgeschwader.

So far German naval activity off Dunkirk had been non-existent; this situation, however, was not to last. In the early hours of 28 May Kapitänleutnant Rudolf Petersen, commanding the 2nd Schnellboote Flotilla in Wilhelmshaven, called his officers together and briefed them for offensive operations in the Channel. Already, on 9 May, Petersen had led four boats of his flotilla in a successful night action north of the Straits of Dover; they had encountered a force of cruisers and destroyers of the British Home Fleet, and in the ensuing brief battle the destroyer HMS *Kelly* had been torpedoed and badly damaged by Kapitänleutnant Opdenhoff's S31.

Now, three weeks later, Petersen's orders were simple: the s-boats were to enter the Channel under cover of darkness, lie in wait and

strike hard at whatever British vessels they encountered, preferably
those homeward bound with their cargoes of troops. Six boats were
to undertake the mission, operating in two relays of three, hugging
the two hundred miles of coast on the outward trip and entering the
Channel after dark.

Accordingly the first three boats slipped out of Wilhelmshaven
that afternoon. In the lead was s25, commanded by Kapitänleutnant
Siegfried Wuppermann, an officer who was later to become one of
the German Navy's small ship 'aces' in the Mediterranean. Behind
him came Leutnant Zimmermann's s30 and s34, under Leutnant
Obermaier. The outward voyage was uneventful, the s-boats entering the Channel on schedule and spreading out, evading the
slender screen of MTBS thrown out by the Royal Navy from Felixstowe and taking up station, engines off, to the north of Ramsay's
cross-Channel routes. Station was kept, from left to right, by s30,
s25 and s34, and after ninety minutes of pitching and waiting on the
Channel swell it was Obermaier in s34 who made first contact with
the enemy. Straining his eyes through night glasses, he picked out a
faint phosphorescence in the distance: the bow-wave of a ship.
Seconds later he made out the vessel itself and positively identified
it as a British destroyer. Starting s34's engines he went quickly to
action stations and closed in. At 00.45 hours, four torpedoes thumped
from the s-boat's forward tubes and fanned out across the darkened
sea.

Among the crew of the destroyer HMS *Wakeful*, the tension of the
day's operations coiled like a steel spring inside every man. Hardly
had the destroyer entered Dover with her first load of troops on the
twenty-eighth when she was ordered out again, and she had sailed
as soon as the soldiers disembarked, still without having refuelled or
taken on fresh stocks of ammunition. On her second trip across the
Channel the Stukas had pounced and *Wakeful* had sustained a hole
in her side from a near-miss, but she had run the gauntlet of the
attack and Commander Fisher had brought her into Dunkirk,
taking on another 640 troops. Now he was taking his ship home
making a steady twelve knots over Route Y, with the light of the
Kwinte Buoy winking away to port.

Turning his eyes away from the flashing light, Fisher scanned the darkened sea to starboard just in time to see the twin trails of s34's first two torpedoes spearing towards him. There was no time for evasive action. The first torpedo streaked across *Wakeful*'s bows; the second exploded amidships, tearing the old destroyer in two. Within thirty seconds she was gone, her broken hull sliding into the depths of the Channel, leaving behind a few islands of bobbing wreckage and a handful of survivors, Fisher among them. Over seven hundred men, mostly troops crammed below decks, went to their deaths with the shattered wreck. Overwhelmed by the terrifying speed of the disaster, struggling in the torrent of water that burst in upon them, they had not stood a chance.

Other vessels in the vicinity observed the disaster and closed in to give whatever help they could. The survivors had been in the water for little over thirty minutes when the first arrived: the minesweeper HMS *Gossamer*, closely followed by the Scottish drifter *Comfort*. By 02.00 the destroyer *Grafton*, the minesweeper *Lydd* and the motor drifter *Nautilus* had also reached the scene, their lifeboats joining the search for the remnants of *Wakeful*'s crew.

A thousand yards away to the east, other eyes were watching the rescue operation. They belonged to Leutnant Michalowski and they were glued to the eyepiece of a periscope in the control room of submarine U-62. Michalowski now focused on the largest of the English vessels, clearly visible in the periscope's graticule as lights flickered across the water among *Wakeful*'s wreckage. A quick check on range, bearing, depth settings and running time, and then Michalowski gave the curt order: '*Torpedo – los!*' For the second time that night, the slender, phosphorescent trails streaked out across the Channel.

The destroyer *Grafton* was lying at rest, her rails crowded with troops who, like her captain, Commander Robinson, were watching the efforts of her lifeboats as they continued the search. At that precise moment U-62's torpedoes struck. One tore away the destoyer's stern like a knife slicing through butter; the other sent an explosion ripping through the wardroom, killing thirty-five officers.

What happened next amounted to panic. The other vessels in the area, their captains aware only that *Grafton* had been subjected to an unexpected attack, began steering in all directions, their crews tense and ready to fire at shadows. On the minesweeper *Lydd*, Lieutenant-Commander Haig saw what looked like the silhouette of a torpedo boat moving south-westwards; *Lydd*'s starboard Lewis gun opened up and bullets danced and sparked over the strange craft's superstructure. *Grafton*, which was still afloat, also opened up with her secondary armament.

It was a fearful mistake: for the target of *Lydd* and *Grafton* was no enemy intruder. She was the drifter *Comfort*, still laden with survivors from the ill-fated *Wakeful*. Machine-gun bullets raked her decks as the *Lydd* closed right in, cutting the drifter's crew to pieces. Minutes later, *Lydd*'s bow sliced into *Comfort*'s hull, tearing her apart. There were only five survivors; among them was Commander Fisher, whom *Comfort* had plucked from the sea when *Wakeful* went down. Fisher spent a long time in the water before he was finally picked up, more dead than alive, by the Norwegian tramp steamer *Hird* at dawn.

Meanwhile *Grafton* was finished. At first light the railway steamer *Malines* took off her survivors, and soon afterwards the destroyer *Ivanhoe* put three shells into her waterline. Ten minutes later she turned over and sank. Over the horizon u-62 and Wuppermann's three s-boats were already well on their way back to base; there could be no doubt that the German Navy had won the first round.

By first light on 29 May the number of craft at Tennant's disposal had grown considerably and the weather continued to favour the evacuation, with fog and drizzle over the beaches. Nevertheless Commanders Thomas Kerr and Hector Richardson were still sending men back to Dunkirk from Bray Dunes at the rate of a thousand every quarter of an hour, and as yet only about 25,500 had been lifted. Because of the heavy swell along the beaches, it had not proved possible to evacuate the anticipated number of men during the hours of darkness, and there had also been a lot of problems along the east mole, where ships had to contend with a fluctuation of fifteen feet between high and low tide. In all seventy vessels had been in operation at Dunkirk and along the beaches during the night of the twenty-eighth to ninth and Ramsay had promised that more were on their way, although it would be some time before the small craft which were being assembled in the south coast harbours could make their full contribution. As yet Tennant was unaware of the tragedy that had unfolded in the Channel a few hours earlier – or that the ordeal was only just beginning.

The evacuation maintained a steady tempo throughout the morning of the twenty-ninth; but from noon onwards, when the mist cleared, thousands of eyes on the beaches were turned apprehensively on the eastern sky. At 14.00 fears were justified when a host of black dots appeared over the horizon, quickly resolving themselves into the menacing, gull-winged shapes of Stukas.

They could not have come at a worse time. Eleven ships were berthed at the east mole, jammed stem to stern, and the French destoyers *Mistral*, *Sirocco* and *Cyclone* were moored inside the harbour; all in addition to the host of other craft at work along the nine miles of beach. There was something terribly fascinating about the sight as, with parade-ground precision, the Stukas split up into sections and peeled off into their seventy-degree dives, plummeting down on the packed mass of shipping and men, the banshee wail of their sirens – a psychologically devastating idea thought up by von Richthofen – drowning the snarl of their engines.

Most of the three Stuka-geschwader involved – a total of 180 Junkers 87s concentrated on the harbour and the east mole, and the havoc they wrought was fearful. Hurtling down through the curtain of steel hurled up by the 4·7-inch and Bofors guns of the destroyers, the 3-inch armament of the armed trawlers, the streams of bullets from the multiple Vickers anti-aircraft guns, the Stuka pilots hunched up in their cockpits, sweating with fear and concentration, and grimly held their stationary targets in their sights. A thousand-pound bomb and two 500-pounders struck the destroyer HMS *Grenade* in a ripple of almost simultaneous explosions. Within seconds the ship was a funeral pyre, ablaze from end to end. Her mooring ropes parted and she swung clear of the mole, striking the fishing trawler *Brock* and drifting helplessly into the fairway, a burning hulk. On the mole Commander John Clouston, the pier-master, hurriedly yelled orders to another trawler to take the stricken destroyer in tow and drag her clear before she went down, blocking the fairway. The trawler skipper obeyed quickly, pulling *Grenade* out into open water and speedily casting off. Not a moment too soon: a minute later the destroyer's magazine erupted in a terrific explosion and the warship disappeared in an awesome mushroom of smoke that was visible from La Panne, ten miles away.

The echoes of the explosion had hardly died away when another heavy bomb burst on the quayside next to the French destoyer *Mistral*. The blast and chunks of white-hot metal scythed away her superstructure, causing severe casualties. Her two sister ships, *Sirocco* and *Cyclone*, were more fortunate; both of them, laden with five hundred troops, were near-missed but undamaged. The destroyer *Jaguar* had just got under way when she sustained a direct hit; fearfully damaged she managed to struggle clear of the harbour, where her captain, Lieutenant-Commander Hine, reluctantly gave the order to abandon ship. HMS *Verity* succeeded in getting clear, with near-misses exploding all around, only to run aground beyond the harbour mouth and suffer damage.

The armed boarding vessel *King Orry* arrived in the middle of the attack, steaming past the charnel house of the ill-fated *Grenade* which miraculously was still afloat, her red-hot plates hissing as the water lapped against them. Within minutes *King Orry* too was hit, a bomb tearing away her steering gear so that she swung out of control and ripped a great gap in the mole, putting it temporarily out of action. Then, as the water poured into her, the *King Orry* heeled over and went down. Berthed beside the mole, the trawlers *Calvi* and *Polly Johnson* both received direct hits. A bomb hurtled down *Calvi*'s ventilation shaft and exploded deep in her vitals, blowing out her bottom; as she began to settle, still upright, her crew scrambled on to the deck of a neighbouring trawler, the *John Cattling*.

Hour after hour, or so it seemed to the dazed, blast-rocked soldiers and sailors, their senses benumbed by the fearful crescendo of wailing aircraft and explosions, the slaughter went on. Like the *King Orry*, the paddle minesweeper *Gracie Fields* took a hit on her stern that wrecked her steering gear; she circled helplessly until she eventually sank, the minesweeper *Pangbourne* taking off her survivors. The personnel ship *Fenella*, with six hundred soldiers on board, survived a near-miss only to have a bomb rip through her deck and burst in her engine room; a shattered hulk, she had to be abandoned.

After the Stukas came the horizontal bombers: the Heinkel 111s and Dornier 17s, along with the twin-engined Junkers 88 dive-bombers of Lehrgeschwader 1. The latter howled down on the biggest merchant vessel to be used in the Dunkirk evacuation, the 6,900-ton Glasgow freighter *Clan MacAlister*, which was laden with landing-craft. Bombs shattered her, setting her on fire and killing a third of her crew as well as many of the soldiers who had recently boarded her; once again the *Pangbourne* came to the rescue, taking survivors from the crippled freighter before the rushing seas extinguished her fires forever.

Six miles west of Dunkirk, Heinkels caught the Southern Railway ship *Normannia* in the open sea off Mardyck; torn apart by the bombs, she settled to the bottom on an even keel. Her sister ship, the *Lorina*, suffered a similar fate minutes later, while the minesweeper *Waverley* went down in that same cauldron, blown to pieces in a concentrated thirty-minute attack by a dozen Heinkels. Hard by the beaches, the old Thames river paddle-steamer *Crested Eagle*, filled to capacity with troops and the survivors of the *Fenella*, was hit by a single bomb and burst into flames. A white-hot furnace, with screaming, burning men leaping overboard into the oily water, she slowly approached the beach under the direction of her skipper, Lieutenant-Commander Booth. At last she grounded and the sur-vivors hurled themselves into the shallows, away from the fearful heat, while the ship flared like a beacon behind them.

Such was the awful toll of 29 May; and, in addition to the ships sunk, many others had been seriously damaged. They included the sloop *Bideford*, her stern a mass of tangled wreckage; the crippled destroyer *Jaguar*, which somehow refused to sink; and the destroyers *Gallant*, *Greyhound* and *Intrepid*, among the Navy's most modern warships of their kind. Yet despite all the destruction, despite the chaos and loss of life, the embarkations had continued even through the worst of the air raids, the vessels' captains taking incredible risks to get the men away – like Lieutenant Edwin Davies, commanding the paddle-minesweeper *Oriole*, who deliberately grounded his ship to provide a kind of jetty over which 2,500 men scrambled to other waiting boats, then managed to free her and set course for home with six hundred troops of his own on board.

As dusk fell on the twenty-ninth, the scene off the beaches at

Dunkirk was one of utter carnage; the whole sea seemed to be littered with blazing ships. Nevertheless 47,310 men had been lifted off during the day, 33,558 of them from the east mole – a fact that underlined that structure's vital importance. Yet now the mole was unusable, its lifeline broken by the luckless *King Orry*, and as the hours dragged on Tennant's anxiety increased: there was no sign of the ships that should have arrived to continue the evacuation after dark. By 21.00 only four trawlers and a yacht had appeared, and the horizon was empty.

Tennant had no way of knowing that the First Sea Lord, Admiral Sir Dudley Pound, seriously alarmed by the day's losses, had already issued orders for the Navy's eight most modern destroyers to be withdrawn from Operation Dynamo. This meant that the burden of the evacuation would now fall on the fifteen elderly destroyers still at Ramsay's disposal, and these would be capable of lifting not more than 17,000 men in the next twenty-four hours.

The night of the twenty-ninth to thirtieth passed with agonizing slowness. Dawn broke at last to reveal the most welcome vista Tennant and his staff had ever seen: the whole length of the beaches shrouded in a chill, dank fog that had rolled in overnight from the Channel. And under its opaque, sheltering veil, the rescue armada patiently assembled over the past days crept out at last from England's south coast ports, coves and estuaries; almost a thousand craft, destroyers, minesweepers, sloops, yachts, ferries, cockle boats, drifters, barges, trawlers, schuits and pleasure boats – all bound for the cauldron of Dunkirk, all with a single purpose: to bring salvation to the waiting thousands, clustered like dark clouds on the sands from La Panne to the burning port. More were coming, too, small craft for the most part, together with volunteers to man them; volunteers such as Lieutenant-Commander Archie Buchanan, RN (Retired), who – not disclosing his previous naval service – signed on as a motor-boat engineer at Lowestoft in response to a BBC radio appeal the previous evening. At nine o'clock in the morning of the thirtieth he was deep in the bowels of his assigned craft, the six-berth estuary cruiser *Elvin*, going over her two 25-hp Highlander Fordson engines enthusiastically. Together with three other cruisers she would sail for Dunkirk twenty-four hours later.

The first wave of small craft arrived off the beaches, still under their blanket of fog, to find a light wind blowing from the east and the surf that had hampered operations on the previous day gone. At intervals engineers were hard at work building improvised jetties from lorries and whatever spare planks and gratings they could find; small craft could lie alongside these, which meant that in some cases troops no longer had to wade out often neck-deep into the sea. Larger craft also attempted in some cases to berth alongside these flimsy structures, with disastrous results; the makeshift piers simply crumpled under the strain and the engineers had to start all over again.

As the fog persisted, the evacuation received an unexpected boost: the First Sea Lord decided to lift his restriction on the use of the modern G, H, I and J Class destroyers. The lifting of the ban was supposed to be temporary, but in the event the demands of Operation Dynamo were to become so pressing over the next twenty-four hours that the destroyers remained committed to the end.

Some of the hardest-worked vessels off the beaches on this Thursday 30 May were the minesweepers. They were able to come much closer inshore than the destroyers, and consequently their loading took place at a higher frequency – which in turn often meant more cross-Channel trips. No ship had a prouder record off Dunkirk than HMS *Locust*, which, together with her sister ship *Mosquito*, was based at Sheerness as part of the Thames Estuary Defence Flotilla. Both vessels had sailed for Dunkirk on the twenty-ninth in company with the Thames paddle steamers *Golden Eagle* and *Crested Eagle*; the rumour circulating round the lower deck was that they were bound for Le Havre to evacuate women and children. Then, as they altered course around the North Foreland, the crews saw for the first time the enormous pall of black smoke that rose from the oil tanks at Dunkirk. As they approached each ship hoisted her battle ensign; the crews knew for certain now that this was something deadly serious.

On the morning of the thirtieth, after taking on troops during the night, *Locust* was given the task of towing the sloop HMS *Bideford* – minus her stern, which had vanished in the explosion of the bomb that had hit her and of her own depth charges. This job was accomplished with great difficulty, the tow home lasting thirty hours. One man who served on *Locust* at the time, E. Clark, recalls: 'As we were getting clear we came under intense fire from the guns at Gravelines, but two of our destroyers covered us with a smoke screen. I have since seen this incident described as one of the epics of the evacuation; maybe, maybe not. All I know is that we were determined to bring *Bideford* home – at any price.'[3] And that is what they did. It was typical of the spirit that gripped the men of the Royal Navy during those terrible days; a spirit probably unmatched since Trafalgar.

HMS *Bideford* had just completed the loading of her troops when the bombers struck. One of these soldiers, F. G. Hutchinson, a signals despatch rider with the 42nd East Lancashire Division, pays tribute to the calm efficiency of the sailors of both *Bideford* and *Locust*:

Down below conditions were fairly chaotic; the accommodation was packed and the gun on the deck above was making a fearful racket. Suddenly, above all the noise there was an almighty crash and *Bideford* seemed to lift right out of the water and then sink back, shuddering. After recovering from the shock those of us below made a scramble for the companionway leading to the deck, the general impression being that we were sinking. However she remained afloat, for by good fortune her bulkheads held even though forty feet had been blown off her stern. A petty officer stopped the rush on deck; he told us that we were in no immediate danger of sinking and that we were to stay put until a vessel arrived to take us off. By this time casualties started coming down, and we were saddened to learn that the sailors had suffered badly. I estimated that there had been about fifty casualties, many of them fatal.

A short while later, we learned that the minesweeper HMS *Locust* had drawn alongside and was going to take us off, so we formed a queue at the foot of the companionway leading to the deck. I was quite far back in the queue and decided that I would just have time to make it to the galley and collect my uniform, which I had taken off to dry out; all my personal possessions were in my jacket pocket, including my paybook. On returning to the queue, which by this time was quite small, I was dismayed to learn that HMS *Locust* had filled to capacity and could take no more. Those of us who were left remained on *Bideford*, knowing that with the coming of daylight all hell would be let loose again; then we learned that *Locust* was going to try and take us in tow.

After several abortive attempts, it became obvious that we were firmly lodged in a sand bank. At one stage during the attempts to move us, all available men were formed up on one side of the ship and on the command we all ran to the other side in an effort to rock her free. We eventually floated clear when the tide came in, and in the small hours, towed by the faithful *Locust*, we limped away from Dunkirk. During all this time a surgeon had been working non-stop below, operating where possible on the wounded. I found a hammock and enjoyed the most perfect sleep I can ever remember.

Even then our troubles were not over, for some time later I was awakened by a petty officer who told me that some French colonial troops on board were expressing strong doubts about our intention of taking them to England, and were insisting on being landed in France. Most of them were armed, and the PO instructed us that in case of mutiny we were to make our way to the bow of the ship where arms would be issued. Fortunately nothing came of this, and we limped on our way towards Dover.[4]

If the men of HMS *Locust* were in the dark as to their destination when they sailed from England, the crews of the Grimsby-based 4th Minesweeping Flotilla were left in no doubts, as W.T. Elmslie, then a seaman aboard the fleet minesweeper HMS *Dundalk*, recalls:

On 28 May 1940 our flotilla, MS4, was berthed in Harwich on a rest day. During the forenoon divisions were held on the quay and the commanding officer of MS4 addressed all hands, advising them that Britain was passing through one of the blackest pages of her history and that very soon we would be called upon to do something which we had never been called upon to do before. It would be dangerous; but he had no doubt that every man would do his duty.

On the following Thursday, 30 May, HMS *Dundalk* – which was now at Grimsby – sailed from that port independently and proceeded south. During the voyage the crew were advised that we were making for the beaches of Dunkirk to evacuate the BEF, and shortly afterwards all battle ensigns were hoisted.

We arrived off the beaches on the evening of Thursday the thirtieth and were detailed to proceed to La Panne, bringing off as many soldiers as possible. The scene on the beaches at La Panne at this time was very depressing, with dark groups of soldiers huddled together in small parties. Through the twilight we could see the oil tanks burning in the distance, and occasional flashes of gunfire lit up the horizon. The boats were lowered, each manned by one sailor; they were towed to the beach by a motor launch and filled to capacity, the troops manning the oars and pulling back to the ship.

This process went on all night. Just before dawn a boatload of wounded came in; as soon as the men were taken aboard one of them, an officer of the Durham Light Infantry, came up to our first lieutenant and asked to be put back ashore, as there were more wounded to be looked after. 'Jimmy' told him that he was very sorry; the ship had taken on her full quota, with every inch of space occupied above and below, and the sooner *Dundalk* could unload her troops in England the sooner she would be back. The army officer pleaded, but to no avail. Suddenly, he turned and wandered away, past the 12-pounder which I was manning. He looked all in and utterly dejected. Then, from round the stern, came the putt-putt of a motor boat. The officer hailed it; it came quietly round the stern and he took a flying leap into it from the afterdeck. The boat disappeared into the night and I never saw him again. As he went I looked at the beach, at the burning oil tanks and the flashing of guns; and I knew that I would not have had the courage to do what that man did that night.[5]

Not all the officers were of the same calibre as this one. Among the hundreds of dedicated men, from subalterns to brigadiers, who brought their men back to Dunkirk and shared their agony with them to the end, there were the inevitable rotten eggs – officers who deserted their own troops, or who had not sufficient will and authority to control exhausted, rebellious men, or who simply broke under the strain and gave up. Such things are inevitable in war, particularly among those who have not experienced combat before. Nevertheless the sight of officers losing their heads is the most damaging blow to morale that can happen in a habitually disciplined army – and it happened at Dunkirk. One of those who saw it at first hand was Corporal Edward Faulkes, DCM, MM – no stranger to action, as his decorations from the First World War testified. At the age of forty-four, Faulkes had re-enlisted in the Royal Engineers; and when his company was sent home from France when the BEF's retreat began he had applied for, and been granted, a transfer to his old regiment, the Royal Northumberland Fusiliers. In the chaos of the retreat he never found them; so, attaching himself to various units and carrying out what amounted to a one-man war against the enemy, he finally arrived on the beaches soaked to the skin and with a two-week growth of beard on his face. As he tried to attach himself to a group of men awaiting embarkation, a captain approached him and said: 'You are not one of my regiment, so bugger off.' At once, Faulkes canted his rifle into the man's stomach and said: 'I'm in the British Army. If your blokes get away then I'm going home with them.'

For tense, interminable seconds the two men stared at each other Then, in Faulkes' own words:

Just then the small boats came in and discipline broke down. Everyone made a rush and soldiers pulled at one another in their haste to get into a boat. Finally, packed to capacity, their gunwales flush with the water, the boats were towed out to a waiting ship. I remember an officer telling me to pass the word that there must be no rushing of the rope ladders once we reached the ship's side. A man next to me shouted: 'Sir, you can go and f—— yourself.' The officer pretended not to hear.

As we approached the ship – she was the destroyer *Scimitar* – I saw that the crew had lowered rope scrambling nets that stretched the length of her side. The officer shouted a hasty 'one at a time!'

then launched himself at the nets. That bastard was first out of the boat; he wasn't going to risk his skin any further. Then, without warning, our boat swamped and went down. I floundered along the destroyer's hull and somehow managed to grab the rope net. The next thing I knew was that a sailor was slipping a rope under my armpits and I was being hauled aboard. The only thought going through my mind was 'Christ, I've lost my rifle – they'll stop nine quid out of my pay for that'[6]

For the crews of many of the small boats that arrived off the beaches on this Thursday – stunned as they already were by the holocaust that unfolded before their eyes – the sight of dirty, wild-eyed men rushing through the surf towards them was an unnerving experience. Time and again, boats were capsized by the onrush of troops laden with field equipment, equipment that dragged them down to a choking death in the water.

Nevertheless in the great majority of cases the embarkations proceeded in good order, despite the fact that the fighting troops who now came pouring into the bridgehead through the perimeter were often crazed with hunger and thirst and every instinct urged them to break ranks and forage in wild bands for water to slake their caked throats and food, however meagre, to ease the cramps in their stomachs.

During the afternoon of the thirtieth the Navy's modern destroyers returned to the fray. Ships bearing proud names – *Harvester, Havant, Icarus, Impulsive, Ivanhoe, Javeline* – they steamed at full speed from their south coast ports across the narrow seas, heading for the beaches at La Panne. Meanwhile the destroyer *Esk* had also arrived post-haste off the beaches, bringing with her a personality who, on the orders of the First Sea Lord, was to co-ordinate the movements of the rescue ships: Rear-Admiral Frederick Wake-Walker. With him came eighty officers and ratings, including Vice-Admiral Gilbert Stephenson. who was to take control of the evacuation at La Panne, and Vice-Admiral Theodore Hallett, who was to be responsible for the Bray Dunes sector. Wake-Walker himself set up his HQ at Malo-les-Bains; from here, with incredible energy, he moved among the rescue craft, transferring his flag no fewer than six times to different ships in the space of twenty-four hours. Captain William Tennant and his exhausted team certainly had some big guns on their side now.

One of the vessels from which Wake-Walker temporarily flew his flag was the destroyer HMS *Worcester*. Later that day she sailed for England bearing two VIPs: Lieutenant-Generals Alan Brooke and Sir Ronald Adam, their task at Dunkirk over. Brooke's departure had been preceded by a moving scene: heartbroken in the belief that his II Corps was to be sacrificed so that the rest of the BEF might escape, he had wept bitterly as he bade farewell to his old friend General Montgomery; now, the fatigue sweeping over him in waves, he collapsed into a bunk on board *Worcester* and found merciful oblivion.

Meanwhile Wake-Walker's primary concern had been to get the east mole operational once more. By 20.30 hours on the thirtieth, following hasty repairs, he judged that the mole was once again fit for use by destroyers and sent a signal to that effect to Admiral Ramsay in Dover. With ships once again working from the mole the number of troops lifted off increased substantially during the evening; by midnight the day's total had reached 53,823, of whom some 30,000 had been taken from the beaches.

On Friday 31 May the task of the evacuation personnel increased a hundredfold, for now the decision had been taken to lift off French troops in equal numbers – and already the evacuation fleet had suffered badly, from collisions, groundings and mechanical troubles as much as from enemy action. Moreover navigation on the approaches to Dunkirk was becoming extremely hazardous because of sunken wrecks; and to make matters worse the wind had risen to Force 3, seriously complicating the task of the small craft in the shallows. Many small boats, laden to the gunwales with troops, set course for home – a move which Wake-Walker desperately tried to stop, for every small craft would be needed that night to ferry men to the ships waiting offshore. For a time, towards noon, boat work off the beaches became virtually impossible, and enemy bombing and artillery fire had become so intense that larger ships could not use the port. The crisis seemed grave: and then, in the afternoon, both enemy activity and the swell decreased, and by the time the day ended no fewer than 68,014 men had been taken off – the highest daily total of the whole operation.

And still the small boats were coming – although for some, it was not easy. Lieutenant-Commander Archie Buchanan, of the *Elvin*:

Skipper Noble took the boat to Ramsgate without any charts, just his memory to go on. He seemed to be able to judge by the look of the water where the banks and the deeps were and if there was enough water to cross a bank. We arrived at Ramsgate about 4pm [on the thirty-first] and Noble went ashore to report to the senior naval officer. To Noble's amazement and fury we were ordered back to Lowestoft, and when he asked about charts he was told: 'You got here without charts – you can go back without them.'

On arrival back at Oulton Broad I went ashore and rang up my wife Ruth at the farm. She said that she had just had a telephone call to say that we were to return to Ramsgate. I asked her to bring my rifle and some other things down with her. We drew charts and provisions for forty-eight hours and had fuel for about thirty-six hours. Ruth brought the rifle and then dashed off to get some Beechams pills, which she dropped into the cockpit as we went under the bridge at Mutford Locks on our way from Oulton Broad to the sea at Lowestoft.

On arrival at Ramsgate about 10 am on 1 June I went ashore with Noble to report to the SNO and we were ordered to go alongside the South Wall – I had the distinct impression that this was where the boats that were not going to be used were sent, and I got into conversation with a Sub-Lieutenant Coates RNVR who told me that his naval motor cutter had broken down and the crew had refused to do another trip in her, so I suggested he took *Elvin*. I collected a spare battery and four rifles and ammunition from store – the latter somewhat unlawfully. As I was walking away, I heard the Lieutenant-Commander in charge protest to the storeman 'Surely you are not issuing rifles to *civilians*!'

In the late afternoon Coates came along and told us that there was an operation taking place that night, so we took him on board. We were fairly well jammed in by other boats, until a kindly trawler skipper gave a kick ahead on his engines to take the lot clear and let us out. We went alongside the East Wall where boats were given their orders. Coates went ashore to report but the commander in charge was very reluctant to let us go – civilian crew, too slow, Red Ensign and so on. Eventually we just took matters into our own hands, letting go fore and aft; as we moved out there came a shout from the petty officer up top and the commander turned away in apparent disgust. A shower of first-aid kits fell into our cockpit and we were on our way.

We had no idea what the operation was, or what we were supposed to do. With our boat darkened, we just followed the general flow of traffic across and then steered straight for the fires of Dunkirk.[7]

The morning of 1 June had dawned brilliantly clear, and at first light the Luftwaffe arrived over the beaches with murderous intent. Bill Elmslie, back off La Panne in *Dundalk* after replenishing in Dover, recalls that even before the arrival of the first wave of bombers, small-craft operations off the beaches were complicated by a heavy swell; coming away from the makeshift jetty in one of *Dundalk*'s whalers with eleven soldiers on board, the boat suddenly capsized and Elmslie and his passengers went headlong into the sea. Somehow they managed to hang together and drifted back to the beach, where they turned the boat over, baled her out and set off once more for *Dundalk*. As they pulled away for a second time Elmslie caught sight of something that made a lasting impression on him: an Army padre, moving up and down the column of patient men on the jetty, directing, helping, encouraging, selecting soldiers for the boats, an inspiration to all by his utter calmness. Elmslie returned to the minesweeper with his boatload, and it was while he was waiting to hook on that the Luftwaffe swept out of the sky.

I glanced back at the beach and saw a German fighter streaking across the sands, his machine guns cutting through those columns of soldiers like a reaper slicing through corn. Our own guns were hammering away furiously. One dive-bomber came hurtling straight at us and we were convinced he was going to hit us, but at the last moment he swerved and his bomb went wide. I think this was due to the efforts of a seaman manning one of our twin Lewis guns, who sent up some very accurate fire against the enemy aircraft.

That morning of 1 June was one I shall remember for a long time. Not very far from us lay HMS *Skipjack*, an oil burning fleet sweeper and a member of our flotilla. She was lying at anchor, still taking on troops, when she took the full delivery from a dive-bomber and went up in a terrific explosion. When the smoke cleared she had vanished; there was simply nothing there any more.[8]

Skipjack went down like a stone with 275 troops on board; there were very few survivors. The bombers now turned their attention to the big fleet destroyer HMS *Keith*, to which Admiral Wake-Walker had recently transferred his flag. The *Keith*'s gunners were down to their last thirty rounds of ammunition, and there was little the warship's captain could do except take violent evasive action. The first attack on her came while she was turning under full port helm and no fewer than nine bombs exploded in a pattern close to her starboard side, throwing her over on her beam ends and causing severe damage to her hull. Helplessly she careered in a tight circle, her rudder jammed, and then the second attack came in. This time a heavy bomb went down her aft funnel and exploded in her boiler room, while near-misses caused further damage. She lost way rapidly, enveloped in clouds of steam, and wallowed to a stop with a 20-degree list to port. Wake-Walker was taken off by an MTB and transferred his flag to another vessel; shortly afterwards the *Keith* was hit yet again by the Stukas and the warship turned turtle and sank.

Meanwhile the dive-bombers had hurled themselves on another destroyer, HMS *Basilisk*, hitting her aft and killing eight men. She survived another attack and began the long struggle back to Dover, but she later had to be abandoned and her survivors were taken off by trawlers, among them the French *Jolie Mascotte*. The shattered hulk of the *Basilisk* continued to float until it was sent to the bottom by a torpedo from the destroyer *Whitehall*.

The massacre went on unchecked. Some vessels, in the act of taking on troops, were powerless to take evasive action; other captains – like Lieutenant-Commander Kirkpatrick of the *Dundalk* – suspended operations and kept their ships on the move, zig-zagging down the coast amid the hail of bombs. On *Dundalk* Bill Elmslie witnessed an unforgettable sight: the fleet destroyer HMS *Havant* forging out into the channel with so many troops on board that her entire superstructure seemed to be covered in khaki. The next instant a full salvo of bombs hit her, killing all her engine-room staff. Immediately two minesweepers closed alongside her and the troops poured from the stricken ships on to their decks. The *Havant* had taken two bombs through her engine room and a third exploded as she passed over it; the minesweeper HMS *Saltash* tried to take her in tow, but it was hopeless. At 10.15, after further air attacks, she sank with the loss of thirty-four hands.

Other ships were more fortunate. The destroyer *Ivanhoe* had a bomb rip through her forward funnel and explode in the boiler room; terror-stricken soldiers scrambled from her lower decks and on to the minesweeper *Speedwell*, which came alongside. Despite her damage the destroyer remained afloat and was taken in tow by the tug *Persia*.

As the vicious air attacks died away, the ships returned to the beaches and the mole at Dunkirk to carry on the embarkation. It was a brief respite. At 13.00 the Luftwaffe returned, the Stukas plummeting down on to the French destroyer *Foudroyant*. Three direct hits and a deluge of near-misses reduced her to tangled wreckage, and she went down within minutes. As her survivors struggled in the water, a defiant voice began to sing 'La Marseillaise' and soon they were all singing as they drifted with the tide among the islands of debris and pools of oil.

Not only the warships suffered, although these were the Stukas' primary targets. The old *Brighton Queen*, a paddleboat converted for minesweeping, had just set out for Dover with seven hundred French troops on board when the Stukas pounced; a 550-pound bomb hit the boat's afterdeck, causing fearful casualties. The survivors were taken off by the minesweeper *Saltash* before the *Brighton Queen* sank. There were casualties, too, on the personnel vessel *Prague*, which was steaming away from Dunkirk with 3,000 French troops on board when she was hit and damaged; her sister ship, the *Scotia*, was also hit while carrying 2,000 French troops, many of whom were drowned when they panicked and rushed the boats. The destroyer HMS *Esk* took off most of the survivors. The *Scotia*, of 3,454 tons, was the largest merchant ship to be lost that day.

On some ships that managed to limp back to Dover the casualty toll was frightening. The old destroyer HMS *Worcester* was relentlessly attacked for thirty minutes by flight after flight of dive-bombers, sustaining damage that reduced her speed to a mere ten knots; yet she limped across the Channel with her pitiful cargo of 350 dead and 400 wounded. During the late afternoon, the French naval vessels off Dunkirk once again came in for severe punishment; at 16.00 Stukas fell on a convoy of French auxiliaries, sinking three of them – the *Denis Papin*, *Venus* and *Moussaillon* – within five minutes.

In all the evacuation fleet lost thirty-one vessels sunk and eleven damaged on that terrible day, a day in which the seaborne units nevertheless managed to lift off 64,429 British and French troops. Most of the stricken vessels had fallen victim to enemy air attack, but it was the German Navy that had the last word; shortly before midnight, Leutnant Obermaier, making yet another sortie into the Channel in Schnellboote S34, sighted two ships and attacked with torpedoes, sinking both. They were the trawlers *Argyllshire* and *Stella Dorado*.

Since the last stretches of beach still in Allied hands, and the shipping offshore, were now being heavily shelled, Admiral Ramsay planned to lift as many men as possible in a single operation on the night of 1–2 June. It had originally been planned to complete the evacuation on this night, but this was no longer feasible; there could be no question of abandoning the French troops who had fought so hard on the perimeter, and through whom the British had passed on their way to the beaches. Ramsay therefore decided to concentrate all available ships after dark in the Dunkirk and Malo areas, from where the maximum lift might be obtained. For this purpose he had at his disposal some sixty ships, together with the many small craft still involved in the operation; the French could provide ten ships and about 120 fishing craft.

One of the little craft which arrived off the beaches that night was the *Elvin*, with Archie Buchanan on board:

We lay off the entrance until first light. We could hear gunfire to the eastward and saw a great pall of smoke over the town and flashes in the inner harbour. As soon as we could see we went alongside the eastern pier where a column of soldiers was drawn up. An officer called out '*Combien de soldats?*', and as I could not remember the French for twenty-five I replied '*Trente*,' but before we could take on the thirty that had been detailed by the officer the sub rushed up from below and said that we were full.

Alongside the pier there was a small open motor boat with an RNR sub in charge and a whaler in tow. He looked to me as if he was taking on a bit more than he could handle. I nipped over to him and asked him what he was going to do with his lot and he told me that he was going to put them on a ship outside the harbour and come back for more. This seemed a good idea and we decided to do the same.

The destroyer had gone when we got outside the harbour, so we chased after some French minesweepers to westward hoping to put our soldiers on board, but they were unable to take them so we decided to set course back to Ramsgate. We had no idea where the swept channel was, but as we drew only three feet six inches and it was not low water we didn't think that there was much danger from mines. This conclusion may have been fortified by memories of the Dover Patrol in 1917, when it used to be said that British mines were so safe that they never went off. I think a large lump of wood would have been far more dangerous.[9]

As *Elvin* puttered back to Ramsgate with her weary passengers – all soldiers of the French 28th Infantry Regiment – the big lift went on. There was no question now of taking off any but walking wounded; stretcher cases took up too much room, and the urgency to evacuate the thousands of fit men still on the beaches was too pressing. Captain Tony Steede of the Green Howards, lying wounded in No. 12 Casualty Clearing Station at Château Rosendael, remembers:

There were so many wounded that they could not be accommodated in the château; stretcher cases were lying all around the grounds in the open air. I personally was in an ambulance, with a dying

Hurricane pilot in the bunk above me. It was far from pleasant. Then we got a message to say that the last boats would soon be leaving Dunkirk, and that anyone who could walk was to make his way down to the beaches. Some managed it, struggling along on improvised crutches made from broom handles, but they were very few. The rest of us knew with terrible finality that we had no hope. All we could do was lie there and wait, and the waiting was bad enough; the French placed a light anti-aircraft gun in the château grounds, and this drew a lot of artillery fire.[10]

By midnight on 2 June a further 26,256 soldiers had been evacuated from Dunkirk. The last British battalion to leave was the 1st King's Shropshire Light Infantry, which had covered the withdrawal of the 1st Division the previous evening. Finally, at 23.30, Captain Tennant made his last signal to Admiral Ramsay. It read simply: 'BEF evacuated.' Then Tennant, together with General Alexander, boarded a motor torpedo boat and set off to make a reconnaissance of the beaches. Sighting no further British troops, they set course for England.

There remained the French: some 30,000 of them, whose resistance against the enemy continued throughout 3 June. The last great effort of Ramsay's evacuation fleet therefore had to be made during the night of the third to fourth, and the resources available to accomplish the task were seriously depleted. Of the forty-one destroyers originally assigned to Operation Dynamo only nine were left, and only five of the forty-five personnel vessels. Nevertheless at 22.15 on 3 June these set out across the Channel, together with a couple of dozen smaller craft, and the last lift began. The ships probed into Dunkirk harbour, lifting men from both the east and west moles, while boats cruised along the beaches and hailed any groups of French troops their crews sighted. Among the vessels which took part in this final evacuation was the little gunboat *Locust*, whose crew during the evening had the unhappy task of placing demolition charges on board their sister ship, the gallant little *Mosquito*, sunk inshore with her decks awash a few hours earlier. Amid all the devastation and carnage, amid the tightly packed column of battle-weary French troops on the east mole, one of *Locust*'s company saw something that touched his heart: a tiny pup, only a few days old, in danger of being trampled underfoot. He rescued it and brought it aboard – and, aptly named 'Dunkirk', it remained the ship's mascot for a year until it found a new berth in a petty officer's home in Gillingham, where it lived out its days.

By 03.00 on 4 June Operation Dynamo was almost over; almost, but not quite. The last French troops capable of being lifted off before dawn had filtered down through Dunkirk, and the last boats were moving in. An hour earlier Admiral Abrial and General Fagalde had both been taken off; it was now left to the incomparable General de la Laurencie, together with General Barthélemy, the commander of the Flanders Fortified Sector, to carry out one final, moving ceremony. It was described by Commander H.R. Troup, RN, who had been conducting the last embarkations: 'About a thousand men stood to attention four deep about halfway along the pier, the General and his staff about thirty feet away; and after having faced the troops whose faces were indiscernible in the dawn light, the flames behind them showing up their steel helmets, the officers clicked their heels, saluted and then turned about and then came down to the boat with me and we left at 03.20.'[11]

Dawn was glimmering in the eastern sky as the last ship left the mole; she was the old destroyer *Shikari*, and her load brought the total for the night to 26,209, all but seven of them French troops. Minutes later British naval parties sank two boats in the swept channel.

At 09.00 on 4 June General Beaufrère formally surrendered Dunkirk to the enemy and went into captivity together with between 30,000 and 40,000 French troops who still remained. The actual number taken prisoner at Dunkirk is uncertain, for the records do not discriminate between this figure and that for the French surrender at Lille.

Later that day, at 14.23 to be precise, the Admiralty announced the completion of Operation Dynamo. In nine days of incredible achievement 198,284 British troops had been brought away; counting the 26,402 'useless mouths' taken off before the start of the evacuation proper, this made a grand total of 224,686 men of the British Expeditionary Force, of whom 13,053 were wounded. The number of Allied troops evacuated rose to 141,445, making a combined total of 366,131.

(It should not be forgotten that the Royal Navy participated in other evacuation operations after Dunkirk. Between 4 and 25 June 1940 British ships carried out a whole series of evacuations beginning at Le Havre, moving west to the Gulf of St Malo, the Channel Islands and Cherbourg, round Ushant to Brest, along the French Biscay coast to St Nazaire and La Pallice, and finally from Bayonne and St Jean de Luz near the Spanish frontier. These operations, collectively known under the code-name of 'Aerial', resulted in the rescue of an additional 191,870 fighting troops and 35,000 civilians. The biggest loss incurred during these operations happened at St Nazaire, when the troopship *Lancastria* was sunk with 3,000 on board.[12])

The cost of Operation Dynamo, however, had been terribly high for the seaborne forces engaged. Of the British ships committed 226 had been sunk out of a total of 693, fifty-six of them large craft such as destroyers, minesweepers and personnel craft. Out of the total of 168 Allied ships involved – mainly French, with a few Polish, Dutch and Belgian – seventeen were lost.

Enemy action against the ships at sea and the beaches resulted in the deaths of some 3,500 British troops out of the total of 68,111 killed, wounded and taken prisoner during the three-week campaign in Flanders. No firm figures can be given for French personnel losses during the evacuation, but they were high: witness the sinking of the French destroyer *Bourrasque*, with 300 drowned out of 800; the destruction of the destroyer *Sirocco*, with 750 men; the loss of 400 on the *Emile-Deschamps*, 300 on the *Brighton Queen* and 300 of the 2,000 on the *Scotia*. It seems likely that the actual combined loss through enemy action may have been in the region of 6,000 troops – and this takes no account of those accidentally killed or drowned or of the substantial naval casualties.

On the afternoon of 4 June, with the seas off Dunkirk empty except for the numerous wrecks, parties of German troops roved through the shattered streets of the town and along the beaches, taking first inventory of the piles of abandoned equipment and rounding up Allied stragglers while Luftwaffe flak units set up their

3·7s and quadruple 20-mm guns on the east mole and other strategic points.

At Château Rosendael the agonizing wait of Captain Steede and the other wounded came to an end with the arrival of a German horsed artillery company, who marched in at dawn on the fourth. To their surprise, the British found these enemy troops friendly and sympathetic; they moved around among the wounded, distributing buckets of water, food and cigarettes. This treatment contrasted sharply with that meted out by the enemy administrative troops, medical officers and orderlies who arrived later in the day; one MO ordered the evacuation of the casualty clearing station in fifteen minutes, a physical impossibility. From then on, according to Steede, the wounded 'were treated pretty callously'. Things only improved when he and other severe cases were transferred to hospitals in Belgium, where they were cared for by Belgian nursing staff who were kindness personified. Weeks later Steede had the demoralizing experience of watching massed formations of enemy bombers assembling over the nearby Belgian airfields before setting course for England; it would be a long time before he learned of the great victory being carved out in filmy vapour trails over the quiet summer fields of Kent.

Homecoming

On 27 May, the day on which the main evacuations from Dunkirk began, few people in Britain as yet had any real idea of the magnitude of the disaster that had overwhelmed the BEF and the French and Belgian Armies in Flanders. Only in the principal south coast ports – and in particular Dover, where base troops and wounded were being landed almost continuously from 20 May – did the populace have an inkling that the Allies might be suffering an overwhelming defeat.

Prior to the main evacuation a joint agreement for the reception and treatment of casualties had been worked out between the Royal Naval Sick Quarters at Dover and neighbouring military and civil authorities; all resources were to be pooled in case of a serious emergency. The first casualties had arrived on 11 May, the day after the German invasion of the Low Countries; they were sailors from HMS *Whitshed*, which had come under air attack while evacuating personnel from Holland. On the fourteenth thirty-seven casualties were landed from HMS *Wivern*; this was the first large batch of wounded to arrive at Dover and it revealed many of the difficulties encountered in dealing with casualties in small ships, such as the inaccessibility of the wounded and the ingenuity required in getting them on to stretchers and transferring them to ambulances on the quayside.

The report of Captain A.P. Fisher, the senior naval medical officer Dover, provides an illuminating insight not only into the reception of casualties, but also into the extent and frequency of the cross-Channel traffic that built up during the nine days of Dunkirk:

By 25 May it was necessary to obtain additional medical staff, two additional ambulances being obtained and a converted motor bus loaned from Chatham. By this time the RAMC had established a medical transport office at the Dover Marine Station, and had organized a service of hospital trains and convoys of motor ambulances. Up to this time we had endeavoured to deal with all naval casualties ourselves, but owing to the fact that all landing stages were being used at the same time this was found impracticable and an arrangement was made with the RAMC that they would deal with all casualties at the Admiralty Pier, and the naval staff with those at all other landing stages.

During this period (25 May–5 June, 1940) 180,982 troops were landed in Dover; of this number 6,880 were casualties requiring hospital treatment. 31 May was the peak day; during this twenty-four hours 34,484 troops were landed in Dover from the following ships:

    25 destroyers
    12 transports
    14 drifters
    14 minesweepers
     6 paddle minesweepers
     5 trawlers
    16 motor yachts and small vessels
    12 Dutch schuits
     4 hospital ships
    21 miscellaneous foreign vessels.

Amongst these troops were approximately 1,200 casualties. Disembarkation went on throughout the twenty-four hours, but was most intense in the middle and morning watches.

All ships carrying wounded were met by one ambulance with a medical officer and two sick berth ratings. The medical officer would board the vessel, ascertain the number of casualties, estimate the amount of ambulance transport required, render first aid when required to the more seriously injured. Injuries of almost every variety were met with and it was impossible to lay down any definite rules for treatment; this depended on the discretion of the man on the spot. Generally speaking, it was deemed expedient to transfer the most serious cases – such as multiple wounds, wounds of the abdomen, chest and head – to hospital without delay. Morphia injections were given, and dressings applied with as little disturbance of the patient as possible, but ensuring the complete covering of all wounds. No elaborate bandaging was used. The patient was kept warm and protected from the elements with blankets . . .

In the ships attended, some forms of first aid had usually been attempted. Destroyers and larger transports carried medical officers, and in these the standard of first aid was usually high, though in many cases the medical officer had not had time to attend all cases, particularly when the ship had been subjected to enemy air attack during the passage, fresh casualties occurring. In the smaller ships the first aid carried out was necessarily more rudimentary, though it was rare to find a wounded man who had not had some sort of dressing applied.

Blood transfusion was never attempted on the quayside. On one occasion, however, in response to a destroyer medical officer's signal the apparatus was taken to Admiralty Pier, but was not used as the patient, who had had an amputation of the leg, was in satisfactory condition and was immediately transferred to hospital. This patient, a petty officer of fine type, after his wound had been treated in hospital overheard the medical officer say that he required plenty of fluid. He asked for a bottle of beer and dispatched it, and an hour later had the other half. Next day he assured me that bottled beer was a better lifesaver than blood transfusion any day.

Casualties arrived in Dover in every sort of vessel which, in the vast majority of cases, were berthed at one of the many landing stages. On a few occasions casualties had to be removed from ships moored in the harbour; also medical assistance was sometimes asked for by ships lying off Dover. The removal of casualties from the ships could not commence until the troops had been disembarked. The medical officer of the ship could usually give an approximate number of casualties, and information as to the more serious ones requiring instant removal to hospital. About sixty per cent of the ships went to Admiralty Pier. This position was the most suitable as ambulances could be parked close by.

The hospital trains were in the station about 200 yards away, and large squads of stretcher bearers were constantly in attendance.

Our work was chiefly concerned with the outlying landing stages. At most of these, steep brows and slippery steps had to be negotiated, the patients being either manhandled or conveyed to the quayside in Neil Robertson stretchers. From these most cases were transferred to Field Service or ARP stretchers and placed in the ambulance. Carrying wounded from the ships to the landing stages, and thence to the ambulances, proved a great physical strain and it was very gratifying to see how eager the sailors were in helping to carry their wounded mates and also the keenness of ambulance drivers to assist ...

One hospital train was kept at the Marine Station, and one in a siding in reserve and a third at a station twelve miles inland. Their accommodation varied from 150 to 250, with a medical officer and nursing staff. All types of casualties, except those urgently in need of surgical attention, were transported by train. This method saved the nearby hospitals from total submersion In all, 4,646 were transported in the trains.

The Royal Naval Sick Quarters, HMS *Sandhurst* Sick Bay and Dover Patrol Sick Bay worked at high pressure during the Dunkirk evacuation. I cannot give even an approximate figure of the number of cases that received first aid here, but 200 cases were admitted for the night. The cases were not all wounded, but included cases of immersion and nervous exhaustion. The cases were only detained for one or at the most two nights, and were then either discharged to the rest camp or hospital as requisite The value of the sick bays was particularly demonstrated in the nervous cases. On one occasion twenty ratings from one crew were accommodated in HMS *Sandhurst*; they all appeared anxious and generally 'jittery'. A bath, a hot meal, a dose of bromide and a good sleep enabled all except two of these to resume duty next day.

Amongst the casualties brought into Dover there were approximately 600 naval casualties, including fifty-four dead ... The casualties included wounds of every description met with in warfare. The main causative agents were high explosive bombs, high explosive shells, Messerschmitt cannon shells, machine-gun bullets, burns from incendiary bombs, ignited cordite and ignited oil fuel. In addition when ships were sunk those in the water were exposed to concussion injuries due to the explosion of bombs, mines and depth charges. Bomb splinter wounds, machine-gun bullet wounds were commonest in that order.[1]

For most of the troops who came away from Dunkirk, the passage homeward across the Channel remains at best a vague memory. The majority collapsed into the sleep of utter exhaustion the moment they found a space on the crowded deck of one of the rescue ships, sharing the experience of Sergeant Bruce of the 7th Field Company RE, who remembers nothing at all after boarding the vessel that took him off the beach. It was a shout of 'Here's some more!' that woke him up hours later, to find that they had berthed in Ramsgate and that a host of willing hands was reaching down to help them from the boat. For Tom Collins, of the 35th Field Battery RA, the sweetest words he would ever hear in his life were, 'Wakey wakey, lads, come on, you're at Dover!' Fatigue shrugged off, he and the others scrambled to the deck of the destroyer that had brought them over and poured on to the quay, pausing only to let the wounded be taken off first.

> Unwashed, unshaven, very prominent in our rags and tatters, we were welcomed it seemed by people from all walks of life; but those who were top of the league in my books were the crew who brought us back, the medical men who attended the sick and wounded – and the wvs, who gave every man a mug of tea, a piece of cake and a cigarette. After we settled down in the waiting train, something happened that has stuck in my mind ever since: a soldier got to his feet and said, 'Boys, I'm thanking God I'm home. Now let's give a thought for the boys we left behind.' And we, all strangers from different units, held a minute's silence in that compartment; and as we travelled through the green fields, I thought that England wasn't such a bad place after all.

For others, the journey to England had the never-to-be-forgotten quality of a nightmare. Bill Elmslie, on *Dundalk*, remembers Frenchmen staring at the receding coastline of their homeland, tears

streaming down their faces, not knowing when or if they would see
France again; and a French officer, passing among the crew and
solemnly shaking hands with each man as he murmured broken
words of thanks. He remembers, too, a young Royal Fusilier
slumped on the deck and weeping as though his heart would break,
sobbing over and over again that his brother was still in there,
somewhere beyond the smoke and flames of Dunkirk ... And the
fifteen other Royal Fusiliers, exhausted beyond description, who
nevertheless fell in on the quay at Folkestone and marched away in
regimental order with rifles at the slope, their officer at their
head.

They were an exception: although the vast majority of troops
who arrived back in England retained their rifles – a not incon-
siderable tribute to the British Army's standard of discipline – three
weeks of battle and immersion in water had reduced their clothing
to a pitiful state. Many had no uniform left at all, and came ashore
dressed in whatever nondescript rags they had managed to pick up
en route; Peter Pring, who landed at Folkestone, remembers one
soldier who shared his train compartment wearing the black-and-
white striped trousers of a French farmer's best Sunday suit, a sack
with holes cut in it for the neck and arms, and – the crowning glory
– a silk top hat.

For those without items of clothing, the people of the debarkation
ports pitched in with whatever spare items they had available. The
British people opened their hearts to the homecoming soldiers and
sailors, as Commander Thomas Kerr describes:

We landed at Margate ... and reported to Dover. The people
were so good to us; they tried to fit us out with boots, fitted up
the sailors and fed them. Richardson and I fed at the pub and
had a rough wash, then we were given a lorry to take us to the
station. The rest of the party got off at Chatham, their depot, and
I went on to London. Somewhere around eight o'clock we
arrived at Victoria. There were crowds and crowds, with police-
men keeping open a lane. I toddled down in my tin hat and
bedroom slippers, haversack and revolver still strapped around
me. Someone shouted 'Good old Navy!' and a woman kissed me

on the cheek. They cheered and I wanted to cry. Then a man got hold of me and said: 'Where do you want to go? I'll look after you.' He led me to a taxi, brought me to the Admiralty and paid the cab off.

Peter Pring, trundling through the countryside in his troop train towards Aldershot, was as puzzled as the other men in his compartment to see suburban gardens festooned with slogans: 'Welcome Home, Brave Lads', 'Well Done, Our Heroes'. To men who had just suffered the most crushing defeat in the history of the British Army, it took some time for the significance to sink in.

'Christ!' said someone in an awed voice, 'They mean *us*!'

The memory of this battered army coming home remains strong in the minds of those civilians who witnessed it. One of them, W.E. Williamson, then a railway clerk at Weymouth in Dorset, recalls:

Slowly they came, bewildered and shocked, yet the faces of hundreds showed the great joy of once again being on dry land, above all their homeland. Even the troops of other nations accepted thankfully the greeting and helping hand from those waiting on the quayside. The bedraggled army was marshalled by Army and Navy personnel, the local Home Guard, the Salvation Army, the Red Cross, coach drivers, police, railwaymen and every possible local organization. Fearing air attack, the troops were encouraged to disperse temporarily in the streets, away from the sea front. They sat on the pavements with their backs to railings and garden walls; men, women and children brought out jugs of tea and plates of food, spared from their own meagre rations. Sodden and bloodstained uniforms were gratefully exchanged for trousers, jackets, shirts and dressing gowns.

The railway station staff were now in top gear. Trains were being marshalled, instructions were issued, control points and railway junctions to other regions were in direct contact, arranging the reception of troop specials and their dispatch to secret destinations. We were all part of this huge effort to get the army away from the coast: railwaymen and RTOs with their red caps and armbands were working together as one team, shepherding the men into railway sidings and yards prior to getting them away.

With some of my railway colleagues, I handed out blank Great Western Railway postcards to the troops. They were asked to write just two words – 'Am Safe' – adding their Christian name and home address. These cards were sent off that day, with no postmark or stamp. I remember we ran out of cards and ransacked cupboards in the stock room for blank railway truck labels. In three days we sent off several thousand, most of them with their messages scribbled by railway staff and other helpers. Many of the troops were dead beat with exhaustion, and we had to lift hundreds into the carriages. A lot of scheduled trains were cancelled to provide extra rolling stock and engine power for the massive movement.

Throughout the southern counties, and Kent in particular, thousands of volunteers, mainly women, worked tirelessly by day and night to supply food and drink to the troops at stations where their trains halted. The whole of Kent was literally ransacked in a gigantic bid to collect all available supplies of food and cigarettes, collection centres being set up at Redhill, Tonbridge, Faversham and Headcorn. Many firms and individuals donated supplies and money in this spontaneous voluntary gesture.

The gratitude of the soldiers was overwhelming. Mons Trussler of the 4th Royal Berkshire, safe at last in Folkestone Hospital after being carried ashore, remembers 'dear old ladies coming in with huge plates of bread and butter, cut very thin, which we devoured like wolves. They looked on in amazement as we cried, every last man of us.'

At Margate, recalls Reg Rushmere of the Royal Signals, 'We had a marvellous reception. There were people handing out oranges, and when we got on the train they came to the carriages with fruit and whatever we wanted.' J.F. Duffy of the 52nd Heavy Regiment RA remembers the people of Margate with affection, too: 'I had no boots and was still soaked. Single-decker buses were awaiting us on the quayside, and we were taken to Margate railway station. It was such a wonderful sight to see the wvs giving out cups of tea and sandwiches . . . we knew now that we were home.'

At camps and reception centres all over the country military and civilian personnel had been standing by to receive the home-coming thousands. There could be no attempt at sorting out the men into their units at the debarkation ports; that task would be undertaken later, when the urgency was over. As far as the railways were concerned, the second phase of Operation Dynamo began when the troops were rested and refreshed and redistributed to regular depots, where units were reorganized and rearmed. This second phase did not begin until 6 June, forty-eight hours after the last troops had been brought across the Channel.

At an army barracks in Cardiff, Mrs B. Bowden – then a corporal cook in the ATS – had waited, night and day for a whole week, with very little sleep, for the arrival of the Dunkirk men assigned to this centre. She was not prepared for the emotional impact of their coming:

Oh, the horror of seeing those poor men arrive, many with hardly any clothes and no footwear, dirty and unkempt – and yet, as they queued up for their first meal in many days, how their faces changed, their eyes lit up! With food inside them and issue of new uniform they became human beings once again. I shall always be grateful that I was able to help in that operation, together with my daughter, who cried over them.

The reorganization and reforming of units proceeded with con-siderable efficiency, a remarkable achievement considering the prevailing chaos. Troop Sergeant Major C.S. Best, of the 20th Anti-Tank Regiment, describes how the scattered units of the 3rd Division were rounded up:

We arrived at Folkestone, where we were put on a train. After travelling all night we arrived at Burton-on-Trent. We were taken to some warehouses belonging to a brewery and were told that we could sleep for as long as we liked. I awoke about 11am, by which time officers were at work taking names, ranks and numbers. I was told that I could get a bath at the public baths down the street, so off I went. The lady at the door wanted to know all about Dunkirk, so I explained as briefly as I could and then had my long-awaited bath. On the way back to the warehouse a lady stopped me in the street and asked me if I had come from France; when I replied that I had, she gave me a shirt and a packet of Woodbines. At a nearby pub I asked if I could phone my wife; the landlord took charge, got the number for me and refused to accept any payment.

Things were organized for us in Burton-on-Trent as though we were heroes. We were taken on a bus tour, had an evening out at a working men's club, were entertained by the bowls club – and all for free. Shortly afterwards, all 3rd Division personnel were sent to Frome in Somerset, where the division was being reformed. From then on we lived a sort of gypsy existence, on the move every fortnight or so all over the south of England until the division was all together once more.

For some Britons, the vague ideas of the disaster and magnificence that had attended the evacuation of the BEF were suddenly translated into stark reality by the appearance of a telegram or postcard to say that a son, husband or brother was safe. Private Geoff Turner of RAOC, who had served with a recovery unit in France, sent a cable to his mother in Middlesbrough explaining that he was all right and on his way home; the poor lady collapsed on the doorstep, believing that the GPO messenger brought bad news.

At his home in the London suburbs, twelve-year-old Charles White had no real idea where Dunkirk was, and it was difficult to understand why the name had suddenly leapt into every newspaper headline. Yet even he was seized by a sense of deep drama, of history in the making:

It was, I remember, a day of brilliant sunshine when an uncle of mine appeared on our doorstep in a dishevelled petty officer's uniform. He looked completely shattered and tired out. We kids were kept out of the house and told to be quiet, for our hero uncle had to rest and recover from whatever he'd been doing in the war. He had been at Dunkirk and we learned later that two ships he had been on had been sunk and a third badly damaged.

I never knew the names of those ships; I only remember the brilliant sunshine, and the petty officer who slept for three days.

And so, in their many different fashions, the thousands came home from Dunkirk.

Epilogue

It may be said truthfully that the evacuation of the British Expeditionary Force from Dunkirk made a greater impact on the British nation than any other military operation, before or since. It may also be said that out of this, the biggest single defeat ever suffered by British arms, grew the shoots of later victory; for Dunkirk and its prelude destroyed the myth that a modern army can fight a war on the same basis as a previous one. That myth ought to have been shattered nine months earlier, when Hitler's tanks rolled across Poland; but the knot of complacency is hard to sever.

During the three-week battle in Flanders the British commanders who were later to shape the destiny of the Second World War confronted their adversaries for the first time – and got the measure of them; in 1942, in North Africa, both Alexander and Montgomery were to apply the principle of armoured mobility and overwhelming tactical air power, a combination that had brought the Germans victory in France, and use it to defeat their old opponent Erwin Rommel.

In short the British Army had gone to France in 1939 untried and untested, composed for the most part of young men; comparatively few of its officers and men had seen action during the First World War, and even they had to relearn the art of war during those desperate days in May and June 1940. The majority went to France with high spirits and confidence, certain in their insular pride that they were a match for anyone and anything; they emerged from Dunkirk battlewise and battleweary, veterans of nineteen and twenty, not disillusioned or embittered, but with a new awareness of the calibre and material efficiency of their opponents. From this awareness, as the battered divisions were reformed and refitted in England to meet an invasion that never came, arose a determination to see this fight through, no matter what the cost. It would be a long, uphill struggle: but these men, with the thousands who were to follow them and the direction of the senior commanders who had slipped through the German net, would later redeem the succession of disasters that seemed never-ending until the Afrika Korps broke at El Alamein.

In the mind of every man who took part in that great evacuation, Dunkirk left its own individual imprint. No one lived through those nine days and emerged without being changed to a greater or lesser degree. Even today Ken Carter of the Green Howards cannot speak without a break in his voice of the boys from Middlesbrough and the surrounding countryside who, like himself, had joined the Territorial Army in search of adventure, who were his friends and who died in Flanders because – not for the first time in history – British soldiers stood firm and fought when other armies broke all around them. For Carter, like so many others, Dunkirk was only the beginning of the road. Ahead of him lay the battles of the desert and, ultimately, the horrors of the death march from Stalag VIIIB in Silesia in the winter of 1944–5; yet it is of Dunkirk that he retains the most vivid memories.

If there is to be a summing-up of the Dunkirk story, let it be in the words of a man who lived it: Mons Trussler of the 4th Royal Berkshire, whose comment on this great episode makes more of a point than a dozen history books.

They talk about the hell of Dunkirk: and I think my God, they should have lived through those three weeks in Flanders to find out what hell was really like. They call Dunkirk a great defeat: and I suppose that it was in reality. But in a sense there was a victory; because for three weeks we held at bay the best the German Army could throw at us. And what were we?

For the most part just young lads with rifles, that was all.

Notes

Chapter 1 **Battle Situation, 20 May 1940**

1 Paul Baudouin, *Neuf Mois au Gouvernement* (Paris 1948), pp 60–61.
2 J.R. Colville, *Man of Valour* (London 1972).
3 McLeod and Kelly (eds), *The Ironside Diaries 1937–40* (London 1962); Brian Bond (ed), *Chief of Staff: the Diaries of Lieutenant-General Sir Henry Pownall* (London 1972).
4 Alistair Horne, *To Lose a Battle* (London 1969), p 439.
5 Personal accounts of Weygand's flight north are provided by both pilots: in Veniel, 'A la recherche de l'Armée française avec Weygand', and Lafitte, 'Sur Amiot jusqu'au Front' in *Icare, Revue de l'aviation française: 1939–40 – La Bataille de France*.
6 Alexander Werth, *The Last Days of Paris* (London 1940).
7 Winston Churchill, *The Second World War*, II, *Their Finest Hour* (London 1949), p 58.

Chapter 2 **Fateful Decisions, 23–26 May**

1 Churchill, p 60.
2 Churchill, p 61.
3 J. Meredith Whitaker, 'The Green Howards in France', part XV, *Scarborough Evening News* (15 March 1950).
4 Churchill, p 62.
5 General Maxime Weygand, *Recalled to Service* (London 1952).
6 Churchill, p 63.
7 Churchill, p 64.
8 Sir Arthur Bryant, *The Turn of the Tide, 1939–43* (London, 1957).

Chapter 3 **Holding Action: Boulogne and Calais, 19–26 May**

1 Heinz Guderian, *Panzer Leader* (London 1952).
2 Peter Verney, *The Micks – Story of the Irish Guards* (London 1970).
3 Verney.
4 Guderian.
5 Cajus Bekker, *Angriffshöhe 4000* (Hamburg 1964).
6 Bekker.
7 Churchill, p 72.

8 Churchill, p 72.
9 Churchill, p 73.
10 Bekker.
11 Churchill, p 73.
12 Churchill, p 73.

Chapter 4 **Dunkirk: the Last Lifeline**
1 Guy Chapman, *Why France Collapsed* (London 1968).
2 General Fournel de la Laurencie, *Les Opérations du* III *Corps d'Armée, 1939–40* (Paris 1948).
3 Lord Gort, *Dispatch* (London 1941).
4 Gort.
5 Michael Howard and John Sparrow, *The Coldstream Guards, 1920–46* (London 1951).

Chapter 5 **'Dynamo'**
1 Captain S.W. Roskill, *The Navy at War, 1939–45* (London 1960).
2 Churchill, p 52.
3 Roskill.
4 O.S. Nock, *Britain's Railways at War, 1939–1945* (London 1971).

Chapter 6 **Fighting Retreat**
1 Much of the material forming the background to the stand on the Ypres–Comines Canal Line is drawn from Major-General H.E. Franklyn's 'Story of One Green Howard in the Dunkirk Campaign', *Green Howards' Gazette* (1966) and from corps, divisional and brigade war diaries.
2 From the personal account of Mr M. Trussler (author's archives).
3 44th Division War Diary (May 1940).
4 From the personal account of Mr Lee (author's archives).
5 44th Division War Diary (May 1940).

Chapter 7 **The Perimeter**
1 From the personal account of Mr K.D. Anderson (author's archives).
2 Quoted in W.G.F. Jackson, *Alexander of Tunis* (London 1971).
3 Chapman, p 224.
4 From the personal account of Mr K.W.S. Carter (author's archives).

Chapter 8 **The Beaches**
1 From the personal account of Mr McWilliam (IWM).
2 M. Trussler's account.
3 K. D. Anderson's account.
4 From the personal account of Captain James, *Western Morning News* (2 June 1965).

5 Mr Duffy's personal account (author's archives).
6 Mr Bruce's personal account (author's archives).
7 Churchill, p 95.

Chapter 9 **The Air Battle**
1 Bekker.
2 Bekker.
3 Graham Wallace, RAF *Biggin Hill* (London 1969).
4 Sqn Ldr D.H. Clarke, DFC, AFC, 'Ghost Fighters over Dunkirk', RAF *Flying Review* (March 1959).
5 Personal account of Mr Ronald Avey (author's archives).
6 Personal account supplied from private source.

Chapter 10 **Last Stand**
1 Field Marshal the Viscount Montgomery of Alamein, *Memoirs* (London 1958).
2 General André Beaufré, *The Fall of France* (London 1967).
3 J. Benoist-Mechin, *Sixty Days that Shook the West* (London 1956).
4 Benoist-Mechin.
5 Major A.E.G. Steede's personal account (author's archives).
6 Mr C.S. Best's personal account (author's archives).
7 Mr Peter Pring's account (author's archives).
8 An excellent account of the French stand at Dunkirk appears in Chapman, *Why France Collapsed*.

Chapter 11 **The Narrow Seas**
1 Personal letters of Commander Kerr (IWM).
2 Bryan Cooper, *The Battle of the Torpedo Boats* (London 1970).
3 Personal account of Mr E. Clark (author's archives).
4 Personal account of Mr F.G. Hutchinson (author's archives).
5 Personal account of W.T. Elmslie (author's archives).
6 Personal account of Edward Faulkes, DCM, MM (author's archives).
7 Personal account of Lt Cdr Archie Buchanan (author's archives).
8 W.T. Elmslie's account.
9 Lt Cdr Buchanan's account.
10 Major Steede's account.
11 Quoted in Major L.F. Ellis, *The War in France and Flanders 1939–40* (London 1954).
12 See Roskill, *The Navy at War, 1939–45*.

Chapter 12 **Homecoming**
1 Report of Captain A.P. Fisher, RN Sick Quarters, Dover (IWM).

Select Bibliography

General Works

Beaufrère, General André, *The Fall of France* (London 1967).

Bekker, Cajus, *Angriffshöhe 4000* (Hamburg 1964).

Benoist-Mechin, J., *Sixty Days that Shook the West* (London 1956).

Blaxland, Gregory, *Destination Dunkirk* (London 1973).

Bond, Brian (ed), *Chief of Staff: the Diaries of Lieutenant-General Sir Henry Pownall* (London 1972).

Bryant, Sir Arthur, *The Turn of the Tide 1939–43* (London 1957).

Chapman, Guy, *Why France Collapsed* (London 1968).

Churchill, W.S., *The Second World War*, II, *Their Finest Hour* (London 1949).

Collier, Richard, *The Sands of Dunkirk* (London 1961).

Colville, J.R., *Man of Valour* (London 1972).

Cooper, Bryan, *The Battle of the Torpedo Boats* (London 1970).

Divine, David, *The Nine Days of Dunkirk* (London 1959).

Ellis, Major L.F. *The War in France and Flanders, 1939–40* (London 1954).

Franklyn, Major-General Sir H.E., *The Story of One Green Howard in the Dunkirk Campaign* (Richmond, Yorks 1966).

Gort, Lord, *Dispatch* (London 1941).

Guderian, General Heinz, *Panzer Leader* (London 1952).

Horne, Alistair, *To Lose a Battle* (London 1969).

Ironside, Field Marshal Lord, *The Ironside Diaries* (London 1962).

Jackson, Robert, *Air War over France, 1939–40* (London 1974).

Jackson, W.G.F., *Alexander of Tunis* (London 1971).

Jacobsen, Hans-Adolf, *Dunkirchen* (Neckargemund 1958).

Laurencie, General F. de la, *Les Opérations du III Corps d'Armée, 1939–40* (Paris 1948).

Liddle Hart, Sir B.H. (ed), *The Rommel Papers* (London 1953); *The Tanks*, II, *1939–45* (London 1959).

Liss, U., *Westfront, 1939–40* (Neckargemund 1958).

Manteuffel, General Hasso von, *Die 7. Panzerdivision im Zweiten Weltkrieg* (Cologne 1965).

Masefield, John, *The Twenty-Five Days* (London 1972).

Mordal, Jacques, *La Bataille de Dunkerque* (Paris 1948).

Neave, Airey, *The Flames of Calais* (London 1972).

Prioux, General R.J.A., *Souvenirs de Guerre, 1939–43* (Paris 1947).

Reynaud, Paul, *Mémoires* (Paris 1960–63).

Roskill, Captain S.N., *The Navy at War, 1939–45* (London 1960).

Smith, Peter C., *The Stuka at War* (London 1971).

Spears, Sir Edward, *Assignment to Catastrophe* (London 1954).

Stoves, Rolf, *1 Panzer Division, 1939–1945* (Bad Nauheim 1962).

Wallace, Graham, RAF *Biggin Hill* (London 1969).

Werth, Alexander, *The Last Days of Paris* (London 1940).

Weygand, General Maxime, *Mémoires* (Paris *1953–7*); *Recalled to Service* (London 1952).

Uni Histories

Anon, *History of the East Lancashire Regiment in the War, 1939–1945.*

Aris, George, *The Fifth Division 1939–1945.*

Barclay, Brigadier C.N., *A History of the Duke of Wellington's Regiment. 1919–1952*; *History of the Royal Northumberland Fusiliers.*

Birdwood, Lieutenant-Colonel Lord, *The Worcestershire Regiment, 1922–1950*

Blight, Brigadier Gordon, *The History of the Royal Berkshire Regiment, 1920–1947.*

Chaplin, Lieutenant-Colonel H.D., *The Queen's Own Royal West Kent Regiment, 1920–1950.*

Cunliffe, Marcus, *History of the Royal Warwickshire Regiment, 1919–1955.*

Daniell, David Scott, *History of the East Surrey Regiment,* IV.

Dean, Captain C.G.T., *The Loyal Regiment, 1919–1953.*

Deedes, Major W.F., *Swift and Bold: the Story of the King's Royal Rifle Corps in the Second World War.*

Ellenberger, Brigadier G.F., *History of the King's Own Yorkshire Light Infantry* VI.

Ellis, Major L.F., *Welsh Guards at War.*

Evans, Major-General Roger, *The Story of the Fifth Royal Iniskilling Dragoon Guards.*

Forbes, Patrick, *The Grenadier Guards in the War of 1939–45.*

Fox, Sir Frank, *The Royal Iniskilling Fusiliers in the Second World War.*

Godfrey, Major E.G., *History of the Duke of Cornwall's Light Infantry, 1939–1945.*

Howard, Michael and Sparrow, John, *The Coldstream Guards 1920–46.*

Kemp, Colonel J.C., *The History of the Royal Scots Fusiliers 1919–1959.*

Kemp, Lieutenant-Commander P.K., *History of the Royal Norfolk Regiment, 1919–1951.*

Kenrick, Colonel N.C.E., *The Story of the Wiltshire Regiment.*

Martineau, G.D., *A History of the Royal Sussex Regiment.*

Masters, Captain J.W.A., *The Story of the 2nd Battalion the Sherwood Foresters, 1939–1945.*

Miller, Major-General C.H., *History of the 13th/18th Royal Hussars, 1922–1947.*

Sellar, R.J.B., *The Fife and Forfar Yeomanry, 1919–1956.*

Sheffield, Major O.F., *The York and Lancaster Regiment, 1919–1953.*

Stewart, Captain P.F., *The History of the 12th Royal Lancers.*

Synge, Captain W.A.T., *The Story of the Green Howards, 1939–1945.*

Ward, S.G.P., *Faithful: The Story of the Durham Light Infantry.*

Williamson, Hugh, *The Fourth Division, 1939–1945.*

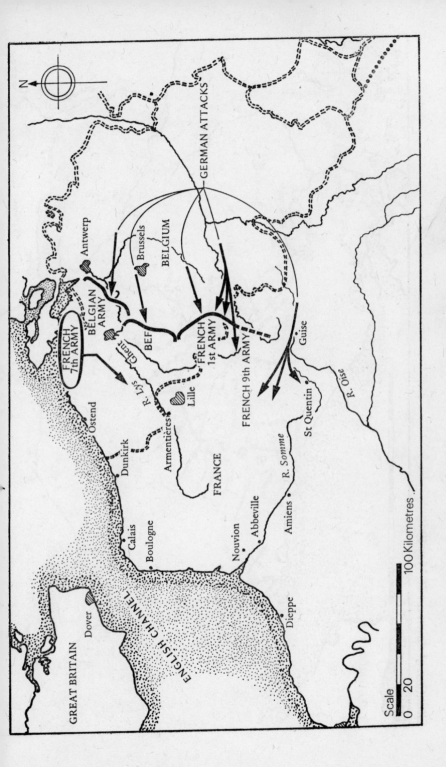

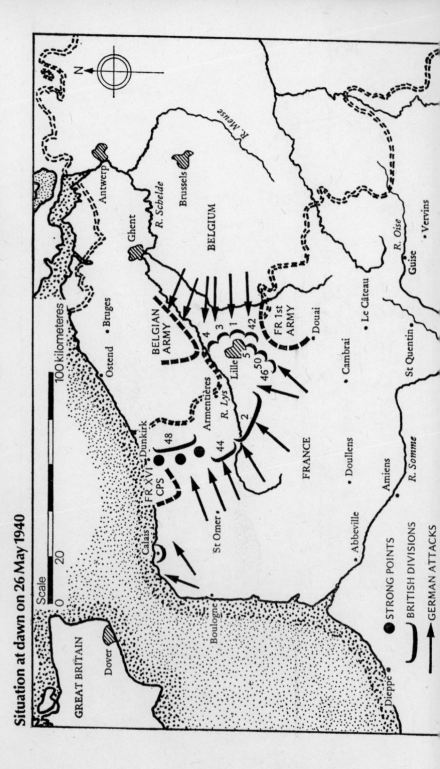

Situation at dawn on 26 May 1940

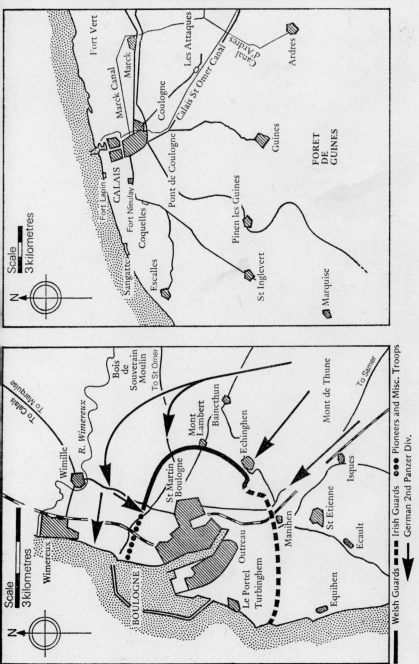

The Ypres-Comines Canal Line, where the British 5th and 50th Divisions made their stand on 27-28 May

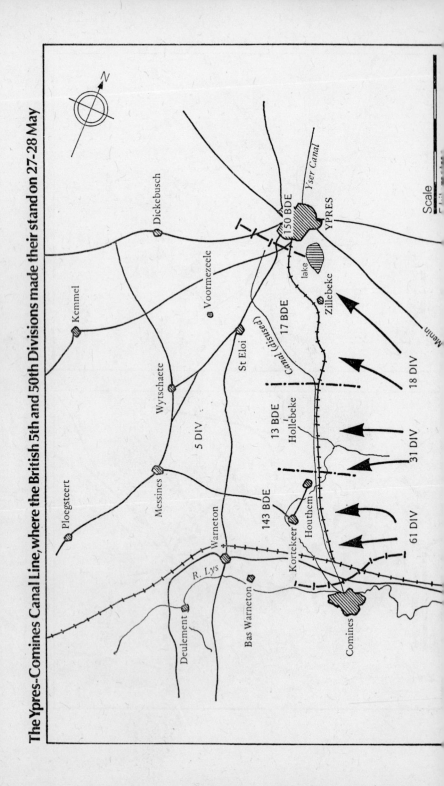

Scale

YPRES
150 BDE
Yser Canal
lake
Zillebeke
17 BDE
18 DIV
Menin
Canal (disused)
13 BDE
Hollebeke
31 DIV
143 BDE
Kortekeer
Houthem
61 DIV
Comines
R. Lys
Warneton
Bas Warneton
Deulement
Messines
Ploegsteert
Wytschaete
St Eloi
5 DIV
Voormezeele
Kemmel
Dickebusch

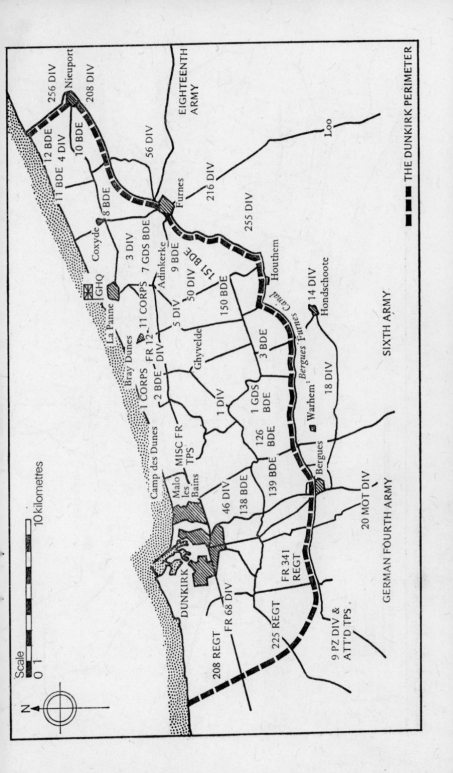

Scale

0 1   10 kilometres

N

THE DUNKIRK PERIMETER

EIGHTEENTH ARMY

256 DIV

Nieuport

208 DIV

12 BDE 4 DIV

10 BDE

11 BDE

8 BDE

Coxyde

56 DIV

Furnes

216 DIV

3 DIV

7 GDS BDE

255 DIV

GHQ

La Panne

11 CORPS

Adinkerke

9 BDE

151 BDE

Houthem

Bray Dunes

1 CORPS

FR 12 DIV

5 DIV

50 DIV

14 DIV

Bergues-Furnes Canal

2 BDE

Ghyvelde

150 BDE

Hondschoote

Camp des Dunes

MISC FR TPS

1 DIV

3 BDE

Warhem

18 DIV

Malo les Bains

46 DIV

138 BDE

126 BDE

1 GDS BDE

139 BDE

Bergues

DUNKIRK

FR 68 DIV

FR 341 REGT

20 MOT DIV

208 REGT

225 REGT

9 PZ DIV & ATT'D TPS

GERMAN FOURTH ARMY

SIXTH ARMY.

Loo

The BEF's last bridgehead at Dunkirk

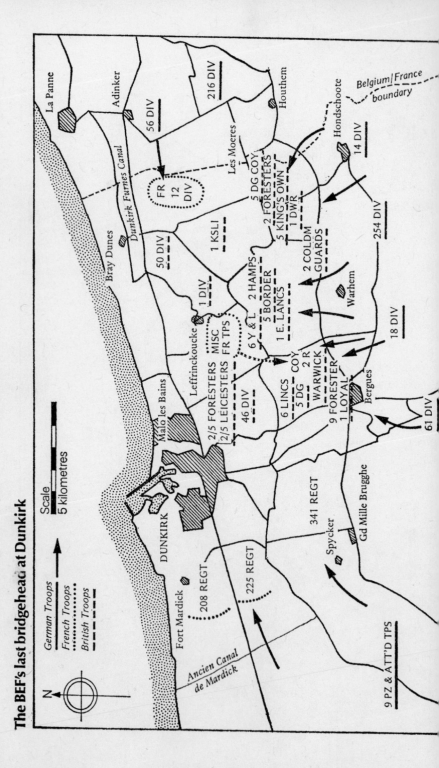

Scale

5 kilometres

Legend:
- German Troops
- French Troops
- British Troops

N

La Panne

Adinker

56 DIV

216 DIV

Houthem

Belgium/France boundary

Hondschoote

14 DIV

FR 12 DIV

Les Moeres

5 DG COY

2 FORESTERS

5 FORESTERS

5 KING'S OWN

1 DWR

254 DIV

Dunkirk Furnes Canal

Bray Dunes

50 DIV

1 KSLI

2 COLDM GUARDS

1 DIV

2 HAMPS

5 BORDER

1 E. LANCS

Warhem

18 DIV

Leffrinckoucke

MISC FR TPS

6 Y & L

2 R COY

WARWICK

2/5 FORESTERS

2/5 LEICESTERS

46 DIV

6 LINCS

5 DG

9 FORESTER

1 LOYAL

Bergues

61 DIV

Malo les Bains

DUNKIRK

Fort Mardick

208 REGT

225 REGT

Ancien Canal de Mardick

341 REGT

Spycker

Gd Mille Brugghe

9 PZ & ATT'D TPS

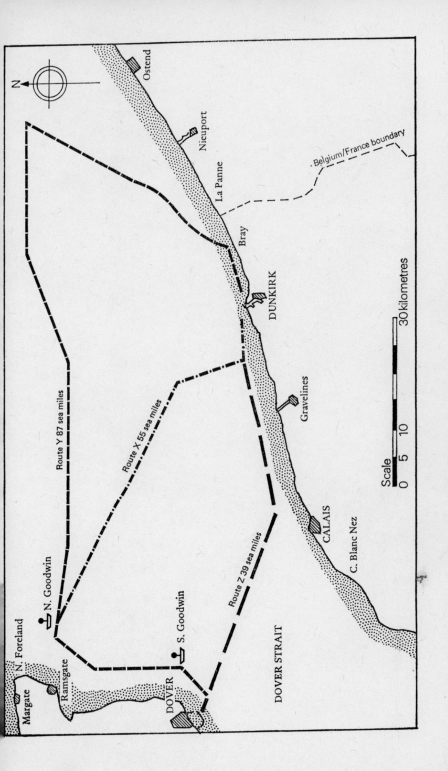

Index